Bethany Sketches and Records

BETHANY

SKETCHES AND RECORDS.

COMPILED AND PUBLISHED BY

W. C. SHARPE. SEYMOUR, CONN

RECORD PRINT. SEYMOUR
1908

PREFACE

This book is intended to put in convenient form for handy reference sketches, transcripts of records and other data which have been collected for some years and which seemed worthy to be embodied in book form The writer is especially indebted to Wallace D Hurriston for assistance in the work While errors may be found in the names and dates it should be remembered that most of them are probably in the original records, as any who have had experience in similar research knows that names are variously spelled at different times, and dates are not always correctly entered as for instance the writer has sometimes found on careful investigation that the date of a marriage license has been recorded in place of the date of a marriage, and a date of burial instead of death

The writer has collected largely of genealogical data of many Bethany families but is unable at present to devote the time necessary to carry them to such a degree of completion as would warrant their insertion here, and the work is therefore of necessity brought to a close

CONTENTS

ILLUSTRATIONS

THE FIRST ECCLESIASTICAL SOCIETY.

Bethany was incorporated as a town in May, 1832, but as an ecclesiastical society it has an honorable record which ante dates the Revolution by twelve years and contribu ed liberally of men and means during that gre it epoch of history

It was in May, 1762, th it a petition was presented to the General Assembly, signed by "Joel Hotchkiss and others, inhabitants of the northern parts of the parish of Amity, in the town of New Haven, praying to be made a distinct ecclesiasti cal society with proper limits and bounds," and a committee was appointed to hear the parties interested and to report at the next session of the General Assembly

At the October session ("on the second Thursday of October") a favorable report was made, and it was enacted that the "inhabit ints of the parish of Amity living north of an east and west line drawn from the south end of the widow Hannah Sperry's dwelling house, as prayed for in said memorial, shall be a distinct ecclesiasti cal society, with all the privileges and powers naturally belonging to such socie ties in this Colony and shall be called and known by the name of Bethany"

The first meeting of the new society was held Nov 13, 1762 The record reads, "At a Lawful Society meeting of the inhabitants of bethany in new haven and milford held at the schoolhouse in sd bethany," etc

Deacon Joel Hotchkiss was elected moderator, James Sherman clerk, and Timothy Peck, John White, Isaac Beech-er, Daniel Toles and Joel Hotchkiss were chosen societies' committee It was "vo ted that the meetings shall begin on the second Sabbath in December and hold until the last in April "

"Vo ed that a ı aight be laid of a penny half-penny on the pound for defraying the charges of preaching the year ensuing "

The next winter the meetings were to begin on the second Sabbath in November and application was made "unto the Rev erand Association for a minister to be set tled among us " At the meeting of the Association of New Haven County, con vened in Waterbury May 31st, 1763, Mr. Stephen Hawley was recommended He was called on probation for the first Wed nesday in June, 1763, for three months, and on the 3d Wednesday in August it was voted "to settle him in the work of the ministry amongst us," and to allow him 200 pounds settlement. "100 pounds the first year after he is first settled, one-half of settlement, and 50 pounds yearly the next two years, with 50 pounds salary a year the first three years, then 65 pounds a year "

"On the second Wednesday of Decem ber, 1767, it was voted that it is necessary to build a meetinghouse " It was also voted to make it 50 ft long and 40 ft wide and a rate of four pence on the pound was laid to defray the expense, "the rate to be laid in flax seed or some other spee she that will answer at New York "

At a meeting of the society held on the last Wednesday of April, 1768, "it was voted that this society will make applyca tion to the honourable general assembly for the one lot purchis in milford bound that lyeth south of the top of beacon hill and also for that part of Darby that lyeth between bethany and nawgetuck river to be annexed to sd Bethany " The petition was granted at the January session of the General Assembly, 1769, in the following words

"Resolved by this assembly, that the said lands belonging to the first society of Milford which lies north of said Bethany south line extending westward un il it came to said Derby east line be, and they hereby are, annexed unto the said society of Bethany and made part thereof "

At a meeting in December, 1768, it was "voted that we will get timber this winter and set up the meetinghous next spring and cover it as fast as we conveniently can Dea Hotchkiss, Dea White, Capt. Hitchcock, Capt Lines, Mr Jesse Bradley, Mr Hez Clark and Mr. Timothy Peck snall be a committee to carry on the building abovesaid "

"Voted, that those that skoar timber for the meetinghous shall have two shilling and sixpence pr day "

"Voted that those that hew shall have three shillings and sixpence pr day "

"Voted that we will apply to the county court for a new committee to start a plase for the me tinghous "

The location finally decided upon was on the hill a little south of where the church now stands There the church was erected in 1769, and enclosed so that services were held in it, though not completed until some years later

"The sum total of Bethany rate book in the year 1776 is £7524 8-1. Then take out ye Churchmen's list, and there remains on the list 6720 11 0, at 2d half penny on ye pound makes 69 17 5, then take out one penny on New Haven side which makes 23 9 3, then remains on ye book 46 8 2."

Lnsign JOEL HOTCHKIS, Collector.

Timothy Ball was one of the committee in 1766 and two years later is referred to as Lieut Ball The use of military terms had become more common in 1778 as shown in the record of the choice of the society's committee, Capt Ball, Capt E Sperry, Ensign Jacob Hotchkiss, Jared Sherman and Ensign Joel Hotchkis A rate of two pence on the pound was then voted At this mee ing it was also "voted yt ye Society shall pay Mr Hawley's Sallery in Provisions, Labor & other Species according to ye first stateing of provisions by ye general assembly, wheet at 3-6 & other things in Proportion. & those yt Dount pay in ye afforsd Species of Provisions &c , shall pay money equivalent "

"Voted yt Deacon Peck, Capt Ball & Ensign Jacob Hotchkiss should be a committee to seat ye meetinghouse "

"Voted yt ye Committee shall have regard to age & what each one has paid to ye building of sd house & according to their discression with all "

A diagram of the church with names of pewholders as assigned in 1791 has been preserved and from it the illustration given herewith has been made The original drawing is 13 3-16x18 inches, on hand made paper 15½x18¼, with two watermarks, one a crown over G R, (Georgius Rex) and the other the name TAYLOR In it the pews are not numbered, the names being written in the space representing each pew, but in the reduced copy given herewith numbers have been inserted and the names are given below

1. Deacons.
2. Widow Ruth Brisco Lydia Peck, Hannah Sperry
3 and 4 No names given
5 Capt Ezra Sperry, Mr. Daniel Tolles, Mr John Thomas, Capt Joel Hotchkiss, Widow Mary Ball
6 Mr. Roger Peck, Lieut Medad Hotchkiss, Mr Valentine Willmott, Widow Sarah Andrews.

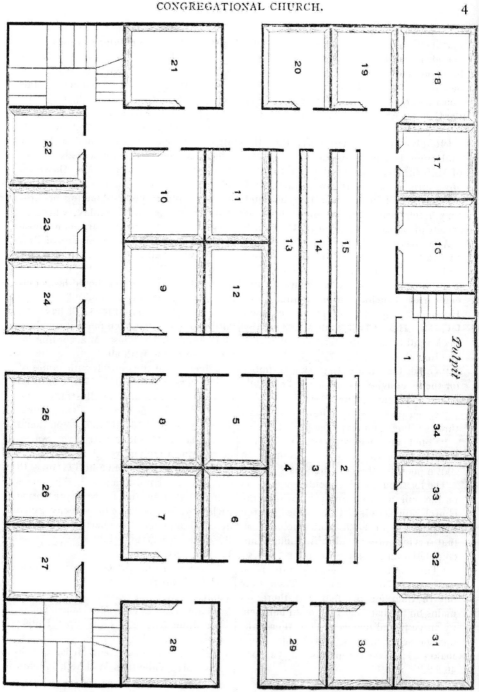

7   Mr Timothy Bronson, Mr Benjamin Hotchkiss, Mr Elam Sperry, Mr. Timothy Lounsbury, Jr, Mr Jesse Terrel

8   Widow Hannah Beecher, Mr Lamberton Tolles, Mr Timothy Ball, Mr Jared To les, Widow Perkins.

9   Lieut Jesse Beecher, Mr. Jared Beecher, Mr Hezekiah Beecher

10   Mr Samuel Hotchkiss, Mr John Russell, Mr Elias Hotchkiss, Mr. Eber Lines

11   Mr Buckingham, Mr Hezekiah Johnson, Mr. Joseph Bishop, Mr Eden Johnson

12   Ensign Jacob Hotchkiss, Mr. Hezekiah Sperry, Mr Nathaniel Tuttle, Mr Joseph Hotchkiss.

13   Messrs. Ezekial Smith, Abraham Pain, Jacob Barnes, David Beers, Jonathan Sackett, Silas Nelson

14   Messrs Stephen Lounsbury, Abel Ives, Joseph Collins, Reuben Bradley, Elihu Sanford, Joseph Woolcott, Stephen Sanford

15   Messrs Isaac Beecher, Valentine Willmott, Amos Hitchcock, John Lines, Sam'll Downs, Abijah Buckingham John Wooding, Jonathan Atwater, Esquire French

16   Rev Stephen Hawley's family

17   Mr Timothy Lounsbury, Mr David Thomas, Mr. Oliver Buckingham, Capt Elijah Sperry

18   Capt Lazarus Tolles, David Sanford, John Alsop Talmadge, Mr. Amos Atwater, Mr Amasa Tuttle, Elihu Sanford, Jr

19   Mr Reuben Sperry, Mr Lucas Lines, Widow Phebe Tirrel, Mr. Caleb Audrus, Mr Demas Sperry

20.   Ensign Garshom Thomas, Mr Amos Thomas, Mr Ebenezer Hitchcock, Mr. Isaac Foot, Mr. John Nettleton, Mr Isaac Sperry

21   Mr Lemuel Alling, Mr. Joel Collins, Mr Joseph Hitchcock, Mr David Atwater, Mr Medad Sperry, Mr Joseph Collins, Mehetibal Sanford

22   Mr Linus Lounsbury, Mr Noah Alling, Mr Nathan Beer, John Russell.

23   Mr Joel Hotchkiss, Jr, Mr Joseph Downs, Mr Felix Downs, Mr Jonathan Sanford

24   Mr Joel Wheeler, Mr. Isaac Hotchkiss, Mr. Aaron Clark, Mr Timothy Hitchcock, Widow Mary Brisco

25   Lieut. Abraham Tolles, Mr Noah Thomas, Mr Saml Peck, Mr Edward Warren, Widow Sarah Nettleton

26   Mr Justus Beecher, Mr Wheler Beecher, Mr Nathaniel Warren, Mr. Elias Lounsbury, Mr John Tirrel, Mr. Thomas Kimbal

27   No names entered

28   Mr Jonathan Smith, Mr. David Willmott, Mr Walter Willmott, Mr Matthew Baldwin, Mr William Hitchcock, Mr. David E Hotchkiss

29   Mr Ebenezer Lines, Mr Uri Sperry, Mr Amos Hitchcock Mr Robert Russell, Mr James I Hotchkiss, Mr. Benjamin Collins

30   Mr Jabez Hotchkiss, Mr. Abraham Hotchkiss, Mr Stephen Hotchkiss, Mr. Elmore Russel.

31   Mr Reuben Perkins, Mr Phenihas Tirrel, Mr Ezekiel Hotchkiss, Mr John Thomas, Jr, Mr Israel Perkins, Mr. William Andrew

32   Capt Hine, Capt Thomas, Lieut Atwater, Eliphalet Johnson

33   Mr Daniel Beecher, Deacons' wives, Capt Sanford

34   Widow Anne Russell, Widow Rebeckah Hitchcock, Widow Sarah Downs

We are told that the meetinghouse was partially surrounded by "Sabbath Day Houses" in which in cold weather fires were built on arrival in the morning After the morning service all left the unwarmed church for these buildings, and ate their dinners in the cheering warmth of the fires in the stone "fireplaces."

The location of the church had been made by a committee appointed by the County Court. Difficulties seem to have arisen, a second application to the Court was made in 1768, and a third in 1769, and at length in May, 1769, it was voted "that we are willing to build a meetinghouse at the last stake set by the Honorable County Court's Committee" On this question there were 29 in the affirmative and 10 in the negative A committee consisting of Isaac Beecher, Ensign Clark and Israel Thomas was appointed to purchase the land of Isaac Hotchkiss

Of the votes taken while the preparations for building were in progress some were recorded which illustrate some customs of the times In December, 1767, it was voted "that we will provide the boards, clapboards shingles, nails and glass necessary for building a meetinghouse the year ensuing" A tax was laid, and it was decided that one half might be paid "in flax seed, or some other species that will answer at New York" The Society fixed the prices to be paid for the different kinds of lumber

In December, 1768, a vote was passed, "that we will get timber this winter, and set up the meetinghouse as fast as we conveniently can" It was ordered "that those that score timber for the meetinghouse shall have two shillings and sixpence per day, and those that hew shall have three shillings and sixpence per day" Deacon White and Deacon Hotchkiss were appointed "to cull the clapboards and shingles for the meetinghouse"

In March, 1769, it was voted "that this Society give free liberty for a belfry to be built on the meetinghouse," but this liberty was not then used In January, 1770, the Society meeting was held in the meetinghouse for the first time

It was customary to appoint particular persons "to tune the psalm" In 1765, the choristers were Valentine Wilmot, Benajah Peck and Stephen Sanford In 1770, on entering the new church, a larger number received this appointment, viz Isaac Baldwin, Joel Hotchkiss, Thomas Beecher, Anan Ives, Lazarus Tolles, Timothy Lounsbury, Nathaniel Tuttle and Nehemiah Tolles. At this time it was voted "that the choristers sit together near the foot of the pulpit stairs"

In 1771 a committee was appointed "to give liberty to people to build pews in the meetinghouse, where they see cause" In 1773 a tax was laid "to color the meetinghouse and case the windows, and to provide boards for the inside of the house" In 1774 a vote was passed "that the meetinghouse be colored blue, and the windows white," but soon a special meeting was called "for the purpose of altering the color of the meetinghouse," and it was decided to color it white In December, 1776 it was voted " to finish the lower part of the meetinghouse, and the front of the galleries"

In 1777 Nathanael Tuttle, Isaac Baldwin, Daniel Tolles and Joel Hine were chosen "to tune the psalm, and sit in the fore seat in the front gallery" In 1778 it was voted "that the Society shall pay Mr Hawley's salary in provisions, labor, and other species, according to the first stating of provisions by the General Assembly — wheat at six shillings, and other things in proportion, and those that do not pay in the aforesaid species of provisions, &c, shall pay money equivalent"

At the same meeting a committee was appointed to seat the meetinghouse — viz Deacon Peck, Capt Ball, and Ensign Jacob Hotchkiss and it was ordered that "the committee shall have regard to age, and what each one has paid to the building of said house, and according to their discretion with all" In December,

1779, a vote was passed "that the committee shall lay out the overplus money of finishing the meetinghouse, on the steps and other ways as they think best"

Thus, at the end of ten years from its raising, the house seems to have been considered finished In 1791 the Society voted "to take up three seats in the square body, and build pews on each side of the broad alley." In 1792 it was re-solved "That the Society may build a steeple to the meetinghouse, if they can get money enough signed to build said steeple" But the steeple and bell were not added until 1803

There were three entrances, north, south and east, the latter being the prin-cipal one and facing the street and opening into the central aisle It will be noticed that the large pews had seats on four sides, except only at the place of entrance, so that some, it is said the children, sat with their backs to the minister There were doors to each pew, as was common until within half a century.

Most of the old churches were not lathed or plastered, but we are told that this was the exception to the rule, but as churches were not warmed in those days, it was cold in winter, and even with the "Sabbaday houses" and their cheerful warmth to resort to before and after service, it must have often been a great trial to endure the cold during the services, notwithstanding the relief to some by means of box frames lined with perforated tin, which were filled with live coals from the fires in the Sabbaday houses and carried into the church for footwarmers

The pulpit was very high, so that the minister could have a fair view of the galleries which extended across three sides of the church and were reached by stairways in the northeast and southeast corners of the church.

The "meetinghouse" of a century ago was often the only place in town suitable for a town meeting, and it was not thought inappropriate to hold within its walls the yearly meeting to arrange town affairs for the ensuing twelve months.

It is interesting to note that there were paid singers a hundred years ago, as we find under date of 1793 an entry of £2 paid Isaac Foot for singing, as well as £1 5s to Eber Lines for sweeping the meetinghouse

THE CONGREGATIONAL SOCIETY

BY W D HUMISTON

Two centuries ago but very few set tlers had sought homes in the vast and almost trackless forest which prevailed in the northern part of New Haven,and what nowcomprisesthe townof Bethany. A few, however, had built rude cabins on the Mattatuck Turnpike, Straits Highway and Downs Street at base of Mad Mare's Hill. These localities are still sometimes called by the names which the early settlers gave them

The first settlers found themselves far from any place of public worship, yet every Sabbath found them wending their way fully armed against the dusky savages, who might lurk in the deep recesses of the forest, to the meetinghouse on New Haven green

A few years later Amity Parish was incorporated, and for over twenty years the inhabitants of the present towns of Bethany and Woodbridge formed but one ecclesiastical society On the Lord's Day and on other occasions our fathers, the hardy pioneers of this forest town, assembled at the meetinghouse of the parish of Amity and offer ed up their devotions as a united body For seven or eight miles in all directions thse men of God descended from the breezy, life-giving hills, to the tem ple down in the valley, to pay this debt of duty to the Supreme Ruler of the Universe. Their affections during these years entwined themselves around the old sanctuary They loved their kind pastor, Rev. Mr. Woodbridge, and the great inconvenience of the remote parts of their parish could scarcely in-duce them to think of forming a new society and forming new church relations.

But at length the time came when it seemed necessary to many to separate from the old society and attempt the formation of a new one And accordingly a memorial was sent to the May session of the General Assembly in 1762. A committee was appointed to view the circumstances and report. This committee, having attended to the duties of their appointment, reported favorably and a distinct ecclesiastical society was incorporated and named Bethany The following is a copy of the original charter

"BETHANY MADE A DISTINCT ECCLESIASTICAL AND CIVIL SOCIETY, SIMILAR TO OTHER PARISHES IN THE COLONY, BY THE GENERAL ASSEMBLY OF THE COLONY OF CONNECTICUT"

"At a General Assembly of the Colony of Connecticut, held at New Haven, on the second Thursday of October, A. D 1762, upon the memorial of Joel Hotchkiss and others, the Inhabitants of the Parish of Amity, living north of an east and west line drawn from the dwelling house of the Widow Hannah Sperry,

Preferred to this Assembly at their sessions in May last, representing the inconveniences they are under in attending the public worship, &c, and praying for said Privileges, a Committee was granted, &c., which Committee having made report to this Assembly of their Opinion, that said Memorialists and Inhabitants dwelling north of said east and west line should be made a Society, &c , which report being accepted by this Assembly,

"Thereupon it is enacted and ordered, That said Inhabitants of the Parish of Amity, living north of an east and west line drawn from south end of the Widow Hannah Sperry's dwelling House, as prayed for in said Memorial, shall be and they are hereby made a distinct Ecclesiastial Society, with all the Privileges and Powers usually belonging to such Societies in this Colony, ...and shall be called and known by the name of .... Bethany, A true copy examined.

"By George Wyllis, Secretary "

The parish of Bethany is one of the oldest in this vicinity, and at the time of its incorporation was bounded on the north by the parish of Waterbury, west by Oxford and Derby, south by Amity and east by North Haven The society began at once to exercise its power by levying a tax "at a penny halfpenny for defraying the charges of preaching the year ensewing.' The parsonage lands lying in Bethany, having been sold by Amity, action was taken at once to recover them A committee was appointed to receive from the Amity committee the bonds for "the three publick lots that they have sold in s'd Bethany and which was a parsonage for s'd Society "

The church now deemed it necessary to settle a suitable minister over the parish, and accordingly, on April 20, 1763, Deacon Joel Hotchkiss and Timthy Peck were appointed to confer with the Reverend Association in order to obtain their advice concerning a candidate. At a meeting of this association convened at Waterbury Stephen Hawley was strongly recommended to the Society. Isaac Beecher and Samuel Downs were appointed to be a Com" to apply unto Mr. Stephen Hawley to call him upon three months' probation in order for settlement." Two hundred pounds settlement was voted. This was to be paid in three years, one hundred pounds the first year and fifty the two remaining years Mr Hawley was to receive fifty pounds salary the first year, and this was to increase with the parish lists to seventyfive On being informed of these votes, the Rev Stephen Hawley sent this reply

"To the people of Bethany

"Hoping that love and unanimity and the grace of our common Lord Jesus Christ may be multiplied among you, I have taken into consideration your public votes and desires that I would settle among you in the arduous employment of the gospell ministry, and also the sett'ement you have offered me, together with the salary for my yearly maintainance, and I think that what you have done for me is both generous and honorable, and I return my hearty thanks for your Christian good will I firmly rely upon it that you will not see me in indigent circumstances and turn off your bowels of tenderness and relief I depend upon it that you will conduct towards me as an embassador and servant of Christ, and yet as a treasure in an earthern vessel and subject to many infirmities

"Upon these conditions I accept of your propositions, and am willing to settle among you unless something very material happens before the ordination

"May the God of Truth guide our hearts into all truth, and by the grace of God may we so behave as that our neighbor societys may see how beautiful it is to dwell together in unity

"STEPHEN HAWLEY

"Bethany, Sept 12, 1763 "

The ordination of Rev. Stephen Hawley took place on Oct. 12, 1663. The ordination services were performed in a field about one mile south of the present church, near the first Bethany meeting house, a small building erected on the corner opposite the home of William Smith, for public worship, but never entirely finished. Several ministers of other parishes were present, among whom was the Rev. Dr. Trumbull of North Haven, the famous historian of Connecticut.

In the early days of which we are speaking the singing was done in the following manner. A person was appointed to act as chorister or "to set the psalm," who selected and "pitched" the tunes, then a line or two was read off, when the whole congregation joined in singing them, and thus proceeding alternately to read and sing the lines until the whole psalm had been sung. By an action taken by the society Valentine Willmott and Stephen Sanford were appointed to tune the psalm.

During the early history of the church rates were levied repeatedly through the year, sometimes being as heavy as two shillings on the pound. These taxes might be paid in provisions, however, if the people so wished.

A word might be inserted here concerning the records of the society. Of the three earliest records dating from 1762 but two are now extant, the bank book and the record of the society meetings. The third, a record of births, baptisms, marriages and deaths in the society for a long period, of prime importance to genealogists is unfortunately missing. The prominent surnames that appear in the early records are given below.

Alling, Andrew, Andrews, Atwater, Baldwin, Ball, Barnes, Beecher, Beers, Bishop, Bradley, Brisco, Brown, Buckingham, Carrington, Clark, Collins, Downs, French, Foot, Grinnel, Hine, Hitchcock, Hooker, Hotchkiss, Ives, Johnson, Kimball, Lines, Lounsbury, Nelson, Nettleton, Pain, Peck, Perkins, Russell, Sackett, Sanford, Sherman, Smith, Sperry, Talmadge, Terrel, Thomas, Todd, Tolles, Turner, Tuttle, Warren, Wheeler, Wilmott, White, Wolcott and Wooding.

In 1756 it was found necessary to build a larger meeting house to accommodate the increasing congregation, and application was made to the County court for a committee to look over their situation and choose a site. Much difficulty was experienced in choosing a suitable situation, and three committees were elected before a location could be agreed upon, and even then ten members opposed. The site was located on the north side of the road leading over the hill from the turnpike near the residence of James Cotter. The meadow on which James Cotter's carriage house now stands was the meeting house green, the church being on the western side. On the north was the mansion of Dr. Hezekiah Hooker, and the south and east sides respectively the residences of Rev. Stephen Hawley and Capt. Ebenezer Dayton.

Capt. Dayton's residence, of Revolutionary fame, is now the only one remaining, although the Buckingham place is built on Rev. Stephen Hawley's cellar. The cellar place of Dr. Hooker's mansion is still visible.

It was voted that the meetinghouse should be fiftyfive feet in length and forty in width, and that material for building it should be furnished during the ensuing year. "Dear Hotchkiss, Dea White, Capt Hitchcock, Capt Lines, Mr Jesse Bradley, Mr Hez Clark and Mr Timothy Peck" were appointed "a committee to carry on the building above said Timothy Ball and Isaac Beecher were soon afterward added to this number. Application was made to the General Assembly to enlarge the parish by annexing the tract of land belonging to the town of Milford "which lyeth south of the top of beacon hill, and also for that part of Derby that lyeth between bethany and nawgetuck river." The exterior of the meeting house was completed in 1769, and services were held in it at this time, although the interior was not entirely finished until several years afterward

The society now had a church edifice of which they might be justly proud, since it was one of the largest and most expensive in the region and consid, ibly larger than either of the churches now at the Center Besides the galleries and choir loft, it contained nearly thirty large square pews, arranged in two central "square bodies," and in a row about the sides, with the exception of spaces reserved for the pulpit and the three entrances The pulpit was on the western side of the church and was reached by a number of steps The whole was surmounted by a huge green sounding board." Beneath the pulpit was a long seat on which the deacons sat facing the congregation The tall white spire of Bethany meeting house was one of the most conspicuous objects that met the sailor's eye as he entered New Haven harbor

In 1783 the parishes of Bethany and Amity united their efforts in trying to secure town privileges, but they could not agree at to the location of the town house After Bethany had made many proposals, none of which were accepted by Amity, it was decided to petition the General Assembly to be made into a separate town, but Amity coming to terms, the two parishes were incorporated under the name of Woodbridge.

Similar attempts were made in 1802 and 1804 to have the parish incorporated a town, and at last successfully in 1832.

The ringing of curfew was observed in Bethany long after it had become obsolete in other parts of the country. The old meeting house bell was rung here until the early part of last century at nine o'clock in the evening, Sundays included. It was a signal for the inhabitants to cover their fires and retire for the night.

Rev Stephen Hawley died July 17, 1804, in the fortyfirst year of ministry and the sixtysixth of his life. For a short period preceding his death he was unable to perform all the duties of his pastoral office

He was an intelligent and honest preacher, exemplary and faithful in all the relations and duties of life. He was twice married and had, it is believed, several children whose names are now unknown, with the exception of Spencer, who died in 1803. Mary Bellamy, his first wife, died in 1791, and his widow, Mehetable Hotchkiss, November, 1827, aged 66. The aged pastor was buried in the old cemetery and there reposes, surrounded by his family and a numerous congregation, slumbering, and many of whom he himself, while living, had followed to the grave As in life he was ever united to his people, so in death they are not divided

At this point in the ecclesiastical history of our town it would be well to glance back on the difficulties which surrounded the lives of the early fathers in the church. Many of them, before coming to this wilderness, had comfortable estates on the other side of the sea, but they came for conscience sake and made light of their privations

It was their aim, in establishing the many towns, to erect churches in strict accordance to Scriptural example and to transmit civil and religious liberty to their posterity. All their acts and designs tended to the accomplishment of this grand purpose, and therefore all persons were obliged to contribute to the support of the church and ministry. All must attend the public worship The Congregational mode of worship was adopted and established by law, but all orthodox persons dissenting could, upon application to the General Court, worship in their own manner. Such persons, however, were beheld with distrust Our fathers, who desired religious freedom and periled all for it, probably had not anticipated that they would speedily be called upon to extend the toleration to others for which they had vainly sought in the mother country, and at first they viewed with alarm any departure from the established discipline or doctrine, yet they had the germ of toleration and developed with more rapidity, it is believed, than any other christian sect can show. In early times the influence of the clergy was much greater than at present The majority of them were wealthy and could help their parishioners out of their financial difficulties. They also were the most highly educated and possessed a large amount of the literature of the colony. They prepared the young men for college and afterwards assisted them in their studies, and in return the people loved and respected them

The Puritan Sabbath began, according to Scriptural injunction, at sunset Saturday, the "day of preparation," and all unnecessary work was laid aside At the sound of the meeting-house bell on the Lord's Day the industrious inhabitants prepared for the journey to the house of God, on foot or horseback as their means allowed The huge old meeting house was built upon the high-est hill at the intersection of roads leading to various parts of the parish and as near the geographical center as possible. But the people went up to the sanctuary though bitter storms were in the air and the wild wind howled drearily about the bleak hill. At that time the possibility of heating the meeting-house by stoves or fire places had never entered the minds of men, and hence the only heat was derived from the small foot stoves which the wealthier matrons carried with them No matter how severe the weather, the worshipper, who perhaps had waded three or four miles through roads drifted with deep snow, sat with heroic fortitude for an hour and a half, and then at intermission repaired to the glowing fires of the parsonage or union schoolhouse, which was rented for that purpose Then another hour and half in the warm meeting-house completed the service of the day, and they were dismissed to the long, cold ride home The remaining hours of the Sabbath were spent in the employments appropriate to the conclusion of the day of rest But the early settlers of long since departed and several generations sleep with them. It is to be feared that many of their valuable customs and precepts have departed with them.

For a short period during the last year of his ministry Rev Stephen Hawley's health did not permit him to discharge all his pastoral duties, and the society found it necessary to install a colleague with him in the person of Mr Isaac Jones Rev Isaac Jones was ordained June 6, 1801 For many reasons he was disliked by many of his congregation, and a wide breach was opened between the two factions. Rev Isaac Jones' actions intensified this feeling, and at last it was determined to dissolve his pastoral relation with the church. The church met many times in order to adjust the difficulty, and finally, after a long debate, the controversy was brought nearly to a close. Before the conclusion of the meeting Col. Joel Hine, the leader of those in favor of Isaac Jones, said, "Now do you not think you ought to make some recantation for what you have said to our party?" David Thom as replied, "No, we think that you ought to acknowledge to us for what you have done." Silence ensued for a few minutes, and then both parties quietly departed and never met again for the same purpose. Soon after Rev. Isaac Jones was deprived of his office by a Council met for this purpose. With about sixty others including the deacons, Phenehas Terrel and Hezekiah Beecher, he "signed off" and united with the Episcopal church, a small body which had been organized a few years previously.

That this sad event did not effect the ruin of the church is due, perhaps, to the spirit of determination to overcome great obstacles which have everywhere characterized the descendants of the Puritans. It deprived the church of nearly or quite one half of its members, but in the following year a large fund of several thousand dollars for the support of the ministry was raised by subscription among the remaining members of the society and added to a fund which had been willed to the church many years before. Donations have been received from time to time until the fund is now nearly double the original amount.

Shortly after the deposition of Isaac Jones Nathaniel G Huntington was ordained third pastor, in which office he continued until 1823, when his health obliged him to resign much to the regret of the parishioners.

Previous to 1824 no stoves were used in the meeting-house, but by the aid of warm clothing, foot stoves and a glowing fire at the parsonage and union schoolhouse at intermission, the congregation seemed unaware of the cold weather. In 1824, however, stoves were placed in the church.

By means of a General Conference convened in this parish, Jan. 17, 1829, a revival occurred and thirtytwo members were added to the church, twentyfive of whom were received in one day, probably the largest number on one occasion since the formation of the society.

Preparations for building the present church edifice were begun by the society in 1830. John Thomas, Silas Hotchkiss, Elihu Sanford, Lewis Thomas, Lewis Hine and Hiram Hotchkiss were appointed a building committee, with the liberty to pull down the old meeting house and to sell the green. From the proceeds of this sale and by subscription the present church was built in 1831 according to plans submitted by Ira Atwater, of New Haven.

Extensive repairs were made on the church in 1851, and a new bell purchased partly by subscription. The old parsonage was sold and the house now occupied by F A. Perry was purchased and used by the society for a parsonage many years. The church was again repaired a few years later and the wide portico which extended across the church was enclosed in order to enlarge the vestibule.

The centennial of the church was celebrated Oct 12, 1862, near the site of the first meeting house. Many clergymen and a great concourse of people from various parts of the state attended this celebration. Rev. Dr. Elwood, who was then pastor, conducted the services, consisting of speaking, singing, etc. The assembly then proceeded to the old cemetery and there wit-

nessed the erection of a tombtone in
memory of Rev. Stephen Hawley,
whose grave had remained unmarked
for nearly sixty years The stone
bears the following inscription

REV STEPHEN HAWLEY,
FIRST MINISTER OF
BETHANY,
PASTOR FORTY YEARS
Ordained Oct. 12, 1763.
Died July 17, 1804,
.E. 66.

A few years since an academy was
conducted by Rev W. L Woodruff in
a large hall which was formerly at
tached to the residence of F A Perry,
Perry's Hall was built to serve as the
gymnasium for the numerous students
Rev W. L. Woodruff was ordained
and installed pastor over the church
April 5, 1876 In many ways he was
unfit for the holy calling, and two years
after ordination a council was called
and the pastoral relation dissolved.

The following is a list of the persons
who have held the office of deacon as
complete as the records show Their
names appear as far as far as possible
in the order in which they were appointed   Joel Hotchkiss, John White,
Benajah Peck, Peter Perkins, Pheno-
has Terrel, Hezekiah Beecher, Jabez
H tchcock, Jesse Bradley, Theophilus
Smith, Clark Hotchkiss, David A
Lounsbury, Edwin N. Clark, Thomas
Horsefall and Clifton D. Rosha

The pulpit is at present supplied by
Rev Mr Case of New Haven He is an
earnest and thrilling speaker, and his
efforts are appreciated by his parishioners

Thus we have traced the principal
vicissitudes of this part of the "church
universal down the stream of time for
over one hundred and forty years   At
times, ever since its incorporation, the
storm and whirlwind have passed over
it, but by the kindness of Providence
it still stands secure and prosperous,
notwithstanding the marked decrease
in the population of Bethany for the
last few decades among its younger
sister churches of the various denominations.

SKETCH BY REV. H. W. JOHNSON

The following historical sketch by Rev. H. W. Johnson published in the Seymour RECORD, Nov. 19, 1896, gives so good a view of the church usages in the olden time, and so many details not before given in the other sketches and compilation, that so much of it is given as is not included in the preceding pages.

There was no preaching here until 1763. There was no meeting house, and as yet no town house. Services were held in the schoolhouse, built 1750, the first one erected in Bethany. * * *

The period of Mr. Hawley's ministry may be said to be the most flourishing and prosperous in the history of the church. It was the period that saw the largest number of influential men. Prominent names were Timothy Peck, Joel Hotchkiss, John White, Isaac Beecher and Daniel Tolles. In piety it was also thorough, even austere, and every action was characterized by fervor and zeal. Religion was pure and hearty. It was a period of strong, intense faith, of firm, unshaken trust, as seen by their persistence during the stress of the Revolutionary War and the years following, but also of good works. There was a jealous care for the things of God, a stern regard for the purity of the church, but also a tender solicitude for one another. The young of the parish were cared for and any delinquent was quickly dealt with. Through the severe trial of the Revolutionary days the faith remained strong and unshaken, and in the face of great hardships they persisted in the work of keeping up preaching and church institutions. During this time the church had paid singers. Expenses were met like modern town expenses by a property rate.

The first church edifice, used for many years until the present building was occupied, stood upon the high hill, just above the house where Mr. James Cotter now lives, and was visible for miles around in almost all directions. It was one of the first landmarks seen by the sailors entering New Haven harbor. It was a rectangular structure, 40x50 feet, with high pulpit, and with benches just beneath the desk for the leading men singers who had places assigned them. The diagram showing the seating arrangements and the assignments is still preserved. About 175 persons were given seats, as many as six or seven in a square pew, showing that at the time the audiences were large. It was voted that a tax of four pence on the pound, payable in flaxseed or other specie acceptable in New York, should be levied. The first meeting was held in it in 1770. It was voted that Isaac Balding, Joel Hotchkiss, Thomas Beecher, etc., should tune the Psalm and that the above choristers should sit together near the foot of the pulpit stairs.

The War of the Revolution made exacting drafts upon the young society. At this time we find the titles Capt., Lieut., Ensign, prefixed to the names of the prominent leaders, and that year (1775) it was voted to pay the salary of Stephen Hawley in provisions, labor or money if wished, the price of wheat being the standard

Later 25 cords of wood was paid as part of his salary. In 1803, being advanced in years, a committee was appointed to visit Mr Hawley and learn on what conditions he would consent to retire Arriving at terms they secured as their next pastor Rev Isaac Jones. A M , evidently a young man of promise and ability as gleaned from his sermons at that time His first sermon after ordination is in print, as also his farewell sermon, preached two years later, in 1806, when a division arising in the church, he was deposed The records contain no statement as to the cause of the difficulty or the charges preferred against him The matter was of such dimensions that the Consociation was appealed to to settle it Charges were made by one Medad Hotchkiss and as the result Mr Jones was obliged to leave the parish and with many others joined the Episcopal church

Tradition has it that certain of the older members and deacons undertook to advise the young man in matrimonial matters, who, rejecting their counsels, married the person of his choice, a Miss Thomas. and brought upon himself their ill wishes which continued to work against him, leading to opposition of his labors and this resulted finally in his deposal

In 1808 about 61 members withdrew There had been a growing difference in religious opinions, other views than those held by the orthodox or Presbyterian church, as this church was then called, and disrupting tendencies began to appear. Those who left joined the Methodist, the Baptist or the Episcopal churches, the latter getting the larger number

About this time effort was made to raise the amount in the church bank as it was called, to $5,000, and a subscription was started, the name of John Thomas heading the list with $750, and Elihu Sanford following with $250, others with amounts from $25 to $200, making it considerably above the amount set as the goal at the start From certain references the church bank had existed for many years. In 1791 the amount in the bank was £430 9s 7d It was increased in 1809

The old meetinghouse having become unserviceable, the matter of building a new one was agitated and finally it was voted to appoint a committee to sell the property known as the old green and add it to amounts raised for the new building It was not until 1832 that the present building was put up In 1866 it was remodeled at a cost of $2,500, and again in 1885 further repairs were made at an outlay of $500

The parsonage for many years was a house not far from the corner to the right of the present church, but in 1850 it was exchanged for the property nearer the church, the society paying $1,600 as the difference in value and also assuming a mortgage for $600, a total of about $2,225

There have been, if I have studied the records aright, four sets of deacons. The first deacons were Joel Hotchkiss and John White, who continued long in office and were strong pillars in the early church These were followed by Dea Jesse Bradley and Dea Jabez Hitchcock These were succeeded by Deacons Clark Hotchkiss and Theop Smith and they by the present incumbents Mr. Oliver Nettleton was clerk when the church records were first kept After him we have Clark Hotchkiss and Theophilus Smith

Faithful in the discharge of all duties, whether town or church, was Mr. Nathan Clark, who for years presided at the church organ, sustaining the musical department of the church efficiently and well

Of the familiar figures of last generation none were more closely identified with every movement in the church and few remembered with more affection as none were held in more reverence than Dea. Clark Hotchkiss and Dea. Theophilus Smith. Elected deacon in 1829 at the age of 85, Dea. Clark Hotchkiss continued the honored officer of the church until his death in 1890, a period of service of over 62 years. In addition to serving as deacon he was also clerk of the church for a major part of his life time. He was a man of thorough piety, modest and retiring though active in anything of general welfare. His name is today the synonym of goodness, virtue and integrity. His religion was of the quiet, retired kind, of thorough purity and deep sincerity. His name was above reproach and everyone was forced to recognize the purity and simplicity of his religious life. Such a life in its consistency could bring only honor to the cause of Christ, as many were led to respect and honor the God of his faith, and the church of his love and labor. While not forward in devising plans for the advancement of the church, he was active in co-operating with any scheme presented which he thought would develop or better it, and threw in his effort to make the plan successful. He died in 1890 at the age of 87, honored and beloved by the community and the church in whose spiritual and material development for over 60 years he had had such part.

His colleague and colaborer, whom the older members remember with an esteem and honor not less great, Theophilus Smith, was equally identified with the church and society. Coming to the town as a young man, he soon showed himself a person of great energy and push, and by reason of his strong character as well as marked efficiency soon took a place of prominence and influence. He was a self-made man, obtaining by hard effort his education. He taught a high school the first in the town, and not unfrequently a person returns from distant parts who sat under him for instruction in those days. He kept a store, and also a tavern, which because of the great amount of travel between the northern villages and cities and New Haven was well patronized. He was a man of wonderful energy and marked vigor. From an active days work he would go to the house and taking up a paper or book spend the evening in the cultivation of his mind. Family worship was constantly kept up in his house. The tavern was never open on Sunday. He was closely connected with the church in many sides of its life and carried with it the same energy and spirit and businesslike ways. He made it the subject of prayer and was constantly anxious for her welfare. His characteristics were great activity and boundless energy, with thorough conscientiousness. His religion possessed the heartiness and fervor carried into his daily life. His life was intense and strong, and though possessing decided opinion and a quiet, active spirit he never dishonored the cause in which he was found a faithful and valiant warrior, ' Moreover it is required in a steward that he be found faithful."

In addition many here will remember the kindly features, the genial paternal bearing of Mr. Amos Hitchcock. Of modest, quiet demeanor he was a man thoroughly conscientious in his discharge of christian obligations. His integrity and the sincerity of his christian life was never questioned. Retiring in habit, he was yet shrewd and keen in mind, faithful in his observance of the Sabbath and by report a true christian.

Closely identified with every movement of the church, deeply interested in everything pertaining to it, and long an officer of the society, was Mr. Justus Peck,

whose faithful attendance at church services and whose constant zeal touching
even the minor matters of her on going are still vividly remembered

During this period the church was served in the ministry by Daniel Butt,
1844-'47, Fosdic Harrison '49-51, Alex Leadbetter '52-'54, Ebenezer Robinson
'54-'60, Seth C Brace '61-'64, and David Elwood '64 '69   During the terms of Mr
Harrison and Mr Mitchell revivals were held which stirred the church and awoke
it to new endeavors and a more earnest, active life

One of the most impressive things in the history is the piety of the early
church   We glean this from the confession of faith, its church covenants and discipline   The confession of faith is remarkably simple and strong   In its broad
and simple statement of view it is more like the liberal creed of today, while in it
there is nothing opposed to the orthodox views of that period   The church covenant is as you will see impressive and solemn.   It reads

"You do now in the presence of God, the dread majesty of heaven and earth,
before angels and men, with the utmost seriousness and sincerity of soul, avouch
the Lord Jehovah to be your God and Supreme Good, through Jesus Christ de-
voting yourself to his fear and service and engaging in dependence upon his
divine and conscientiously and perseveringly to keep his Holy Commandments
You do also solemnly covenant with His church that so long as you remain a
member of it you will walk together with it in christian fellowship in all Gospel
ordinances, and in a conscientious discharge of all christian duties, constantly de-
pending on the Lord Jesus Christ for that gracious assistance which may be need-
ful and sufficient for you"

After neglecting to keep up the society interests for some years, in 1828 a
petition was sent to the General Assembly, which is noteworthy for its expression
of humility and deep contrition   It abounds in statements of regret and remorse
and confession of neglect and deadness   "They have been a stumbling block to
sinners"   "They have failed to manifest brotherly feeling and tenderness among
themselves."   "They have neglected the children of the flock who have been publicly dedicated to God, and have left the sins of their brethren go unreproved"
"They thus seek the forgiveness of the christian brethren, and of the High, Holy
and Heavenly Father"

In discipline under Mr Hawley they were exact   One Jesse Lounsbury appeared and upon refusing to observe the ordinance of the Lord's Supper according
to the rules of the church, it was voted that they obey the command of Christ and
let him be as a heathen man and a publican and that the watch and care of the church
be withdrawn from him   Also voted that "Whereas Rhoda Hotchkiss has given
satisfactory evidence that she has exercised sincere repentence for living a long
time in neglect of christian duty, and for dishonoring the cause of true religion, and
wishes to be received, that she be again cordially received"   One Allen Thomas
makes a confession to the church in these words   "Having been for some years
a member of this church and having lived unworthy of my christian profession I
desire to humble myself before God and his people this day concerning my sins"
Then followed a statement that he has neglected seasons of prayer, absenting
himself from the table of the Lord and the company of his people   "I now repent
of my sins and ask Christ's forgiveness and of the members of the church whom I
have offended"

In many ways the pure and sincere religion of the early church, their tender solicitude for one another, their care and watchfulness over the young of the parish, and their responsibility over the errant members, stand as an example for the church of today. The devotion and loyalty of the older members seems a solemn call to the same firm faith, pure and honest piety and thorough devotion to the church and kingdom of our God and His Christ.

In 1783 a committee was appointed "to assist the Church of England Committee to find a place for them to set a church on."

In 1779 the Society began "to confer with Amity about being made a town." This subject was one of much discussion and negotiation and of some strife in regard to the place of a town house. The town of Woodbridge was incorporated in 1784 and was named in honor of the first minister of the Amity church. The separation of Bethany as a town began to be agitated in 1803 but was not accomplished until May, 1832.

Other names of those who acted in Society business before 1800 are, (placing them in order of time) Jesse Bradley, William Wooding, Deacon Isaac Johnson, Josiah Lounsbury, Deacon Peter Perkins, John Lines, Timothy Hitchcock, Ephraim Turner, Abraham Carrington, Ezra Sperry, Daniel Beecher, Jonathan Andrew, Reuben Sperry, Amos Hitchcock, Jonathan Tuttle, Deacon James Wheeler, Jacob Hotchkiss, Jared Sherman, Edward Perkins, Jesse Beecher, David French, Raymond Sanford, David Thomas, Lamberton Tolles, Roger Peck, John Russell, Medad Hotchkiss, John Thomas, Hezekiah Thomas, Caleb Andrews, Elihu Sanford, Jr., Reuben Perkins, Hezekiah Johnson, Lucas Lines, Jared Tolles, John Wooding, Darius Beecher, Deacon Hezekiah Beecher, Jared Beecher.

In 1804, (Feb 2d), it was "voted that we will give Mr. Isaac Jones, Jr., one hundred pounds annually for three years and then rise five pound a year until it shall amount to one hundred and twenty pounds, to commence at the time of his ordination and to continue as long as he shall continue to supply the pulpit as a minister of the Gospel in this place."

Feb 8, 1804, it was "voted to give Mr. Hawley the interest of the minister's Bank in this place beginning the first of March, 1803, and to continue during his natural life, upon his giving the Society a full discharge from any other demand on sd society from the first day of March 1803."

At the May session of the General Assembly in 1809 the following resolution was adopted:

Whereas, it hath been represented that the members of the Ecclesiastical Society of Bethany, in Woodbridge, have had no legal society meeting for several years. Resolved by this Assembly that John Thomas, Esquire, be, and he is hereby authorized to give said Society six days warning by posting up the same on the Sign Post in said Society before the first Monday of June next, to meet at the meetinghouse in said Society on the said first Monday of June, at 2 o'clock in the afternoon, and when met, to preside in said meeting, and lead said Society to the choice of a Societies' Committee, Clerk and Treasurer, and to do and transact any business proper to be done at said meeting.

At the meeting so called Timothy Hitchcock was chosen clerk and treasurer, and the following society's committee was chosen: John Thomas, Esq., Medad Hotchkiss, Isaac Hotchkiss, Jabez Hitchcock, Jesse Atwater, Demas Sperry.

John Terrell, Silas Hotchkiss and Jesse Bradley were chosen bank committee, and a tax of one cent and five mills was laid on the list of 1808, to be paid by the first of July.

In 1828 there was a great revival, and from March 1st to October 1st thirtytwo were received into membership on confession of faith.

The list of officers and committees elected at the annual meeting held March 1, 1837, is as follows: Theophilus Smith, moderator; Lewis Hine, clerk; Grant Hitchcock, Levi Wooding, Ebenezer Platt, society's committee; Miles Hitchcock, auditor; and Theophilus Smith, first chorister; Hiram Hotchkiss, second chorister; Clark Hotchkiss, third chorister; Clark Hotchkiss and Oliver Nettleton, singing committee.

The church today (1896) has about 50 members. The present officers were elected as follows: Dea. Horsfall in 1883; Dea. Rosha, 1895; church clerk, Edwin N. Clark, 1890.

THE PRESENT CHURCH, BUILT IN 1831.

"RECOLLECTIONS OF EARLY DAYS."

Edwin Buckingham many years ago narrated his "Recollections of Early Days," which were taken down for the Seymour Record, from which we take the following:

"The old meeting house which I first remember, stood on what used to be called "Meeting House Hill," on what is now called the "Shun Pike Road," in contradistinction of the "Turnpike" on the east side of the town It was a large building—larger by far than the present Congregational church—but yet not too large for the attendance, as it was the only church in which constant services were held in that section of the country, and the inhabitants were by law compelled to attend church. This old church was torn down the year 1830, and the timbers were used in building the present church on the hill north of it.

"This old church was built of large heavy timbers, with a belfry on the north end. The interior had plastered walls, a box pulpit in the west end high enough to permit the preacher to look into the gallery, and box pews with heavy doors, both in the gallery and on the floor. The seats were bare and straight-backed, and such a thing as a cushion on a church seat would have been looked upon as a mortal sin.

It may not be uninteresting to the reader to recount a few incidents here which illustrate that human nature has not materially changed in seventy years even in New England. Some of the young folks desired to have some fun at the clergy-man's expense, and so they drove a large flock of geese belonging to Squire San-ford, into the church early Saturday evening, and up into the pulpit and carefully closed the door. In due time, on Sunday morning, the congregation assembled and the minister with solemn tread marched down the aisle, ascended the steps and

INTERIOR OF THE CHURCH.

opened the pulpit door. Immediately a hissing and quacking sound filled the church, and the frightened dominie sprang backward and aside as down the steps and up the aisle marched the geese with a gabble that was perfectly deafening. The dea-cons assisted in driving the geese out of doors, and after awhile order was restored and the service proceeded with. Great efforts were made to find out the perpetra-tors of this act, but without success. Nevertheless the neighborhood was satified who were the parties concerned in the act, and, if he has not recently died, one of them is still living in New Haven.

Another circumstance connected with the church was the stealing of the tongue of the church bell and hiding it under Dr Castle's haystack. In the spring when he fed to the bottom of the stack the tongue was found. A court of inquiry was held to inquire into the case and half a dozen of the boys of the town were arraigned on the charge, among whom was Jehial Castle son of Dr Castle, Edson Sperry, and Harry Tolles, son of Daniel Tolles. But no one was convicted.

"Tithing men" were annually elected, whose duty it was to see that order was kept in the church. They were usually the most austere men of the society, and we boys looked upon them with an eye of dread and dislike which they at times seemed to heartily return. If a boy whispered to another in church behold there was the tithing man at his side in a moment, with scowling face and threatening words, and if he smiled during the services he was sure of an admonition from them immediately afterward. One of the most austere of these officers was Deacon Tolles, living a little way south of the church. He was quite an elderly man and wore a wig with a long cue hanging behind. He was the terror of the boys. One Sunday quite a number of them were in a pew alone, and the Deacon suspecting they meant mischief went into the seat with them, carrying along a short riding whip. The boys were quite good until they threw the Deacon off his guard, and then one of them managed to tie the end of the whiplash to his cue. This accomplished they were quiet for a few minutes, and then began a concerted noise which caused the Deacon to flourish his whip, and immediately the congregation were edified by seeing a wig flying through the air and the Deacon standing and feeling his bald pate in a most bewildered manner.

CHRIST CHURCH.

On the 26th day of August, 1785, the Rev Bela Hubbard, rector of Trinity church, New Haven, began missionary work in Bethany by conducting divine service and baptising seven infants in the "Church House," a small building situated on what is now an unfrequented road, about a mile east of Bethany center The people were too few in number and too poor to finish this building, so that it was never lathed and plastered Through cracks in its walls the wind whistled and the snow blew And yet, without heat from any source except from foot stoves, which a few had who could afford them in the coldest of weather, on the Lord's Day as many were gathered together to worship God as could find sittings on the rude and backless benches

At noon they went to a near neighbor's to warm themselves, eat dinner, take out of their foot stoves the dead coals and put in live ones for the afternoon service Although Mr Hubbard continued to officiate in this churchhouse until the end of his rectorship in New Haven, it seems that no steps were taken to organize a legal society of the Episcopal church in Bethany until Nov 29th, 1799 Then twentytwo persons, including four whose names were Tuttle, affixed their names to the following

We, the undersignors, professing ourselves Episcopalians and claiming the privileges of the afore mentioned laws, do designate ourselves by enrollment, and are hereafter to be known by the name of Bethany Episcopal Society, holding the right to transact all matters in our own body agreeable to law "

On April 1st, 1800, in answer to a summons issued by a justice of the peace, the signers to this declaration met at the churchhouse and elected a clerk and a committee for the society They were then ready to do business as a religious body according to law, and their first act was to vote to tax themselves one cent on a dollar for the support of religious services, the tax to be laid on the grand list of 1799   It is quite surprising to us in these days to find how ready and willing they were that their religion should cost them something

Until taxation for the support of public worship was abolished by act of the legislature, they continued to tax themselves, nearly all the time, three cents and sometimes four cents on the dollar, so that one of their number, whose property was assessed at $1,000, had to pay for religious purposes $30 and $40 a year

The first wardens were Uri Tuttle and Daniel Hotchkiss, elected April 17th, 1800   On the 16th of December, 1800, it was "voted that we keep church in the schoolhouse near Ely Todd's," the grandfather of Street, Dwight and Jasper B Todd, who came from Northford in 1783 and lived near the present home of J B Todd Evidently the interior of the churchhouse had become too windy for services in cold weather   Soon after this the old churchhouse was sold, and the proceeds of the sale were kept to apply toward the building of a new house   Public worship was then held all the time in schoolhouses, laymen reading the services when no clergymen could be had

On the 9th of January, 1808, the society decided to build a church near the house of Roger Peck, now F A Perry's place, 48 feet in length and 36 feet in width, with a cupola   In the year 1809 one fourth of an acre of ground was deeded to the society by Roger Peck, for which they paid him $50, and on which the church, represented in the accompanying picture, now stands

On the 2d of May, 1809, Alling Carrington was appointed by the society as an agent to present to the General Assembly a petition asking that body to grant them a lottery of $2,000 to finish the church   But there is no evidence that, in this case, this then quite customary plan of getting money for religious and charitable purposes was ever carried into effect   The desired amount appears to have been raised by subscription and promissory notes   Perhaps it was the pressing need of money that caused the appointment of a committee at this time to sell tallow and candles belonging to the church

At a meeting of the society on the 6th day of November, 1809, it was "voted that this meeting consider Isaac Jones a person worthy and well qualified for a gospel minister, and wish that he

may be introduced into the Episcopal order agreeable to the rules
in such cases made and provided." This vote of recommendation
was the outcome of a sensational event which took place at about
this time among the Presbyterians.

Isaac Jones, their pastor, for the offense of coming among
them a bachelor and marrying one of their number, and for various

CHRIST CHURCH AND RECTORY.

other reasons, was disliked by some of them. So intense did the
feeling against him grow to be, that it even entered that indispen-
sable thing of uncertainty—the country choir, and affected it to
such a degree that it refused to open its mouth in praise to God,
when Mr. Jones was present. Every time after he had given out a
hymn and read its verses, the choir was silent. Then it was that
the good Deacon Phinehas Terrill immortally distinguished him-

self as a soloist; for he arose, and going to the front in the choir
loft, sang the whole hymn through alone   The result of this
trouble was that the Rev. Isaac Jones, with his two deacons, Phinehas Terrill and Hezekiah Beecher, seceded and went over to the
Episcopal church, taking with them sixty Presbyterians

This accounts for the fact that since that time the Episcopal
society has been the strongest religious body in Bethany, and for
many years the only one able to support a resident clergyman
Mr Jones was rector of the church here in 1810 and 1811

The frame of the present church edifice was raised May 12th, 1809.
While this church was being built regular services were held
in Darius Beecher's hall, or ball room, as it was then called
This building still stands on the "Shun Pike" road, just north of the
churches, and was later owned by Orrin Wheeler

On the 18th of April, 1814, the society voted to hire preaching
three fourths of the time   When there was no minister, Archibald
Perkins and Reuben Judd were appointed to read the service, and
the following to read the sermon   Timothy Ball, Lysias Beecher,
Roger Peck, John Russell, George Peck, Eber Lines and Hezekiah Thomas

On the 16th of January, 1810, a committee of seven men was
elected "to seat the church, on the list of 1808, showing such respect to age as they shall think proper "   The debt of respect due
from all to the aged was always paid in full in those days   Thus
sittings were assigned to members of the congregation from time to
time, until on the second day of June, 1828, it was voted to sell the
seats annually to the highest bidders   The society then purchased
one half of a ship and gave it to Archibald Perkins for his services
as chorister   The church received its name, Christ church, on the
2d of September, and was consecrated on the 19th of September,
1810

Near the beginning of the last quarter of the 19th century, so
long a time had elapsed since any repairs had been made on the
building that it had become almost dilapidated   It was estimated
that $2,000 would be needed to put it in fair condition,   The people
were determined not to get into debt for their house of worship
The society met time and again to consider ways of raising money
It seemed impossible to get the amount required   S R Woodward had done hard and faithful work as collector, but had secured

INTERIOR OF CHRIST CHURCH.

only $1,500   It was believed that no more could be obtained   S.
G Davidson, at the request of the society, then undertook the task
of collecting, and the $1,500 soon increased to $2,300   Then work
was begun

The two tablets, on which were inscribed the Creed, the Lord's
Prayer, and the Ten Commandments, were taken from the chancel
wall and stored in the woodroom of the rectory   These tablets had
come from England, found a place in Trinity church, New Haven,
when it stood on Church street, and when Trinity church was built
on the Green they were given to the church in Bethany   They
were returned in 1885, and are now to be seen, bright with new
gilding and varnish, in the vestibule of Trinity church

These tablets and the galleries and windows are the only
objects that still exist to show how the interior of Christ church
looked before its renovation in 1875   Then its high pulpit, with
stairway, was torn down, new flooring was laid over the old,
new and most inviting pews and cushions were put in position, new
carpets laid, a beautiful and costly stained glass window placed
over an appropriate scriptural sentence in the chancel, and the
walls, ceiling and woodwork were tastefully kalsomined and painted.
And when all was done, on the 14th of September, 1875, a great
gathering of the clergy from all parts of the state assembled here,
with a crowd of people, and the church was reconsecrated to the
worship of God

Again in the year 1875 the building was a in deplorable condition
for want of paint   At the same time there was urgent need of an
organ to take the place of one which had been given to the church
many years ago by Seymour Tuttle   Some desired that an effort
should be made first to raise money to paint the church, and then that
a small sum should be expended for a reed organ   Others wanted a
pipe organ, but cared not for the paint   S G Davidson declared
that it would be easier to raise the money needed to paint the building, if at the same time subscriptions were solicited for a pipe organ.
He was appointed collector, and within two weeks he obtained
$1,600   The church building was then thoroughly painted, all neces-
sary repairs were made, and an organ purchased from Hook &
Hastings of Boston, at a cost of $1,200

Christ church stands a monument of the piety and self-sacrific-
ing spirit of men and women of past generations, and of generations

still living, who were and are the really great ones of the town, for
the day of judgment will show the great ones here to have been
those who have faithfully worked for God's honor and glory

The present officers of this church, February, 1901, are

Lewis F Morris, rector

F W Beecher, clerk

T D Davidson, treasurer

Noyes Wheeler and J B Todd, wardens

S G Davidson, E O Pardee and George Selleck, vestrymen

(ABOVE BY REV L F MORRIS)

The following entry was found in the parochial record of Trinity
Church, New Haven, the entry having been made by Rev Bela
Hubbard, then rector of Trinity church "Bethany, Woodbridge,
August 26th, 1785, opened ye Episcopal church by ye name of X
church and preached, &c , and baptized 7 infants "

The following list of Bethany names found in the above men-
tined parochial register under the heads of baptisms, marriages and
burial, show which were the families then included in the church

Beecher - Anna, Benjamin, Betsey, Comfort, Eli, Elizabeth,
Trasene, Grace, Hannah, Thompson, John, John Dunlap Laban
Smith, Mary, Mariner, Moses, Moses, Jr , Rachel, Wealthy,
Wealthy Ann, William, Parmelee, Wilmot

Tolles—Abram, Chauncey, Dan, Deborah, Elizabeth, Elnathan,
Francis, Hannah, Henry, James, John, Lydia, Martha, Patty, Sarah,
Thomas, William

Todd —Charlotte, Law, Eunice, George, Joseph, Lowly, Lucinda, Hansel, Michael, Sarah, Thaddeus

Perkins—Archibald, Arch, Abner, Hulday, Sarah, Samuel, Uri

Sperry -Dan, David, Dennis, Eber, Esther, George, Isaac,
Joel, Lois, Lyman, Mary, Miles, Parmelee, Sarah, Susan Zynni,
Margaret, Mary, Peggy, Polly, Richard, Samuel, Sarah, Stephen,
Thomas, Uri, William, Zeruiah

Tuttle—Abigail, Abraham, Amin, Miles, Asahel, Bethel, Bethia,
Charles, David, Dorothy, Elizabeth, Hannah, Eunice, Fannie,
George, Harriet, Henrietta, Henry, Hopkins, Hezekiah, Isaac,
Jane, Catherine John, Todd, Jotham, Julia, Lucy

The original 'church-house" was on the hill south of the residence of Frederick Beecher, on the corner as the road runs east-

ward, which is known as the church corner   The following have
had ministerial charge of the parish.   Rev Bela Hubbard of New
Haven, Rev Isaac Jones, (1809–1811,) Rev Mr Ives of Cheshire,
Rev. Mr Prindle of Oxford, Rev Joseph Clark, during whose
pastorate of four or five years the rectory was built, Rev Mr
Curtis-, Rev Mr Rouse, Rev Mr Potter, who during a pastorate
of two years devoted great energy toward clearing the incum-
brances which weighed so heavily upon the society, succeeding
before his departure in showing a clean balance sheet, Rev Mr
Zell of Litchfield, Rev Josephus Tragitt, and Rev L F. Morris

TOPOGRAPHICAL AND HISTORICAL

What is now the town of Bethany was in colonial times included in the towns of New Haven and Milford If a straight line be drawn on the map of Bethany along the Round Hill Road to where it would terminate at Beacon Cap it will represent the line which formerly was the boundary between New Haven and Milford. The parish of Amity was incorporated in 1739, and included the present towns of Woodbridge and Bethany This parish was divided in 1762, and the parish of Bethany was incorporated, covering nearly the same area as does the present town of Bethany

Bethany Center is about ten miles from New Haven and twelve from Waterbury It is beautifully located on a plateau six hundred feet above the sea level, overlooking an irregular but continuous valley reaching to the lowlands along the seashore. Directly to the east the hillside drops several hundred feet to a wooded valley, beyond which the verdant hills rise again to a considerable height, their sides but sparsely dotted with farmhouses To the westward there is but a slight rise to a broad stretch of arable land including some of the finest farms in the town

Bethany Center includes the two older churches, the Congregational and the Episcopal, the latter with a rectory, the Hall, once the Bethany Academy building, the fine old residence now owned by Frederick Perry, and until recently the old Sperry homestead, which had long been falling into decay A little south is the Hitchcock house, in which the postoffice was kept for many years, the residence of James Megin, the district schoolhouse and the Center Cemetery, and a little farther south the residence of James Cotter, the Capt Dayton house of Revolutionary times To the north are the residences of Deacon Thomas Horsfall and the fine old mansion now owned by the Misses Wheeler, described on pages 99-101 A little farther north is the famous Lebanon Hill, over which the main road leads and on which are several fine old residences. From this hill a view of Long Island Sound may be obtained

Near the foot of the northerly slope of this hill formerly stood the noted Perkins hotel, formerly the principal place of rest and refreshment on the turnpike from New Haven to Waterbury

The eastern boundary of the town is formed by a natural barrier, West Rock Ridge Should one walk a mile or two from where the summit of the ridge is crossed by the Woodbridge town line, he will find an object of interest in the lonely mountain road which winds over the hills On the north side of the road the mountain rises abruptly and the summit is crested with a grove of pines which fact has given it the name of Pine Ledge About a mile beyond this point the mountain is crossed by a deep ravine, known as the "Gap " Across the Gap the ridge is called Mad Mare's Hill It is over eight hundred feet in height and from its crest a fine view may be obtained

Farther to the north is Gaylord Mountain, and at its foot another road finds its precipitous way over the hill A mile or two farther brings one to the highest peak of the whole ridge, Mt Sanford, over 900 feet in height, and upon its summit the towns of Bethany, Hamden, Cheshire and Prospect meet From this summit there is a superb view in every direction

Leaving West Rock Ridge a series of hills known as the Beacon Mountains begin and extend in a westerly direction to the Naugatuck river, where in conjunction with the hills on the opposite side they form a deep gorge through which the river flows These hills abound with localities historically interesting, and many a quaint legend is attached to its deep gorges and wild glens

Perched on the highest point of the mountains is a huge, anvil-shaped boulder called Beacon Cap, which was probably left there during the glacial period In early colonial times it was known simply as the "Beacon " That it was well known and pointed out by the settlers as a prominent landmark before the close of the seventeenth century is shown by the frequent mention in the records of that time It has formed a natural bound for several of the older towns of the county, and at present is a boundary stone between Bethany and Naugatuck In troublous times with the Indians it was included in a system of signals maintained by the colonists, and fires were built upon it, from which fact the mountains derived their name The rock is frequently visited for the beautiful view which may be obtained from the summit It is difficult to climb the rugged mountainside, the way leading up a steep, narrow gorge down which a rill winds its tortuous course. This gorge terminates in a circular, rock-walled space, a difficult path up its steep sides bringing the view-seeker nearly to his goal where the Beacon Cap looms up before him, and the summit once gained repays one for his exertions. To north, south, east and west the view extends, and perhaps the prettiest of all is the Beacon Valley in which lies the village of Straitsville.

THE PERKINS HOTEL.

The only large natural lake which Bethany can boast is that of Lebanon, and that is fast dwindling in size. It is however one of the interesting features, and is situated in the center of a large swamp in the northern part of the town. The swamp is deeply fringed by tall and stately white cedars, so that it is necessary, in entering the swamp, to pass through labyrinth of trees as tall and straight as the pillars of a vast cathedral, branchless to a considerable height, where they branch out into heavy foliage, which casts a deep gloom upon the vaulted avenues of the forest, where silence is broken only by the echoes of the voice or the distant cawing of the crows. Traversing this swamp is somewhat difficult since it is necessary to leap from the moss-covered roots of one tree to the next over pools of murky water But if one perseveres until he emerges into the open space within the circle of the cedars he will be well repaid for his trouble as a scene breaks upon the vision which will never be forgotten Before the visitor, stretches a level plain of peculiar yellow moss into which the foot sinks to the knee at every step, and this soft carpet is dotted with many species of the much sought for pitcher plant, many botanists visiting the swamp to obtain specimens of this remarkable plant

Near the center of this mossy plain is a lake of blackest water, the home of countless turtles who are continually thrusting their heads above the water, while beyond is a background of the tall cedars which encircle the mossy plain Long ago John Thomas owned the swamp and kept a boat upon it for pleasure parties The number of Indian relics which have been found in the fields adjoining the swamp lead one to believe that it was a favorite resort of the aborigines Visits to the swamp are attended with danger and should only be made by those experienced in such places or in parties who can rescue one another in case of mishap

There are however several large artificial lakes in the town, made for the purpose of reservoirs for supplying water to the city of New Haven Among these is Lake Bethany, situated in the eastern part of the town, on West River The dam was built in 1892, by the New Haven Water Company, and forms one of the largest reservoirs in the water system of that city The next in size is Lake Chamberlain, which is situated about a mile west of the former

The northern section of the town is drained by the Beacon Hill river and Lebanon Brook. The former is one of the largest streams in Bethany, and several mills have been built along its banks At the point where it flows through the Straits, a narrow gorge through the Beacon Mountains, it is very picturesque

In the eastern part of Bethany is West River Its source is at the base of Mount Sanford, and it flows into Lake Bethany For two or three miles beyond the lake its course is through a deep ravine From thence it flows across the plains of Woodbridge toward Long Island Sound Sargents River, a tributary of West River, flows through the center of the town Lake Chamberlain is on this stream Bladens Brook forms a part of the southwestern boundary and has a branch called Hopp Brook These streams have furnished power for sawmills, gristmills and cidermills.

Among the early industries of the town was the manufacture of wool. The fleeces from the sheep upon our hills were in part worked up at the homes of the people. At first yarn was spun on the spinning wheel and knit into warm stockings and mittens, and in some cases was woven on hand looms by the industrious wives and daughters of the farmers who had cared for the sheep on whose backs the wool had grown.

ANOTHER VIEW OF THE PERKINS HOTEL.

But as time fled on some more rapid method of manipulating the wool was sought, and a woolen mill was established in North Bethany, where the wool was carded by waterpower, and the homespun woolen cloth was "dressed." This mill was purchased by Bennett Twitchell from the estate of Jonathan Stoddard about 1844. Mr. Twitchell carried on the business until his death in 1853, and his oldest son, George B. Twitchell, then carried on the business for a few years.

Since the incorporation of the town in 1832, there have been only six town clerks, Hezekiah Thomas, 1832-44; Edwin Lines, 1845; Asa C. Woodward, 1846-50; Jason W. Bradley, 1851-54; Nathan Clark, 1855-79; and Edwin N. Clark, since 1879.

The selectmen have been Andrew Beecher, Harry French, Lewis Lines, Miles French, P. B. Hine, Enos Perkins, Darius Driver, Sidney Sperry, Justus Peck, Miles French, Ezra S. Sperry, Andrew T. Hotchkiss, Marcus W. Bradley, Dennis Beecher, Robert

Clark, Guy Perkins, Milo Beecher, Edwin Buckingham, Henry E. Lounsbury, Dwight N Clark, Buel Buckingham, Edwin Pardee, Jason W Bradley, Henry E Lounsbury, Theophilus Smith, E. O Pardee, Horace Tolles, Anthony H Stoddard, Abel Prince, Leverett Shares, Guy Perkins, Dennis Beecher, Robert Clark, David Carrington, Andrew J Doolittle, Adrian C Rosha, Samuel R. Woodward, Samuel G Davidson, Charles C Perkins, David Carrington, Jasper B Todd, Frederick W. Beecher, Dwight L Humiston, Harry F Peck, Arthur H Doolittle, Jerome A. Downs, Noyes Andrew, Wm L Wooding, Edwin G Pardee

Jason W Bradley was Judge of Probate from the formation of the probate district in 1844 until the fall of 1856, Andrew Beecher 1856 to 1863, Nathan Clark 1863 to 1879, and Edwin N Clark since 1879

THE CHURCH BELLS

The bells which have called the people to services in the two churches at the center have each done duty for about half a century High in their towers they have rung in times of peace, in war, or to spread the alarm of fire They have spoken at one time to tell of a happy wedding, and at another to sadly toll out the death of an inhabitant The bell of Christ church probably weighs nearly half a ton It was cast in a foundry in New Haven in 1858. It is said to have been recast from the old bell which was placed in the church a century ago

The bell of the Congregational church, which is the older of the two, has a very clear, loud tone, that can be heard in all parts the town On the bell is the following inscription, made when the bell was cast —"A Meneeley & Son, West Troy, N Y., 1851 1015 lbs, Key B Congregational Church, Bethany, Conn "

This bell succeeded the old one, which had been used for nearly one hundred years In the Revolutionary War it had been rung by Dr Hooker's negro slave, Scipio, to alarm the inhabitants of Bethany Parish, March 15, 1781, the morning after the raid of Alexander Graham and his tory soldiers from Long Island, this signal having been previously agreed upon in case of danger

The following is from the "Recollections of Early Days," by
Edwin Buckingham, published in the SEYMOUR RECORD in 1881.

"In my early days for an individual to transgress church rules
or state laws with any approach to the impunity with which they
are now violated, would be to subject himself to fines and imprison-
ments, and unbearable social ostracism The real "Blue Laws,"
so called, (not the exaggerated counterfeits which have been so
extensively circulated), were yet quite rigidly enforced, and though
many of them were repealed about the time I arrived at manhood,
I can remember when the mere mention of any change in them
sufficed to bring a storm of pulpit rhetoric that was sure to squelch
the offender Furthermore, the opinions of the clergy were heeded,
and most generally accepted by the whole community as the
correct way of looking at things It is hardly necessary to speak
of the change seventy years has wrought in this respect Then the
clergy were right around with and among the people, visiting and
praying with them daily, and inquiring concerning and giving
council about all the common things of life and I have often
thought that this was the source of their influence, and their failure
to continue their labors zealously in that direction the cause of the
decline of church power

"An incident which I remember will illustrate the zealous
manner in which the church executed the laws which the state had
enacted through its influence. It was a statute that every man
must attend church somewhere a certain number of times during
the year, and failing to do so, the deacons of the Congregational
church were empowered to cite him before them, try him, and in-
flict such fine or imprisonment as they found the case demanded
My father's near neighbor, Hezekiah Hotchkiss was a pretty good
sort of a man, but did not attend church anywhere in particular
and was therefore presumably by law under the spiritual super-
vision of the Congregational deacons A tally of his delinquences
having been kept by these falcon-eyed keepers of public morals, it
was discovered at the close of the year that he had fallen behind
the required number of attendances, and he was accordingly cited
to appear before them The case was duly tried, and not being
able to disprove the charge he was severely reprimanded and fined
quite heavily Hotchkiss made a strong appeal against the judge-
ment, but the inexorable deacons turned the screws right down on

him, and brought him to time and made him pay the fine.   Shortly
afterwards he called at my father's house, and being joked about
the circumstance declared that this proceeding had decided him
never to enter a church again except to comply with the letter of
the law and avoid being fined

"Another instance which I remember is this —The statute provided that all the laws touching the observance of the Sabbath be
applied to Fast Day, and the annual proclamation announced that
"Labor and vain recreation is by law prohibited."   There were
two grand jurors, Abel Lines and Minot Collins, strict churchmen,
who lived in our part of the town, who took it upon themselves to
see that the law was carried out.   One Fast Day a number of boys
got together and went down into a back lot to play ball, fully half
a mile away from the nearest house   Somehow Collins learned of
the fact, and the boys were all summoned before his terrible
presence   To such as appeared he administered scathing rebukes
for their Godless conduct, and he imposed and collected heavy fines
upon those who did not appear.

"Notwithstanding the rigidly of those laws and the uncom-
promising manner in which they were executed, I am free to con-
fess that I believe they produced a more beneficial result than the
lax manner in which they are at present administered   There was
little of the lawless brawling, so common now, to be found anywhere then, and what did occur was visited with quick and unflinch-
ing punishment.   Honesty and uprightness were virtues expected
from every man, and there was no winking at a vice because a man
gave liberally to the church   Young men were brought up to
believe that loafing, not labor, was dishonorable , and a girl was
not considered so much better than her mother that she was
allowed to dawdle in the parlor while the latter slaved in the kitchen , good hours were the rule, and courtships did not require a
secrecy which shut both father and mother from confidence.   In
short, if my notions are not too old fashioned for modern belief,
the puritanism of my early days made better men and women than
the average of the present day "

MARRIAGES.

FROM THE RECORDS OF CHRIST CHURCH:

1836

April 17, Wm H Turner of New Haven and Jane Mix of Hamden.

Nov 13, Jobamah E Gunn, Waterbury, and Rebecca A Hotchkiss, Bethany

Dec 18, Alonzo Warner, Hamden, and Ruth Chatfield, Bethany

1837.

Jan 1, Elias N Clark, Waterbury, and Minerva C Mentes, Bethany

Feb 12, Newel Lounsbury and Jennette Hungerford both of Bethany

July 23, Willet Bradley of Courtlandville, N. Y , and Harriet T Hotchkiss, Bethany.

Sept. 2, Amri B Peck and Minerva Nettleton, both of Bethany.

Sept 10, Stephen Hotchkiss, Jr , Bethany, and Abigail Hotchkiss, Prospect

Oct 8, Willis Doolittle, Hamden and Abigail Hitchcock, Woodbridge

Oct 21, Howel Beecher and Adaline Burnham, both of Bethany.

1838

Jan 1, Allen B L Meyart, Auburn, N Y , and Huldah Perkins, Bethany

Jan 7, Henry A, Smith and Catherine E Bradley, both of Bethany.

Jan 21, Edmond B W. Hitchcock and Angeline Terrell, both of Bethany

March 14, Alonzo Sperry and Rebecca Hotchkiss, both of Bethany

March 15, Joseph Hale, Suffield, Mass , and Juliette Hicock, Woodbridge

March 20, Enos Beecher and Lucy L. Russell, both of Bethany.

Sept 16, Stephen Wooding and Mira Kimball, both of Bethany

Sept 15, John Tucker, Waterbury, and Maria Perkins, Bethany.

Dec. 24, Charles Perkins, Bethany, and Mary A Meriam, Waterbury

1839

Jan 13, Jarias B Hotchkiss and Eunice Russell, both of Bethany

Jan. 25, Stephen Bradley, Prospect, and Thirza Gibbard, Waterbury.

June 26 Noah N Perkins and Maria Lounsbury, both of Waterbury.

Sept. 3, Thomas N. Taylor of Granby and Polly P Allen of Woodbridge

Sept. 26, Jesse Hotchkiss and Caroline Lounsbury, both of Bethany.

Oct 6, Beecher D. Hotchkiss and Betsey Perkins, both of Bethany.

Oct. 16, Timothy Lounsbury of Bethany, and Sarah Newton of Westville

Oct. 27, Albert Driver and Harriet A Allen, both of Bethany.

1840.

Jan 5, Daniel Wilmot of Waterbury and Gertie O. Handry of Hamden

April 13, Benjamin A. Clarke of Middlebury and Mary Gaylord of Hamden.

April 17, Francis Rhub of New Haven and Harriet L. H N. Rhoska of Bethany.

April 11, Timothy Fowler of Woodbridge and Mary E. Stevens of Bethany

Sept. 13, Edwin Lines and Mary A. Castle, both of Bethany.

Sept 13, Jared Hotchkiss of Bethany and Amy French of Prospect.

Oct 11, William F Gilyard of Derby and Wealthy A Hotchkiss of Bethany

1841.

March 14, Samuel French of Waterbury and Charry Bradley of Bethany

April 4, George Hotchkiss and Laura Sperry, both of Bethany.

Sept 14, George H Durrie of New Haven and Sarah A. Perkins of Bethany

Sept 20, Lucius Russell and Elizabeth L. Thomas, both of Bethany.

Nov 7, Wales F Perkins and Eliza E Tolles, both of Bethany

1842

March 29, Jeremiah Collins and Nora N Lounsbury, both of Bethany

1843

Jan 19, D. W. Russell and Henrietta M Collins, both of Bethany.

April 2, Buel Buckingham and Henrietta Beecher, both of Bethany

April 10, Harmon Allen and Rebecca Lounsbury, both of Bethany.

Sept. 25, Henry Judd and Hannah French, both of Prospect

Oct. 1, David Ford of Westville, and Sarah M. Umberfield of Bethany

Oct. 9, Nathan Prince of Bethany and Hannah Sherman of New-
town

Nov 13, Burton Mallery of New Haven and Mary Beecher of
Bethany

1844.

Sept 18, Richard Day of Illinois, and Frances N Thomas of
Bethany

Oct 6, Benjamin Bronson of North Carolina and Polly J Perkins
of Bethany

Dec 25, Wm C White and Harriet Prince, both of Bethany

1846.

Feb 22, Guy Beecher and Sarah Ann Chatfield, both of Bethany.

Aug 2, Geo W French of New Haven and Ellen S Scott of
Naugatuck

Dec 7, David Clark and Charlotte Seeley, both of Bethany

Dec 25, Adna Hotchkiss and Elizabeth Perkins, both of Bethany.

Dec 25, Isaac Perkins and Emily Todd, both of Bethany

1847

Nov 7, Samuel Todd of North Haven and Pamelia I Chatfield of
Bethany

1848.

March 5, DeWitt C. Castle of Humphreysville, and Sarah F
Hotchkiss of Bethany

May 17, George H. Alling of Orange, and Martha Sperry of Bethany.

Sept 16, Edwin Terrill and Eveline Smith, both of Naugatuck.

MARRIAGES BY REV HENRY ZELL

Oct 9, Wales F Perkins of Bethany, and Maria L. Clark of Woodbridge

Oct 22, Noyes Wheeler and Charry S. Tuttle, both of Bethany.

1849

July 29, George Northrop of Bethany and Laura E. Truesdale of
Humphreysville

Oct. 21, Charles A Smith of Orange and Julia E. Sperry of Bethany

Nov 11, John M Sperry of Woodbridge and Harriet Jane Sperry
of Bethany

Dec 11, Benjamin P. Chatfield and Sarah E Judd, both of Bethany.

1850

June 16, Nathaniel Langdon Proctor of Woodbury and Elizabeth
Tyrrell of Bethany

June 16, David A. Burnham of Bethany and Emily G. Downs of Woodbridge

Nov 10, Geo. L. Woodruff of Woodbridge and Margaret Burnham of Bethany.

Nov. 21, Joseph William Bradley and Mary J Neal, both of Woodbridge.

1851.

Jan. 19, Joseph O Hubbell of Oxford and Lucy Ann Beach of Cheshire.

April 14, Andrew Johnson of Humphreysville and Ann Elizabeth Davis of Bethany.

April 18, Verus Candee of Naugatuck and Mira Wooding of Bethany.

May 4, Orange W. Race of Hamden and Mary L. Downs of Bethany.

May 4, Silas Wilmot, Jr., of Wallingford, and Mrs Laura Brooks of Bethany

Oct 22, William S Beecher of Prospect and Mary A Sperry of Bethany.

1852.

Feb. 15, Harpin N. Hotchkiss and Charlotte E. Alling, both of Bethany

April 18, Dennis Beecher and Mary Jane Clark (adopted daughter of Nelson Clark).

April 25, William I Pierpont of Waterbury and Mary Grace Beecher of Bethany

May 6, David A. Lounsbury of Bethany and Susan M. Doolittle of of Hamden

May 9, Amasa B Brooks of Cheshire and Elizabeth M. Wooding of Bethany

Nov 14, Jarvis Bronson of Derby and Lucy L Beecher of Bethany.

Nov 18, Jacob W Wilcox of New Haven and Charlotte E. Hulburt of Waterbury

1853

Jan 10, Eli H. Wakelee of Derby and Eunice A Chatfield of Bethany

Feb 8, Wales C. Dickerman of Hamden and Cecil Todd of Bethany.

Feb 20, Charles C. Perkins and Jane B Perkins, both of Bethany,

April 17, Henry N. Johnson of Westville and Sylvia Northop of Woodbridge.

Oct 13, John H. Sherwood of Fairfield and Selina P Beecher of Bethany, (by the Rev John M Guion)

VITAL STATISTICS. 53

1855.
MARRIAGES BY REV CHARLES J. TODD.
May 20, Archibald A. Perkins and Mrs Minerva Scoville, both of Bethany.

1856
April 5, John Russell and Hannah Hotchkiss, both of Bethany.

1857.
MARRIAGES BY REV. JAMES ADAMS
Feb 7, Street B Todd of New Haven, and Sarah Ann Hotchkiss of Bethany.

1858
MARRIAGES BY REV. F B WOODWARD
Aug 19, Levi Marks of Bethany, and Mrs Emeline Pierpont of New Haven.

Sept. 25, George W Woodward and Margaret L Sperry, both of Bethany

1859.
Feb 3, Theodore A Shepard and Ellen L. Ramsdell, both of Chatham

June 10, Albert Sperry and Grace Russell, both of Bethany.

June 10, Dr E P Woodward and Eliza D Sperry, both of Bethany (by Rev Mr. Coley of Westville)

July 10, Franklin B Atwater and Elizabeth Barnes, both of Bethany.

Dec. 22, Charles Austin, Bethany, and Laura C Tuttle, New Haven

1860
Jan 15, W Herbert French and Mary S Carrington, both of Bethany

April 29, Charles E Wooding and Elvira C Clinton, both of Woodbridge

—— Militus Huxford of Ansonia and Kate L Hale of Woodbridge

Oct 7, Lewis Hitchcock and Valma Hine, both of Woodbridge.

Nov 12, Lauren E Cook of Cheshire and Caroline E Perkins of Bethany

1861
May 15, Henry M Tuttle and Nellie M Sears, both of Woodbridge

1862
June 15, Martyn P. Merrill of Orange and Hannah A Brown of Bethany

Aug 13, Charles W. Tyrrell of New Haven and Mary A Norton of Prospect.

Aug. 24, Seth Woodward and Nellie J. Sackett. both of Bethany.

1863

—— Abner Warner of Hamden and Laura A. Hitchcock of Bethany.

BY REV. H S ATWATER.

June 2, George L Smith and Martha E. Lines, both of Naugatuck.

1864

Jan 17, Theron Eustice Allen and Rosella R Russell, both of Bethany.

March 12, Thomas Palmer and Jennett Wooding, both of Bethany.

Dec 24, Horatio N Clark of Prospect, and Laura DeE H Perkins. of Bethany.

1865.

Jan 18, Charles Tucker and Mrs Harriet Taylor, both of Harwinton.

Sunday before Easter, April 9 George Herbert Allen of Hamden, and Almeda E. Buckingham of Bethany

April 9, Henry A Doolittle of Hamden and Emma L. Doolittle of Woodbridge.

July 8, Hobart B. Marks of Milford, and Cynthia Maria Sanford of Prospect.

Oct 15, John Lucius Driver and Mrs Jane D. Kane, both of Bethany

Nov 12, Evelyn O. Pardee and Martha L Sperry, both of Bethany

1866.

Jan 1, Edward Beecher and Christina E. Tolles, both of Bethany.

April 4, Silas E. Jeralds and Julia A Chandler, both of Prospect.

April 29, Miles F. Williams of Prospect, and Mary E Wooding of Cheshire

Oct. 18, John W. Brooks of Ansonia and Carrie Scheifferdecker of Bethany

Nov 15, George F Umberfield and Mrs Catherine Warner, both of Bethany, (married at Beacon Falls).

Nov 22, Richard H Griffing and Celia R. Haskins, both of Bethany.

1867

April 20, Frederick A Parker of New Haven and Anna M Donnell of Bethany

June 5, George B Twitchel of Bethany and Juliette A. Payne of Naugatuck

Oct 20, Hanford L Plumb and Betsey Devine, both of Bethany

BAPTISMS.

1836

May 15, Daniel Harison and Lucy Loisa, ch of Daniel and Lucy Thomas

Sept 4, Joseph Lockwood, son of Joseph and Nancy Bradley.

4, Rebecca Simmons, dau of Ransom and Alma Jeiles

15, Frances Harriet, dau of Harry and Mayant I. Thomas.

1837.

March 20, Ada Maria, (col) dau of Philip Sampson.

May 11, James Theodore, son of Return and Janet Durand

June 4, John Mather, son of Abram and Harriet Beecher.

4, Edwin Abijah, son of A P and Sarah R Judd

4, Dwight Eley, son of Leonard and Julia Todd

4, Edward, son of Henry A and Samantha Carrington

4, Hobart, son of E S and Loisa Sperry.

4, Sylvia Maria, son of Jesse A and Mary Ann Doolittle

Sept 17, Franklin Kirk, son of A T and Mary Beecher

17, Frederic (Humphreysville), son of Isaac and Susan Prince

Dec 17, Harison Smith and Charles Leonard, ch of A L and Mary S Judd

1838

Feb 8, Lucia Angeline, dau of Harry and Lucy Hicox

8, Eliza Ann, dau of David Allen

July 22, Laura, dau of Andrew and Hannah Beecher

22, Wales Herbert, son of Charles and Julia French.

Aug 26, Polly Salina and Harry Russell, ch of Beri E and Mary Beecher.

26, Jesse Burton, son of Jesse A and Mary A Doolittle

Oct 14, Mary Grant, dau. of Rev. J H and Mary A Rouse.

14, Mary Samantha, dau of Harry A and Samantha Carrington

1839

March 4, Leonard Lewis, Cyrus, Nancy Maria, and Cloe, ch of Cyrus D and C. Carrier, (col)

29, Isaac Leverett, son of Allen B and Laura Curtiss

1842

March 24, Harriet Emily, dau of Sidney Downs

24, Laura D Perkins, dau of Guy and Laura Perkins.

24, Julia Ann Judd, dau of wid S R Judd

March 24, Henry Hooker, son of Jared and Amy Hotchkiss.

24, Lewis E. Doolittle, son of Allen and Mary Ann Doolittle.

1843.

March 27, Harriet Amanda Hoadley.

June 18, Margaret Celia Thomas, dau. of Hez and Margaret Thomas

18, Jasper Bryan Todd, son of Leonard and Julia Todd.

Aug 13, Evelyn Ogilvie Pardee, son of Edwin and C Pardee.

13, Sarah Victoria and Cloe Cordelia Tuttle, ch. of Charles and S. Tuttle.

13, Urban Evander, son of George and L. H. Hotchkiss.

13, Nelson Newton, son of Beri E and Mary Beecher.

13, Eunice Amanda Chatfield.

1844

Oct. 13, Caroline Ella Perkins, dau. of Guy and Laura Perkins

13, Homer Guy Perkins, son of Wales and Eliza Perkins.

13, James Seymour Tuttle, son of Chas Tuttle and wife.

1845

Henry Allen Doolittle, son of Allen and Mary Doolittle

1846

Feb 8, Hannah Sherman Prince, son of Nathan and Hannah Prince

July 26, Julia Almira Sampson, (col.) dau of Philip and Betsey Sampson

Oct 4, Lines Prince, son of Hannah Prince.

1847

March 1. Guy, son of Mary and Silas Woodin.

Decr 29, Princetta Maria, dau. of Edwin and Caroline Pardee.

1848

June 4, John Fan, (b. Aug 15, 1845,) William, (b Oct. 30, 1846,) ch. of William and Louise Weightman

July 16, Isaac Lewis, (b May 24, 1837;) Ellen Jane, (b. Oct. 24, 1838,) and Catherine Emily, (b Aug 15, 1842) ch of Enos and Rosetta Sperry.   Parents and Sponsors

Sept 3, Mary Adelia Sperry, (b Jan 30, 1831,) Lydia Maria Sperry.

3, Dolly Eliza Sperry, (b Sept 6, 1834,)   "   "   "

3, Martha Louisa Sperry, (b Aug 8,1837,)   "   "   "

3, Margaret Lydia Sperry,(b Dec.31,1840,) "   "   "

3, Allen Sperry, (b Jan 9, 1839.)   "   "   "

3, Amelia Marilla Sperry, (b, Sept. 8, 1842,) " "   "

Herbert Willard, b Jan 31, 1839, Lysias and Lucy Beecher, grandparents, acting as sponsors

Frederick Beri, b Nov 1, 1846, Beri E and Mary N Beecher

Leonard Wales, b March 3, 1847, Jesse A and Mary Ann Doolittle

Robert Horace Tolles, b April 4, 1840

Frank Wooster Tolles, b August 29 1844

                              Caroline Tolles and Edwin Pardee
              Sept 3, 1848

Josephine Adelaide, b July 31, 1842, dau of Chas and Hannah
    Thomas, the mother standing as sponsor

Eunice Hotchkiss, adult	Children of Jairus and Eunice
Philo Delos, b Dec 7, 1839	Hotchkiss, the mother stand-
Edward Lester, b Dec 11, 1840	ing as sponsor, with her sister,
Juliet Christina, b Aug 21, 1843	Rosetta Sperry, who was also
Jane Dealt, b Sept 5, 1845	her witness

Henry D Beecher, b May 10, 1839
Frances A Beecher, b 1841   Lucy I Beecher
Emerette A Beecher, b Feb 3, 1843

Anna Eliza Clark, an adult, her brother, C F Clark, witness
              Oct 8, 1848

Charry E Beecher, b Jan 14, 1845   Lucy I Beecher

Ellen Josephine Smith, March 9, 1841 Grandparents, Pulaski and
    Amanda Chatfield, sponsors

Mary A Judd, b Dec 1, 1842, Asahel Leonard and Mary Eliz-
    abeth Judd

Dennis Nehemiah Wooding, b Oct 5, 1834   Mary Wooding
Charles Edwin Wooding, b Feb 11, 1838   "   "
Caroline Lucina Hotchkiss, b Dec 1844, Jared and Amy Hotchkiss
Sarah Jennett Perkins, b May 15, 1840   Mary Ann Perkins
Mary Grace Perkins, b December 28, 1847   "   "
Julia Ella Perkins, b March 5, 1848   Isaac and Emily Perkins
Oct 11, 1848, By the Rev Jacob L Clark of Waterbury and the
Rev David Sanford of Oxford, at the request of the Rector of Ch Ch
William Wrightman Zell, b Aug 10, 1848   Henry and Mary Zell

Nov 19, Lowly Jane Sanford, an adult   A A Perkins and Mrs
                              Jesse Doolittle standing as witnesses
Aug 19, 1849, Samuel Herbert Beecher, b March 25, 1849,
                              Beri E and Mary M Beecher

Lucius Russell, an adult
Elizabeth L Russell, an adult
Grace Ermina Russell, b Dec 27, 1842 } Children of Lucius and
Adelia Ann Russell ,b Nov. 19, 1848, }   Eliz L Russell.
Dwight Collin Lines, b May 14, 1845.
Harriet Amelia Wheeler, ch of Orrin and Mary A Wheeler
Nancy Ellen Hitchcock, b Feb 17, 1838,

Ira Perkins and wife, grandparents.
Watrous Tolles, b Feb 23, 1846   Julia A Tolles
Otis Bird Beecher, b. Nov 13, 1848, Guy and Sarah Ann Beecher

Oct 15, Eliza M Tolles, b Feb 21, 1840,

Isaac B and Maria Tolles.

1850

Feb 17, Mary Louisa Prince, b. July 6, 1849.

Nathan and Hannah Prince.
April 6, Wales C Perkins, b. Aug 8, 1849

Wales F. and Maria L Perkins
April 21, Marcia L Perkins, an adult   Guy Perkins and his wife
April 21, Lovenia Sperry, an adult   G. Perkins and Mary Zell
Sept 9, Eugene Walter Nettleton, b March 22, 1850,

R C Nettleton and his wife Louisa
Sept 22, Jennett Frances Wheeler, b June 6, 1850,

Noyes and Chairy S Wheeler
Sept 22, Eliza Emily Perkins, b July 28, 1849,

Isaac and Emily Perkins
Sept 22, Almeda E Buckingham, b May 7, 1844
Olin Dwight Buckingham, b Sept 23, 1847.

Buel and Henrietta Buckingham
Dec 23, John Wells Wheeler, b Oct 18, 1850,

Orrin and Mary A Wheeler
Sept 22, James Burr Perkins, b Oct 3, 1841   Mary Ann Perkins
Thomas Charles Perkins, b Jan 27, 1844 "   "   "
1851.
August 10, William Hasen Perkins, b. April 16, 1851

Wales Ford, and Maria L Perkins
August 10, Jane Ella Hotchkiss, b March 8, 1851

Anna and Elizabeth Hotchkiss

Parents Sponsors and Witnesses

Aug 31, Walter Augustus Pinkham, b Mar 12, 1851, son of Nathaniel J and Elizabeth Pinkham
The mother and Wm Paterson sponsors.

May 9, 1852, Henry Morrison Hull, b Oct 30, 1851 Morrison C. Hull and wife and Edwin Pardee

August 22, Frederick Willie Beecher, Nov 24, 1851. Beri E. and Mary M Beecher

August 22, Marion Cornelia Tuttle, b Nov 13, 1851 Charles and J Tuttle

May 2, 1853, Laura McClure, b 20 Feb 1853, William and Hannah McClure

| Amasa Brooks | Mi B | Morrison C Hull |
| Wales Dickerman | Mr D | Beri E Beecher |

1854

May 16, Mary Grace Pierpont, (private sick adult) Mother and Mrs H Townsend, witnesses

June 25, Edward Scovill Morrison Perkins, mother and M C Hull sponsors

June 25, Mary Jennette Bronson, b. Oct 24, 1853 Parents and M C Hull sponsors

June 25, E   Perkins   Parents and

August 13, Foster Beecher Hull, 9 mos old, Parents and Edwin Pardee

August 13, Amelia Carrington Perkins, 2¼ yrs old   Parents and Edwin Pardee

August 13, Howard French Perkins, 4 mos old   Parents and Edwin Pardee

Oct 22, Mary Jane Beecher, adult   Husband and Mrs Nelson Clark witnesses

BAPTISMS DURING THE RECTORSHIP OF REV JOHN ADAMS

1851

March 27, Helen Josephine, Ellen Justine, b March 11, 1848, twin daughters of Samantha Carrington Sponsors, the mother and Mrs Theophilus Smith

May 31st

Carrie Eliza, b July 17, 1856
The parents, Morrison C and Eliza T Hull

Parents Sponsors and Witnesses

Jane Rebecca, b June 23, 1856, Wales F. and Maria S Perkins
                          Sponsor, Mrs Laura Perkins
Sheldon, b Sept. 21, 1855. The parents, Charles and Anna Clarke.

Mary Maria, b April 24, 1853 ⎱ The parents, Orrin and Mary A
Celia Ella, b Oct 14, 1854 ⎰ Wheeler and Mrs A L Judd
Christina Jane, b July 27, 1856

Adna Todd, b May 21, 1856   The parents, Isaac and Emily Per-
    kins, and Samuel Todd
Julia Abby, b Aug 8, 1856   Daughter of Charles and Mary Ann
    Perkins   Sponsor, the mother
Almira Downes, wife of Eben Downes, an adult
                          Witness, Mrs Enos Perkins.
Amra Clark, wife of C F Clark, an adult
                          Witness, Mrs Charles French

George Warner Woodward, an adult. ⎱ Dr A C Woodward, Ed-
Edward Prindle Woodward an adult ⎰ win Pardee, Mrs Wood-
Lewis Dexter Lounsbury, an adult ⎰ ward, A A Perkins, Mrs
Leroy William Tuttle, an adult   J A Lounsbury and Gil-
                                      bert Davidson

Mar. 6, 1858

James Edward, b Feb 18, 1858   Son of William and Hannah Mc-
    Clure (in private, being ill.) (Private office)

June 10, 1860

Sarah Ann, wife of Street B Todd.
Addie Maria, infant daughter of Street B and Sarah Ann Todd
                          Witnesses, parents and wife of Leonard Todd.
Seymour Gilbert, infant son of —— Baldwin of Madison

Feb 11, 1861

Francis, infant son of F Breekle, (private bap) Woodbridge

June 30th

George Truman, son of Chas F Clark   Parents sponsors
George Bird, son of Geo Hotchkiss   ''   ''
Lillie May and Kate Alice, daughters of Mrs Emma Patterson
                          Mrs Camp and Mrs Patterson sponsors
Richard, son of Wm McClure, parents sponsors
Adeline Julia, daughter of Orson Wheeler   Parents
Kate Augusta, daughter of F S Woodward and granddaughter of
    the Rector   Mrs F B Woodward and Miss L Beecher

Mary Jane, daughter of Lucius Russell   Parents

Frank Beecher, son of G B Johnson   Parents, E Pardee

Clifton Tolles, son of De Ette E Downs

        E Pardee, Polly Tolles, De Ette Downs

Margaret Benecia, daughter of Noyes Wheeler   Parents

Oct 13, 1861

Emma Almira, daughter of F S and Helen Woodward   Parents

May 4, 1862

Marietta, daughter of Sylvia M Doolittle   Mother, L Perkins and
                              Mrs F B Woodward

Dec 25, Mary Jennett, daughter of Henry R and Esther Beecher
                       Parents and Mrs A Woodward

In Christ Church, Sunday, August 20th, 1865

Frederick James, b 4th April 1861, son of Anne Melissa and James
  H Holmes   Sponsors, S Gilbert Davidson, Henry R At-
                      water, and the mother

Henry Todd, b May 16, 1861 son of Maria Lucinda and Wales F
  Perkins   Sponsors, Guy Perkins and the parents

Geo Theodore, b Sept 26, 1858, son of Lucy Lovisa and Jarvis
  Theodore Bronson   Sponsors, Charles F Clark, Wm B
                   Dickerman, and the mother

Mar 7, 1869

Lydia Amanda, b, Mar 25, 1866, daughter of George W and Margaret L Woodward

        Sponsors, parents and Miss Sarah L Atwater

Ella Sarah, b Sept 11, 1866, daughter of Street B and Sarah A
  Todd   Sponsors, the parents and Mrs Orrin Wheeler

Mar 21, 1869

Maud Genevieve, b Oct 18, 1868, daughter of Horatio Nelson and
  Laura De Etta Clark, of Prospect

  Sponsors, Mrs Sarah L Atwater, the mother, and Guy Perkins

1870

June 5, William Irvng, son of Leroy Wm and Lovena Maria Tuttle
         Sponsors, parents and Mrs Sanford

June 5, Lucy Irene, daughter of Stiles C Williams

                   Sponsors, parents

June 5, Fannie Grace, daughter of Evelyn O and Martha L Pardee
      Sponsors, the parents and Mrs Lydia N Sperry

Parents, Sponsors and Witnesses

Aug 14, Charles Willard, son of Edward C and Lucy E. Culp of Norwalk, Ohio, b Jan 1, 1869

Sponsors, Mrs Esther Punderson and the mother

1871

April 16, Theodore James and Minnie Amelia, children of Wales Clark

Sponsors, the mother and Evelyn O. and Martha L Pardee.

April 30, Polly Maria Talmage, an adult

Witnesses, Mr Geo Hotchkiss and Mrs Martha L Pardee.

May 12, 1872, Mary Amelia Beecher, an adult.

Witnesses, Evelyn Pardee, Mrs. Sperry, Mrs. Evelyn Pardee.

ADULTS BAPTIZED IN CHRIST CHURCH SINCE EASTER, 1836

May 15, 1836, Daniel Thomas, at his house

1837

Feb. 28, Mary Ives, wife of Lewis Doolittle

March 20, Bennett Whiticus, (col)

June 4, Hulda Allen.

Oct 8, Sarah Robbins, wife of A P Judd

Jennette, wife of Newel Lounsbury

May 28, 1843, Lucy Hoadley, wife of Garry Hoadley , Elizabeth Perkins, Pamelia J Chatfield

1844, Julia Ann Chapman, Chas F. Clark, Lucy Louisa Beecher

Oct 17, 1846, Ira Perkins, Laura Hotchkiss, Lucretia Lines, Emily Castle, Julia A Castle, Hannah I Perkins, Angeline Hitchcock

May 28, 1859, Henry W Brown

June 10, 1860, Sarah Ann, wife of Street B Todd

June 30, 1861, Anna Eliza Deming, Laura Anna Hitchcock, Huldah, wife of G Beecher Johnson, Deette Eliza Downs

April 27, 1862, Estella Augusta Driver, Polly Teressa Stidman (col)

May 22, 1864, James Harlen Craw, Lovena Maria Tuttle

Aug 13, 1865, Mrs Martha Lucinda, wife of James H Craw

Louisa, daughter of Ezra Stiles

Juliet Elizabeth, daughter of Louisa Sperry

Aug. 18, 1865, Annie Melissa, wife of J H Holmes

June 13, 1866, Charles Thomas, aged 66 years   Clinic baptism, he being confined to the bed with sickness

April 28, 1866, Belinda Catherine, wife of Andrew T Hotchkiss,
    Christina Elizabeth, wife of Edward Beecher, Rosette Amanda
    and Kate Emeline, daughters of Dr A C Woodward, Sarah
    Jane, wife of S Gilbert Davidson

May 5, 1867, Mrs Hannah, relict of the late Major Lounsbury,
    Sarah Jane, daughter of William Burnham

Sept 20, 1868, Eveline Augusta, daughter of Frederick and Rhoda
    Tuttle, born July 28, 1850

Sept 26, 1868, Mrs Rosella, wife of Theron Allen

March 14, 1869, Edson Jesse, son of Howel Beecher

1872

June 16, Agnes May Tuttle, dau of Leroy W and Lovena M Tuttle

June 16, Herbert Goram, son of Eneas and Alice Goram

June 16, Walton Perkins Clark, son of Horatio N and Laura De
    Ette Clark

June 26, Tyler Daniel Davidson, son of Gilbert S and Sarah Jane
    Davidson

Dec 7, Adelia May Hotchkiss, daughter of Harpin and Charlotte
    E Hotchkiss

Dec 7, Fanny Maria Baldwin, child of Polly and Henry T Bald-
    win

1875.

Mar 21, Ray Carrington French, son of Herbert French

BAPTISMS BY C W COLTON

N B —The infant and adult baptisms are from this date included in the same list

1876, Jan 16, Grace Emma Bradley, daughter of Henry B and
    Polly Maria Bradley

1877

April 8, Martha Grace Sperry, adult, daughter of Allyn and Grace
    E Sperry

May 20, Ida Sarah, daughter of Stiles C and Ellen H Williams
    Walter Stiles, son of Stiles C and Ellen H Williams
    Leta Tolles, daughter of Edward and Christina Beecher
    Ida May, daughter of Henry W and Mrs Sarah B Brown

1878.

April 21, Emma Aminta, daughter of Frederick A and Celia E
    Perry

June 9, Mary Ann Beecher, an adult, daughter of Wm and Elizabeth Basham

Nathan French Mansfield, an adult, son of Stephen and Amy Mansfield

Georgiana Bunnell, an adult, daughter of George and Jane Bunnell

Sept 15, Lilah Lydia, daughter of Dennis and Sarah V Tuttle

Charles Seymour Tuttle, son of Dennis and Sarah V Tuttle Megin

Nelson Newton, son of Henry R and Esther J Beecher

Edwin George, son of Evelyn O and Martha L Pardee.

Clarence Garry, son of David F and Amelia M Smith.

William Sperry, son of David F. and Amelia M Smith

1879

May 4, Katie Irene, an adult, daughter of Harpin H and Charlotte E Hotchkiss.

Ida Estella, an adult, daughter of Harpin H and Charlotte E Hotchkiss

May 5, Monday, Helen Matilda, daughter of Clarence W and Cora D Colton   Baptized by the Bishop, the Rt Rev J Williams, D D , L. L D , at his visitation of the parish   The first baptism in the new Font, which was placed in the Church this day

Oct 19, Rollin Frederick, son of Frederick W and Mary A Beecher

June 6, Jennie Frances, daughter of Frederick A and Celia E Peiry

1880

June 27, Daisy Etta, child of Samuel A. and Charlotte F Woodward

July 25, Rachel Prindle and Grace Sylvia, children of Dr J N and Rachel P Parker, Woodbridge

---

FUNERALS ATTENDED IN THE PARISH OF CHRIST CHURCH, BETHANY, SINCE EASTER

1836

April 10, Juliette, daughter of Levi Peck, 13

April 20, Catherine French, 8

April 26, Rebecca Collins, 43

July 17, Laura Tolles, 32
Aug 16, Ery Lounsbury, 64
Sept. 23, James E , son of Eli Carley, 2
Oct 3, Abber Lines, Jun , 44
Oct 19, Jay, son of Jared Allen, 3
Dec. 2, Noyes Sperry, 34
Dec 15, Sarah Jane, daughter of Eli Terrell, 4

1837

Jan 10, Cloe Bradley, 55
Jan 22, John Ferdinand, son of the Rev J H Rouse, 1½
Jan 24, Jane, child of Lewis Tolles, 1
Jan. 25, Nancy Johnson, 38
March 19, Obadiah Lounsbury, 42.
April 1, Betsey S Hotchkiss, 71
April 24, Nancy Terrell, 39
May 12, Nathan Beers, 75
June 3, Jennette Durand, 21
June 8, Burton, son of Silas Wooding, 5.
June 15, Isaac F , son of Jared Pritchard, 4
July 1, Lucy Lounsbury, 34
Sept 22, Enoch Newton, 65

1838

Jan 15, Reuben Hicox, 42
March 10, Sally Hotchkiss, 70
        23, John Wilmot, 60
May 1, Caleb Doolittle, 65.
Sept 16, Nancy Bradley, 15
Oct. 12, Ezra Sperry, 72
        15, Henry Sanford, 41
Nov 21, Wallace, son of Stiles Russell, 1

1839

Jan. 17, Thankful Terrell, 88
March 24, Cyrus D Carrier, Col C, 38
April 10, Rhoda Doolittle, 64
        13, Allen Thomas, 49
        24, Hannah Lounsbury, 69
June 9, Mary Castle, 29
        20, Leonena Lewis, dau. of C D Carrier, 11.
July 9, Elisha Hotchkiss, 72

July 13, Cyrus, son of C D. Carrier, 9
Oct. 13, Lucy Sperry, 51

1840

Jan 8, Wm D Purdy, 80.
    28, Nancy Maria (colored), 7
May 17, Maria Sperry, 28
July 4, Reuben Judd, 69
Nov. 10, Dolly Chatfield, Mrs , 56

1841

Jan. 12, Daniel Thomas, 57.
April 14, Mary Hawley, 53
    23, Sarah Buckingham, Mrs , 77
May 12, Jared Tolles, 89
July 19, Clarissa Doolittle, 60
Dec 28, Abijah P Judd, 37.

1842

Feb. 12, William H Thomas, 18
March 2, Archibald Perkins, 83
    4, Ephraim L Perkins, 32.
May 29, Pena Lounsbury, 68.
    Stephen Hotchkiss, 42
Aug 29, Silliman Hotchkiss, 57.
Sept 24, Juliet Sperry, 4
Oct 9, Jesse Hitchcock, 47
    L. B Whitticus (colored), 26
    Mrs Silliman Hotchkiss, 53

1843

Feb 6, Mrs Harmon Allen, 49
    13, John Woodin, 70
    15, David Downs, 57
March 11, Julia Morris, 48
    12, W H, Burnham, 11
    Daniel Russell, 67
    Wm Woodin
April 7, child of Edwin Lines, 1 yr. 9 mo
    Wid Russia (colored), 80
Sept , Capt Chauncey Tuttle, 72.

1844

Feb 1, Elizabeth Brown, 70
    8, Isaac Sperry 84

Feb 11, Mrs Felix Downs, 79
    22, Eber Lines, 89
    22, —— Whitticus (colored), 63
May 18, Miss Polly Hitchcock, 61
       Calvin Tuttle, 57
Sept 8, Wid Patience Judd, 89
      Ezra Kimberly, 81
      Jehiel Castle, 34

1845

    Wife of Noyes Hotchkiss, 20 or 21
April 7, Enos Beecher (suicide), 32
    15, Hez Thomas, 53
    Mrs Major Hotchkiss
Aug , Benjamin Perkins
      Child of Horace Tolles
      Child of Nehemiah Tolles
      Anna Doolittle
      8, Child of Sheldon Allen, 17 months
      24, Child of Curtiss Tolles, 8 months
Sept 9 Hezekiah Brown, 67
Dec , Child of Jesse Hotchkiss, 5

1846

Aug 29, Stiles Hotchkiss
Sept 28, Sarah Perkins
Oct 4, Luther Smith, 48
    7, Lines Prince, Infant,
Nov 21, Edwin Lines, 31
Dec 31, David Beecher, 56.

1847

Jan 11, Sarah Smith, 24
Feb 22, Phenetta Andrew, 37
    28, Hannah Hotchkiss, 80
March 12, Eli Todd, 75
April 30, Sally Lounsbury, 77.
May 29, Chloe Tuttle, 5
Sept 12, Adelia Thomas, 18
    19, Horace Tolles, 46
    29, Reuben Doolittle, 76
Oct 16, Abel Prince, 57

Nov 5, Stephen Hotchkiss, 88.

 Ellen Tolles, 15 months.

Dec 6, Eliza Perkins, 27

1848

Feb 5, Felix Downs, 89

May 6, Jane Kimberly of Woodbridge, 31

 21, Lyman Tuttle of Hamden, 86

 27, Betsey Underville (colored), 39

July 13, Garry Sperry, 40

Aug 23, Isaac B Brooks, 27

Sept. 21, Rebecca Perkins, Hamden, 68

 29, Benjamin Beers, 77.

Dec 11, Nathan R Morris, 57

 20, Sarah Beecher, 63

1849

Jan 23, Eliakim Smith, child of Mr Dickerman of Cheshire, 19 m

March 10, Abigail Sperry, from Oxford, 79

April 20, Solomon Hotchkiss, 93

 29, Israel Thomas 65

May 2, Eunice Perkins of Hamden, 73

 18, Asaph Umberfield, 22.

 23, Amos Hitchcock, a Congregationalist, 87

July 26, Rebecca Umberfield, 69

Aug 8, Anna Perkins, a Congregationalist, 78.

 16, S Bird Woodward, son of Dr. A C Woodward, 7

 31, AlansonTuttle of Hamden, 49

Sept 5, Mrs E Russia, 48

 9, Howard Wales, son of Wales F. Perkins, 20 months

 18, Lewis Lines, 57

Oct. 1, S E Collins, daughter of Jeremiah Collins, 5

 16, Jeremiah Sperry, 60

 17, Eliza M Tolles, daughter of Isaac B. Tolles, 20 months

 19, Major D Collins, son of Jeremiah Collins, 6.

 25, Sally Morriss, 59

Nov 23, Stephen Wooding, 64

1850

March 1, Hobart B. Tuttle, 20

April 3, Amarilla Sanford, 70

 5, Patty Sperry, 65

April 7, Benjamin Collins, 83

    8, Wales G Perkins, son of Wales E Perkins, 8 months

May 4, Charles Johnson, 30

June 25, Frederick Beri, son of Beri F Beechei, 4

July 30, Jane R Perkins, 27

Sept 11, Eugene Walter, son of R O Nettleton of N H, 6 months

Oct 3, Watrous Tolles, son of Curtis Tolles, 5

Nov 11, Sarah Johnson, 63

1851

July 1, Major Hotchkiss, 63

August 16, Child of Allen Hitchcock, 8

Sept. 20, Frank S Alaby, child of Mrs Harrison Thomas, 2

    22, Augustus Castle, 44

Oct. 14, Lyman Downs, 72

Nov 15, Anna Eliza Clark, 25

    28, Eber Hotchkiss, 55

1852

Jan 17, Levi Peck, 71

Feb 14, Infant child of I Ford, 1 month

March 5, Orrin Hine, 51

    7, Jeremiah Camp, 60

    9, Fanny Prince, 58

    29, Eliza A Hitchcock, 40

May 2, Caroline Hotchkiss, wife of Jesse Hotchkiss, 34

    22, Truman Terryll, 67

    23. Betsey Bradley, 33.

August 6, Lois Perkins, wife of A. A Perkins, 51

Sept 21, Mrs Race, 26

Nov 21, John Andrew, 22

Dec. 11, Maria Lyons, 46

1853.

Feb. 12, Jane Eliza Beecher, daughter of Milo Beecher, 13

April 20, Dr Jehiel Castle, 81

May 17, Anna Wooding, 79

July 5, Nancy Sanford, 76

Aug 26, Harriet French, 62

Sept. 14, Nehemiah Tolles, 43

Oct 18, Celia Sperry, 21

Oct 30, Silas Wooding, 50

FUNERALS ATTENDED BY THE REV H. TOWNSEND.

April 1, Widow Anna Woodin, 92

May 7, Widow Rhoda Wheeler (Congregationalist), 72

    9, Lysias Beecher, wife of Allen Doolittle

July 4, Mrs Mary Ann Doolittle, buried July 6, 40

    25, Mary Grace Pierpont, wife of W. S Pierpont, 20, d July 25.

August 4, Alexis Rosha (Mulatto), 55, d 3d

August 8, Emerit Brown, daughter of Mrs Eunice Brown, 27, d. 7th

    25, Jared Hotchkiss, 50, d 24th

    27, Mrs. Wd Lucy Beecher, relict of Lysias B , 71, d 26th.

Sept. 1, Tenta Lines, wife of Abel Lines, 68, d Aug 31st.

    1, Mary E , daughter of Geo. Driver, West Haven, 14 months

    12, Mrs Polly A Sackett, wife of —— Sackett, 80, d. 11

Oct 5, Mrs Anna Lines, relict of Abel Lines, 95 years and 11 months, d 3d

    26, Josephine L Hubbell, child of Joseph O Hubbell, 15 months, d 25th

    30, Emma E , child of Joseph O. Hubbell, 3, d 28th

Nov 2, Mrs Huldah Sperry, wife of Chas Sperry, 68, Woodbridge, d Oct 31st

    16, James Driver, 77, d 14th

Dec 20, Frederick, infant son of Neh'h Andrew, 10 months, d 19th

———————

FUNERALS DURING THE MINISTRY OF REV CHARLES J. TODD
1855

Feb. 28, Jane A Scoville, daughter of Chester and Minerva Scovill, 23, d 26th

March 1, Edward Charles, son of Charles and Hannah Thomas, 23.

April 3, Frances May, daughter of Isaac and Emily Perkins, 3

    27, Rhoda Hotchkiss, wife of Spencer Hotchkiss, 52

    16, Julia Ella, daughter of Isaac and Emily Perkins, 7.

    18, Zephaniah Downs, 72

    23, Samuel Herbert, son of Beri E and Mary M Beecher, 7

May 24, Jane Ella, daughter of Adna and Elizabeth Hotchkiss, 6

August 24, Howard French, infant son of Wales French Perkins and Maria Lucy Perkins, 1 year and 4 months

Sept 9, Henry A Carrington, 47

    24, Seymour Tuttle, 71, d 23d

Nov 24, Dennis Beecher, son of Andrew Beecher, 31, d 22d.

Nov 26, Mary Hitchcock, wife of Isaac Hitchcock, d 22d
Dec 8, Mrs Thirza Lines, 64 -
    24, Hoel Beecher, son of Jesse Beecher, 45

1856

Jan 3, Ichabod Umberfield, 71
    11, Polly Russell, wife of John Russell, 54
Feb. 10, Jesse Doolittle 78, d 8th
March 16, Albert J. Craw, son of James H and Frances J Craw, 8

FUNERALS DURING THE RECTORSHIP OF REV JAMES ADAMS, COM-
MENCING OCT 7, 1856

Oct 14, Harriet Maria, daughter of Daniel W and Henrietta Rus-
    sell, 18 months

1857

Feb. 10, Asaph French of Prospect, aged 72
March 15, Mrs Deming, 50
    31, Mabel Morris wife of Chauncey Morris, 29
May 13, Ira Perkins, 68
August 15, Sarah Ann Beecher, wife of Guy Beecher, 32
    23, Harriet Thomas, wife of Leveret Thomas, 56
Oct 5, Dorcas Judd, 96
Nov. 2, Mary A Beecher, wife of Wm S Beecher of Prospect, 27
    7, Bede Todd, mother of Leonard Todd, 78
Dec 21, Verus Candee, 76

1858

Jan. 15, Mrs Esther Marks, 64
    30, Asena Perkins, 91
Feb 20, Allen Hitchcock

FUNERALS BY F B W

    Child of Daniel Tolles (Woodbridge)
    Charles Thrall (Prospect), 53
July 18, Philo Hotchkiss, Bethany
Sept 26, Julia A Sampson (colored), 14

1859

Jan. 7, Mary Lounsbury, 83
March 11, Eliakim Smith, 74
April 21, Lydia Nettleton, 63
May 29, Joseph Bradley, 77

Oct 1, Jeremiah Tuttle, 44
Nov 12, Calvin Downs, 22

1860

Jan 16, Isaac Terrill, 60
     18, —— Northrop, 25.
March 28, Harley Hotchkiss, 70
May 19, Harry French, 68
June 20, Charles L Judd, 24.
Nov 20, Martha J Beecher, 25
Dec 16, John Clemens, 51

1861

Jan. 26, Abner Warner of Hamden, 93.
Feb 7, Sheldon Wooding, 76
     20, Micah Sperry, 80,
     28, Frank, son of Beecher Johnson, 7
March 15, Mrs Olive Austin, 72
     16, Francis, infant son of F Breekle, Woodbridge, 2
     17, Friend, son of Anon Atwater, 19
April 14, Melinda, relict of David Beecher, 69
     18, Jane E Doolittle (at Seymour), 25
May 19, Mrs Elizabeth Driver, 66
     29 Wid. Hitchcock, the mother of Beri E. Beecher, 84.
June 14, Henry B Lounsbury, 2
August 25, Adna Hotchkiss, 44
Sept 22, Samuel Pelton, 26
     24, Irvin Lounsbury, 18
Oct. 3, Mary L Prince, 12.
Nov 18, Son of Noyes Johnson, 10 weeks
     20, Mrs Eunice Hotchkiss, 88
Dec 1, Wid Ira Perkins, 70

1862.

March 3, Capt Jesse Beecher, 77
     10, Mrs Caroline Tolles, 56
April 16, William Donnell, 20.
May 2, Althea Buckingham, 43
     22, Leverett Thomas, 62.
July 27, Alva Gaylord, 72
Sept 22, Wid Harvey Hotchkiss, 77
     27, Albert Eugene, son of James Craw, 5.

Oct 18, Mrs Isaac Doolittle, 60

26, Wid Mary Castle

29, Ellen Kimball, (Prospect) 19

Nov 16, Mrs James Patterson 38

21, Mary S, wife of Herbert French, 25

1863

Jan 6, Benjamin M Collins. 72

16, Henrietta, wife of D W Russell. 39

21, Edson Hotchkiss. 32

Feb 8, John Wooding, 50

27, Orrin Hitchcock, 51

May 3, Major Lounsbury, 69

June 26 Isaac Hitchcock, 88

29 Nelson Newton Beecher, 20 yrs, 8 mo, died at Annapolis Md, soldier 27 Reg C V

Sept 22, Roenna E Thomas, 8 years, dau of Daniel Harrison Thomas

Oct 3, Betsey Perkins, wife of Beecher Hotchkiss and dau of Guy Perkins, 42

14, Henry French, 53

27, Marion Cornelia 11 yrs, 11 mo, 13 days, dau of Charles Tuttle

Nov 3, Enos Perkins, 70, nearly

10 Lucy, 51, wife of Garry Hoadley

18, Horace Preston, 55

1864

Mar 9, Abel Linds, 76

12, Patty Hotchkiss. 81, sister of Abel Linds

13, John Hitchcock, 26

29, Patty Harris Hotchkiss, 71

29, Isa Annett, 11 years, dau of Andrew Hotchkiss

May 6, Delia E, wife of John Wesley Weed, 36

17, Laura Woodin, dau of Andrew and Hannah Beecher, 26

25, Cornelia Ella, wife of Henry Edward Lounsbury, 29

June 19, Netty, dau of Charles Preston of Prospect 6

Aug 19, Ada Whitneus, (col'd) 88

Aug 20, Abigal Hitchcock, 91

Oct 5 Laura E Doolittle, dau of Alfred Doolittle, 40

1865

Jan 27, George Hotchkiss, 2d 31

Feb 19, Stan Sperry, son of Ezra Stiles Sperry, 24

Mar 1, Daniel Lynes, 65, a native of Ireland

13, Eugene Burton Castle, 18

17, Oliver Buckingham, 82

18, Alfred Crittenden, infant son of (late) Stan and Mary D Sperry, 4 1 2 months

Apr 9, Philip Sampson (col'd) 66

18, Laura May dau of Wales French and Maria Lucinda Perkins, 11 mo

May 3, Ezra Stiles Sperry 66

Aug 3, Eden Johnson, 85

38 Henry A Doolittle of Woodbridge 20 married 9th Apr. last

Oct 2, Mary Jane, dau of Charles and Laura Austin, 5

22 Charity, wife of Wm H Lounsbury, dau of Oliver Buckingham, 52

Dec 18, Mrs Charlotte Woodin, 78, relict of the late Sheldon Woodin

1866

Feb 15 Noyes Hotchkiss, 51

July 6, Mrs Dolly Eliza, wife of Dr Edward P Woodward 31 y,10 mo

Sept 2, Freddie, son of Frederick and Harriet Amanda Warner, 3 y, 9mo

13, Jennett, wife of Newel Louns bury, 63

26, Lemira Sherman, 85

Oct 31, Beecher Hotchkiss, 52

Nov 20, Mrs Hannah Peck, 77

Feb 18 Mrs Huldah, wife of Ebenezer P Parker in Woodbridge, 72

May 23, Esther, dau of the late Oliver Buckingham 61

June 27, Antoinette, wife of Dr Edward P Woodward, 28 Ten weeks after marriage

Sept 29, Mrs Sarah, relict of the late David Downs, 85

1868

Jan 2, Mrs Betsey, relict of Jessie Doolittle, 86, d Dec 31, 1867.

5, Alice Louisa dau of Andrew C and Ruth Ann Brown, 2 yrs, 6 mo Died 3rd

Feb 5 Amanda, wife of Pulaski Chatfield, 74

Mar 4 Elizabeth, relict of the late Jeremiah Camp of Prospect 71

5 Israel Schofield, d Feb 29, 53 years, late of Paris N Y

Apr 29, Charles Seymour Tuttle, 52, d 27

May 24 Mrs Clarinda, wife of Albert Hoadley 78

24, Mrs Fanny, relict of the late Amasa Brooks of Prospect, 82

July 18, Clark Seeley 66, d 17th

Dec 19, Isaac Doolittle, 68, d 17th

22, Merrit Sanford, 71, d 20th

1869

Jan 13, Abner Archibald Perkins, 84 yrs, 4 mo, 24 days, d 10th

BURIALS BY MARTIN MOODY

May 2 Mrs Lucretia Gorham, wife of Eneas Gorham, 43, d Apr 30

July 23 Wm McClure, 58, d 21st

Aug 19, Winthrop Dudley Wooding, 9 days, d 18th

Nov 28, Mrs Mary French

1870

Feb 2 Mrs Huldah Johnson, wife of A Beecher Johnson, d Jan 31st

Dec 28, Mrs Elizabeth Andrew, 45

1871

Jan 22 John Russel, 84 nearly d 19th

Apr 13, Mrs Nancy Bradley, 86 Funeral at the house of her son Marcus Bradley, d 10th

16, Tubal Sanford, 83
Charles Thomas

Aug 17, Ella Isabel Hotchkiss, 3 y, 7 m

17, Clara Louisa Robertson, 6 m, 9 d

Dec 15, William Belany Dickerman, 63

31, Lucy Kimberly, 95

1872

Jan 14, Horace Bushnell Osborn

Feb 22, Ann Downs, 85 Funeral at the house of Alfred Doolittle

Mar 11, Chancey Burritt Tuttle, 73

July 14, Albert Hoadley, 81. Funeral at the house of Harpin Hotchkiss Agnes May Tuttle

Oct 6, Leroy W Tuttle, 34

Nov 8, Diantha Pitcher

Dec 5, John Jackson Donell

11, Charley E Donell

1873

Jan 4. Adella May Hotchkiss

May 13, Mrs Sarah E Tolles, 66

14, Mr Alonzo Sperry, 59

26, Mrs Celestia Terrill, 63

June 29, Mrs Thirza Bradley of Prospect, 81

July 7, Charles Gay Lounsbury, 44

25, Grace A Woodin, Woodbridge, infant daughter of Lambert Woodin, 6 mo, 1 d

29, Mrs Abigail B Umberfield, Prospect, 65

30, Minnie Sarah Williams, infant daughter of Stiles C Williams

Sept 1, Wales Henry Perkins, son of Homer Perkins, 9 mo

1874

Jan 25, Eber E Downs, Woodbridge, 58

Feb 17, Orin Wheeler, 60

Apr 5, Mrs Laura Perkins, wife of Willis Perkins, 64

22, Jared Allen, '81

May 9, Mrs Louis Andrews, relict of Job Andrews, 77

Aug 13, Merit Wooding, of Straitsville, 53

17, Mrs Augusta Smith, 64

Nov 2, Mr Curtiss Towles, 56

Dec 21, Mrs Sarah B Carrington

27, Mr Lyman Sperry

1875

Jan 26 Star Bradley Dickerman, son of
Wales C Dickerman 2

Mar 13, Charles Preston, 53

28, Ray Carrington French, 15

FUNERALS BY C W COLTON

Aug 18 Jessie dau of Charles A Rob
ertson 11 days

1876

Jan 28 Andrew Beecher 75

Mar 7 Mrs Hannah Lounsbury widow
of Major Lounsbury, 77

April 8 Leonard Todd 76

21, Anson Perkins d April 10 80

May 22 Mrs Ruth N Brown d May 20 38

June 4 David E son of Abram Carring
ton d June 2 1 year 6 months

June 16 Elizur Young d in Prospect
June 14 aged 46

Oct 7 Mrs Harmon Allen d Oct 6 82

Dec 9 Andrew I Hotchkiss d Dec 7
aged 58

1877

Jan 18 Mrs Betsey Adams d Jan 15
aged 108

Feb 16, Mrs Crownage Lounsbury, d
Feb 14 aged 66

Mar 6 Mrs Sarah B Smith d Mar 3
aged 86

June 8 Nathan Prince d June 6 82

July 28 Daniel Norrison Thomas d
July 2 aged 54

Aug 26 Mrs Russell Chatfield d Aug
24 aged 83

Oct 7, Mrs Dorcas Sperry d Oct 6 85

Nov 11 Mrs Annie Clark d Nov 9 79

1878

Jan 8 Alanson Morris d Jan 5 aged 64

Mar 13 Eddie Sanford son of T L and
Lottie M Sanford d in Water
bury, Mar 12, aged 2 mo , 1 d

14, Garry Hoadley d Mar 12 71

July 10 Russell Chatfield d July 8, 90

20, Marshall E , son of Seymour
Russell d July 19 aged 9 mos

Aug 30, Mrs Alma Perkins d Aug 28,
aged 80

Sept 4 George Hotchkiss, d Aug 2, 69

Nov 14 Mrs Emily Y Buckingham, d
Nov 19 aged 54

1879

Jan 7 Carrie Luella Bronson, dau of
Edward Bronson d Jan 4 11 2 m

18 Mrs Ellen McClure d Jan 16 90

Mar 4 Crownage Lounsbury d Feb
28 aged 76

Apr 4 McDonald Fisher d April 2 63

May 26 Mrs Julia A Tolles, d May 24,
aged 66

July 19 Archie N son of Charles A
Robertson d July 17 aged 10 mo

Aug 4 Mrs Elmira Doolittle d Aug 1,
aged 77

Sept 21 Harmon Allen d Sept 19, 93

Oct 22 Mrs Chloe Tuttle d Oct 20 93

Dec 27 Mrs Eliza Davidson d Dec 25
aged 71

1880

Feb 19 Mrs Almeda E Allen d Feb
16 aged 85

23 Levi Marks d Feb 21 88

Apr 9 Lewis Tolles d April 7 aged 75

21 Birdsey Allen d Apr 19 23

May 25 Enos Sperry d May 23 aged 79

Aug 5 Emily T Perkins wife of Isaac
Perkins d Aug 3 aged 55

Sept 17 Betsey Ann Samson wife of
Lines Leneer d Sept 16 aged 41

27 Chas E Clark Beacon Falls d
Sept 25 aged 52

Dec 3, Mrs Lucy Thomas 78

11 Jeremiah Collins d Dec 9 69

1891

Rev J Tragitt Rector

Dec 21 Mrs Sarah Downs d Dec 19 72

25 Marcus Austin d Dec 23 63

From the Records of Trinity Church, New Haven.

Rev Bela Hubbard, who was rector of Trinity church, New Haven, from 1767 to 1812, frequently came to Bethany and held services and performed the rites of baptism, marriage and burial. The following data of services performed in Bethany have been carefully gleaned from the Trinity church records

April 18th, 1770 At a lecture at Bethany baptized Alley, Jesse, Elizabeth, Rayment, James and David, children of —— Carrington, Benajah Peck and Sarah his wife, sponsors

At a lecture at Bethany Jan 30th, 1776, baptized Sarah, daughter of Abram and Rebecca Carrington The above children with proper sureties

At a lecture in Bethany September 26th, 1780, baptized Uri, Dennis, Zimri, Lyman, Dan, Sarah, Lois, children of Isaac and Mary Sperry, Rosana, daughter of Mansfield and Elizabeth Peck, Charles, son of Abram and Rebecca Carrington, Elizabeth and Hannah, daughters of Ebenezer and Hannah Bishop

Baptized at Bethany January 10th, 1781, George Frederick, son of Mansfield and Elizabeth Peck, sponsors, Benajah Peck, Elizabeth Beecher, Sarah Peck

At a lecture in Bethany, May 1781, married one couple, and on Sunday, April 22d, 1781, gave the sacrament of the holy Eucharist to 17 persons

Married, January 29th, 1781, Ebenezer Umberville to Esther Downs, both of Bethany

February 16th, 1782, baptized at Bethany, Esther, wife to Samuel Gilbert The same Esther communed for the first time

September 22d, 1782, baptized at Bethany, 17th Sunday on Trinity, Joseph, son of Abner Bradley Sponsors, Benajah Peck and parents

October 21st, 1782 Burial of a child of Eber and Abigail Downs

June 29th, 1783   Baptized one infant , and Isaac, Polly, David and Betsey, children of Eber and Abigail Downs

1784   Baptized Archibald Perkins, Hulday, Sarah, Samuel 1784   Baptized Lola, daughter of Thaddeus Todd, and Archibald Abner son of Archibald and Hulday Perkins

November 27th, 1784   Baptized Samuel, Miles, David, Joel and Esther, children of Joel Sperry

November 28   Baptized Samuel, son of Abner and Comfort Bradley , Chauncey, son of Cyrus and Sarah Wooding

November 29th   Baptized Stephen, Daniel, Enoch, William, Rachel, Mabel, Amos, John, Mary, children of — —Russell

DATE OF OPENING CHRIST CH , BETHANY

Bethany Woodbridge , August 26th, 1785, opened ye Episcopal church by ye name of X church and preached, &c , and baptized 7 infants.

(Parochial record of Trinity church, page 153)

May 29th, 1787, baptized Nehemiah, son of Allen and Hulda Carrington   September 16th, buried wife of Umberfield , buried ye wife of Abram Tuttle, aged 65 years

Married January, 1793, Uri Tuttle to Margaret Munson

New Haven, Thursday, December 17th, 1795, at the home of Mr David Cook, joined in marriage David Thomas of Woodbridge with Rebecca Cook of New Haven

New Haven, Sunday, June 28th, 1807, published ye banns of marriage between Nathan Prince of Milford and Mary Ann Elizabeth How of New Haven , and on same day at the house of — —York joined them in ye banns of matrimony

THE HILLS OF BETHANY.

BY REV L F MORRIS, MARCH, 1905.

We live on the hills of Bethany,
Where few of human kind we see,
Where few of human sound we hear,
Where nature's voices charm the ear,
 On the hills of Bethany.

A very lonesome place, you'll say,
In which to pass the time away ,
And yet in city's swarming hive
None better live than we, and thrive,
 On the hills of Bethany.

We're nearer heaven here than there,
Where men are worn by carking care
And here less vices are allowed
Far from the city's ''madding crowd,''
 On the hills of Bethany

And fresh and sweet the air e'er comes
Untainted by the city's slums,
And, what is best, the atmosphere
Of social life is pure and clear,
 On the hills of Bethany

The proud coal barons send a chill
Through cities, when at their sweet will
The prices rise , but their demands
We heed not on these wooded lands,
 On the hills of Bethany.

No great coal strikes, have pinched us yet,
For wood is plenty and easy to get,
And lacking coal, not one need freeze,
Though Boreas blow his coldest breeze,
     On the hills of Bethany

We hear the voice of uncaged birds
A-singing these exultant words,
"The city's prisoned air we scorn
As free as eagles we were born
     On the hills of Bethany "

We hear the crow with hungry maw
Proclaim his want with loud caw ! caw !
And robins, singing on the lawn,
Make known the rise of rosy dawn
     On the hills of Bethany

The bobolink carols on the wing,
When winters cease to threaten spring,
And sweet the orioles chants ascend,
As they hang their nests on the long limbs' end,
     On the hills of Bethany

Our eyes are gladdened by living green,
Which in the town is little seen ,
And plants and flowers for all find room
To grow and blossom and shed perfume
     On the hills of Bethany

From these fair heights we look afar ,
And might see Bethlehem's guiding star,
If that were where it once was seen,
And centuries did not lie between,
     On the hills of Bethany

Still to us is divinely given
To see the broad expanse of heaven ,
To see the stars coming trooping out,
And the moon pursue his nightly route
     O'er the hills of Bethany

And we can see the sun arise,
And glorious gild the morning skies,
And that the far horizon gets
Unrivalled pictures as he sets,
    On the hills of Bethany

Ten miles off is the shining sea
Which Indians called Matowaksee,
Where islands keep concealed Kidd's gold—
This sheet of waters we behold,
    From the hills of Bethany

O ye, by city's walls shut in,
And who would purest freedom win,
Move out and try our country life,
With all most useful blessings rife,
    On the hills of Bethany.

MARRIAGES.

FROM 1852 TO 1896, FROM THE TOWN RECORDS

BIRTH RESIDENCE AND MARRIAGE IN BETHANY UNLESS OTHERWISE STATED

1852.

Nov. 7, George Sanford, joiner, and Ann Johnson, m. by Miles French, Esq.

Nov. 14, Jarvis F. Bronson, b. Derby, and Louisa P. Beecher, m. by Rev. Henry Zell.

Nov. 18, Jacob W. Wilcox, printer, b. New Haven, r. Waterbury, and Charlotte E. Hurlburt, b. Hartford, r. Waterbury, m by Rev. H. Zell.

1853

Jan. 10, Eli H Wakelee, mason, b and r Derby, and Eunice A. Chatfield, m. by Rev Henry Zell

Feb. 8, Wales C. Dickerman, farmer, b. and r Hamden, and Celia Todd, teacher, m by Rev. Henry Zell

Mar. 20, Charles O Perkins, farmer, and Jane Perkins, m. by Rev. H. Zell

Apr. 17, Henry N Johnson, founder, b. and r. Westville, and Sylvia Northrop, teacher, b and r Woodbridge, m. by Rev. Henry Zell.

Oct. 13, John H. Sherwood, farmer, b. Fairfield, r. Southport, and Selua Beecher, by Rev John M. Guion

Oct. 16, Alva K. Munson, farmer, b. and r Hamden, and Betsey Hitchcock, m. by Rev. Alexander Leadbetter

Nov. 20, George A. Hall, carpenter, b. Maine, r. Meriden, and Eliza A. Griswold, b and r. Rocky Hill, m by Rev Alexander Leadbetter.

1855.

May 20, Archibald A. Perkins, tanner, and Minerva Scoville, m. by Rev Charles J. Todd.

Nov. 18, David F. Smith, b. and r. Woodbridge, and Delia E. Northrop, m. by Rev. S. H. Elliot of New Haven.

Dec. 31, David French, farmer, and Sarah E. Fuller, b. Oxford, m. by H. B. Munson, Esq., Seymour.

1856.

Jan. 1, Henry E. Lounsbury, farmer, and Cornelia A. Doolittle, b. Hamden, r. Wallingford.

Apr. 5, John Russell, farmer, and Hannah Hotchkiss, m. by Rev. Charles J Todd.

June 8, Stephen Mansfield, farmer, b. and r. Seymour, and Amy Hotchkiss, m. by Ezra S. Sperry, Esq

June 29, Azariah Andrews, farmer, and Sarah A. Pardee, b and r. Orange m. by Rev. O. L. Holcomb.

1857.

Feb. 7, Street B. Todd, farmer, r. New Haven, and Sarah A. Hotchkiss, m by Rev. James Adams.

May 10, John J. Sperry, farmer, and Elizabeth A. White, b. Seymour, m. by Rev J. Guernsey, Woodbridge

Nov. 29, Donald Fisher, farmer, b Middletown, and Eunice Brown, m. by Rev. E. W. Robinson.

1858.

Feb. 26, Elbert Downs, farmer, and Catherine A. Bailey, b Woodbridge, m by Rev. E. W. Robinson.

Apr. 24, Isaac Bradley, farmer, and Fannie A Castle, b. and r Woodbridge, m. by Andrew T. Hotchkiss, Esq

Aug. 19, Levi M. Marks, farmer, b Milford, and Emeline Pierpont, r. New Haven, m. by Rev. F. B. Woodward.

Sept. 25, George W Woodward, farmer, b Litchfield, and Margaret L Sperry, m. by Rev. F. B. Woodward

1859

Feb 1, Jacob Muller, b. Germany, and Licetta Friedman, b. Germany, m. by Rev. Samuel H. Smith, Naugatuck.

Feb. 3, Theodore A. Shephard, b and r. Chatham, and Ellen L. Ramsdell, b. and r. Chatham, m. by Rev F. W. Woodward.

July 10, Franklin B Atwater, farmer, and Elizabeth Barnes, b. Meriden, m. by Rev F. B. Woodward

Nov. —, Mark Sperry, joiner, and Harriet H. Elder, matchmaker, b. Plymouth

Dec 22, Charles Austin, farmer, and Laura C. Tuttle, b. Paris, N. Y., r New Haven, m. by Rev. F. B. Woodward.

Dec 22, Henry W. Perkins, blacksmith, and Emily Sanford, b. Hamden, m in New Haven by Rev. Wm Weed.

Dec. 22, Edward Buckingham, farmer, and Emily Castle.

1860

Jan. 7, Charles T. Baily, farmer, b Hamden, and Emily S. Davis, b Bristol, m. by E. W. Robinson.

Jan 15, W. Herbert French, wagonmaker, and Mary S. Carrington, m by Rev. F. B. Woodward.

Mar. 25, Gilbert R. Doane, farmer, b. and r. Westbrook, and Catherine J. Russell, m. by Rev. Alex. D. Stowel

Jan. 25, Rollin J Bunce, mechanic, b. and r. New Haven, and M. Jane Sanford, m. by O. Evans Shannon, rector of Trinity church, Seymour

Apr. 7, Darius Collins, farmer, and Catherine McClure, b. Ireland, m by Andrew Hotchkiss, Justice of the Peace.

Apr. 29, Charles E. Wooding, farmer, r. Woodbridge, and Elvira O. Clinton, b. and r. Woodbridge, m. by Rev. F. B. Woodward.

May 27, Edward P. Woodward, physician, b. Litchfield, r. Cheshire, and Eliza D. Sperry, m. by Rev. James E. Coley, Westville.

1860.

June 10, Allen G. Sperry, farmer, and Grace E Russell, m. by Rev F. B. Woodward.

June 18, Miletus Huxford, mechanic, Wolcottville, r. Ansonia, and Kate L. Hale, milliner, b. Woodbridge, r. Ansonia, m. by Rev. F. B. Woodward.

Aug. 19, Abel Wilcoxson, farmer, b. Oxford, and Maria Nettleton, b. Watertown, m by Rev. S. P Perry, Seymour.

Sept. 26, Bennett T. Abbott, minister, b. and r Middlebury, and Fanny A. Coe, m. by Rev. T. B. Chandler of Naugatuck.

Oct 7, Lewis Hitchcock, farmer, and Valina Hine, b. and r Woodbridge, m. by Rev. S. B. Woodward.

Aug. 19, Abel Wilcoxson, farmer, b. Oxford, and Maria Nettleton, b Watertown, m. by Rev. L. P. Perry, . Seymour.

Nov. 12, Lauren E. Cook, farmer, b. and r. Cheshire, and Caroline E. Perkins, teacher, m. by Rev. S. B. Woodward.

1867.

Nov. 30, Dr. Edward P. Woodward and Mary A. Atwood, New Haven.

Dec. 22, Leroy William Tuttle and Lovena Maria Tuttle.

1868.

Jan 8, Ely Sanford and Anjennette Caroline Tuttle.

Jan. 31, Otis B. Beecher and Eliza Perkins.

June 17, Henry F. Bishop, Woodbridge, and Kate E. Sperry.

Sept. 6, Daniel Willis Russell and Mary A. Brooks.

Dec. 1, Thomas B McClure and Lucretia Beecher.

1869

Feb. 27, William W. Scoville and Mattie E. Talmadge, Prospect.

May 23, John Henry Westropp, Albany, N. Y., and Mrs Laura Brooks.

June 2, George Washington Davis, Seymour and Martha Harriet Hitchcock.

June 27, Charles Alex. Robertson, Tennessee, and Hannah Sherman Prince

July 12, Charles William Shelton, New Haven, and Eleanor Root Atwater, New Haven.

Oct. 14, Herbert William Brockett, New Hazen, and Eliza Alice Hitchcock, New Haven.

Nov. 14, Wales Franklin Sackett, Oxford, and Sarah Jane Burnham

Dec. 4, Lester Eugene Tyrrel, Naugatuck, and Mary Patterson, Naugatuck.

1871.

Feb. 21, Garry Beecher Johnson and Polly Tolles.

Sept. 5, John Henry Twitchell and Anzonetta Adaline Goodell, Prospect.

Nov 23, Hiram Judson and Lydia Tuttle.

Nov 29, Lucius Leroy Goodell, Ansonia, and Lilian Eliza Nichols, Naugatuck

1872

Feb. 24, Frank Pierce Marsh, Woodbury, and Susan Zilla Atwood, Woodbury

Mar. 19, David F. Smith and Amelia Marilla Sperry

Aug. 11, Dwight L. Hitchcock and Martha Ford, Oxford

Oct. 16, Samuel R. Woodward, Watertown, and Charlotte F. Bigelow.

Dec 28, Charles D. Allen, Hamden, and Celia A. Lounsbury.

Jan. 1, Frank L Doolittle, Woodbridge, and Hattie E. Beecher.

Jan 15, Albert Beardsley, Berlin, and Marietta Lounsbury, Hamden.

June 10, Solon E. Roswell and Ruth A Roswell, Southbury.

June 17, Everard B. Clark, Milford, and Princetta M. Pardee

Oct 1, Frederick H Brown, New Haven, and Kate E. Woodward.

1875.

Jan. 5, George Lounsbury and Mrs Mary Jane Phelps, Prospect.

Feb 4, Charles E. Ball, New Haven, and Mary S. Woodruff.

June 21, C. W. Colton and Cora Dickerman, m. by Rt. Rev. J. Williams, D.D.

Oct. 5, George F. Davis and Fanny H. Dickerman, both of Hamden, m. by Rev C. W. Colton.

Nov 4, Frederick A. Perry, New Haven, and Celia E. Wheeler, m. by Rev. C W Colton.

Dec 16, Ellis O. Warner, Westville, and Georgiana Woodruff, m. by Rev. C. W. Colton.

Dec 27, Richard L. Warner, Hamden, and Josephine French, Beacon Falls.

1877

Jan. 3, Frederick W. Beecher, and Mary A. Basham.

Dec. 24, in Woodbridge, Dwight E Todd and Mrs Catherine E. Bishop, Woodbridge

1879.

Oct. 16, in Woodbridge, Limas Lencei, New Haven, and Betsey Ann Sampson, Woodbridge.

Dec 10, Dwight O Hull and Georgiana Bunnell.

1880.

Jan 28, Frederick S. Hitchcock, Derby, and Martha G. Sperry.

Nov 28, William H. Downs of Hamden and Mrs. Loveina M. Tuttle, in in Woodbridge by Rev. F. B. Woodward

Dec. 4, Horatio N Smith, Middlebury, and Mary N. Wright, Albany, N Y·

1896

Nov. 22, Lewis W Russell and Annie Stephens, Scotland

THE TODD FAMILY

This family is descended from Christopher Todd, who was born in Pontefract, England He was baptized Jan 11, 1617, and came to Boston in 1636 and in 1637 he was in New Haven, where he had a gristmill where Whitney's gun factory now stands This was long known as Todd's Mill

Christopher Todd married Grace Middlebrook, and had a son Samuel who married Mary Bradley and had also a son Samuel Samuel, Jr, married Susannah Tuttle, and had a son Stephen, who married Lydia Ives and had a son Jonah, who moved from Northford in 1783, and bought a large tract of land in the northeast part of Bethany then Woodbridge This tract of land, with additional tracts, has been held and occupied by the Todds down to the present time

Jonah the fifth in descent from Christopher Todd, was born in Wallingford April 28 1731 He married Lowly Harrison of Branford and had six sons, Charles, Thaddeus Thelus, Ambrose, Jonah, Jr and Ely He died in Bethany and was buried in the Carrington Cemetery

Charles married Lydia Ives The late Major Theron A Todd of New Haven came through this branch, being a son of Alfred, who was a son of Albert, who was a son of Charles

Thaddeus was a soldier in the Revolutionary War He married Penina Brockett of North Haven and had eleven children

Thelus married Irene Rogers of Northford His granddaughter Delia married a brother of the late Rev L F Morris of Bethany

Ambrose was an Episcopal clergyman He married Lavina Jarvis of Cheshire Two sons, Ambrose and Charles Jarvis, were also Episcopal clergymen The latter preached in Bethany in the fifties

Jonah, Jr , married Mary Tuttle, daughter of Uri and Thankful (Ives) Tuttle of Bethany   They removed to Plymouth, Conn

Ely, the youngest child of Jonah and Lowly (Harrison) Todd, married Bede Todd, a daughter of Seth and Mary Todd of North Haven

Lowly, wife of Jonah Todd, Sr , died July 17, 1775, in her 45th year, and was buried in Northford   Jonah Todd. Sr., married for his second wife Abigail Crittenden, widow of Dr Hopestill Crittenden   Their children were

Lucy, m. Daniel Hotchkiss and removed to Andas, Delaware Co , N Y

Hannah, m Alex Milmine and removed to Lebanon, Madison Co , N Y

Chauncey, m Susan Hotchkiss and removed to Butternuts, N Y

Russell Todd, son of Chauncey, an Episcopal clergyman, is living in Lansing, Mich , aged 76   Chauncey Todd's daughter Lucy married Norris Gilbert, and their son Mahlon Norris Gilbert, now deceased, was a bishop of the Episcopal church in Minnesota

Loly, daughter of Jonah Todd, Sr , married David Perkins of Bethany She died March 13, 1814, aged 88 years   Nancy Perkins, daughter of David and Loly (Todd) Perkins, married Abraham Lounsbury of Bethany   Their daughter, Sarah Loly Lounsbury, married Nathan Clark of Bethany

Ely Todd, son of Jonah Todd, Sr , born June 29, 1772, settled down on his father's estate and occupied it until his death Mar 10, 1817   He married Bede Todd Jan 8, 1797   She was born Dec 2, 1774, and died Nov 5, 1857   Three children blessed their union   Louisa, born Oct 11, 1797, married Amos Peck, Leonard, born Nov 8, 1800, and Mary Ann, born Oct 11, 1814, married Jesse Allen Doolittle of Hamden   She died July 4, 1854

Leonard remained on the farm in Bethany   He married, Dec 24, 1821, Julia Bradley, daughter of Elam and Lowly (Dickerman) Bradley, of Hamden, born Nov 21, 1800   Seven children blessed their union.

Grace, b Apr 1 1823, m Rev F B Woodward, d June, 1898

Emily, b June 1, 1825 d Aug 3, 1880

Margaret, b Mar 16, 1828, d Mar 15, 1886

Celia, b July 23, 1830

Street Bradley, b Aug 9, 1832, d Mar 12, 1906

Dwight Ely, b Sept 11, 1834, d Jan 3, 1901

Jasper B , b Sept 9, 1842

Emily Todd married Isaac Perkins of Bethany, son of Enos and Alma (Doolittle) Perkins   Their children were

Julia Ella, d Apr 15, 1855

Francis May, d May 1, 1855.

Eliza E , b July 28, 1849, m Otis Beecher   Both are deceased

Adna T

Margaret Todd, daughter of Leonard and Julia Todd, married Chauncey Tolles Beecher, son of Lysias and Lucy (Tolles) Beecher   Children

Irving Chauncey Tolles, b Mar 27, 1856, d in California Dec , 1902

Lillian L , b May 22, 1859, m Samuel W Chapman of Waterbury, d Feb 16, 1881

Lysias b Sept 5 1860, d Aug 19, 1890

Mary, b Feb 5, 1862 m George Meachem

Angelia, b Oct 13, 1865 d Sept 22, 1890

Dr Hesper Beecher, b May 11, 1871, d Feb 7, 1903

Celia Todd daughter of Leonard and Julia Todd, m Feb 8, 1853, Caleb Dickerman of Hamden b June 12, 1831, the son of Enos and Harriet (Doolittle) Dickerman of Hamden Both are living They celebrated their golden wedding in 1903 Their children are

Francis Harriet, b Mar 6, 1854 m George Davis of New Haven

Kate Julia, b May 2, 1757, m David Andrew

Fred Wales, b Mar 6, 1859, m Emeline Atwood, residence Hamden

Elizabeth Celia b Feb 22, 1862, m Fred Peck

Burton Street, b June 12, 1864, d Feb 24, 1888

Edward Todd b Apr 19, 1866, m Bertha Davis

Alta May, b May 5, 1868, m Willford Clark of Straitsville

Bennett Jasper, b May 15 1871, m Ruby Russell of Orange, r Mt Carmel

Stair Bradley, b Mar 1, 1873, d Jan 23, 1875

Street Bradley Todd, son of Leonard and Julia Todd, m Feb 7, 1857, Sarah A Hotchkiss, residence Bethany until fall of 1905 Children

Addie M , b Aug 4, 1858, m Joseph Kelly of New Haven

Ella S , b Sept 11, 1866, m John Crofut of Naugatuck

Dwight Ely Todd, son of Leonard and Julia, m Catherine Sperry daughter of Enos and Rosette (Russell) Sperry of Bethany, and widow of Henry Bishop of Woodbridge Children

Leonard Enos, b May 10, 1880, residence Woodbridge

Julia Rosette, b June 24, 1886, residence Woodbridge

Jasper Bryan Todd, son of Leonard and Julia, resides on the old Todd homestead, married May A Moody, daughter of the late Rev Martin Moody, rector of Christ church, Bethany, in the 70 s Child

Mary Elinore b Mar 7, 1892

The name Todd is from an old Scottish term for fox, hence the representation of a fox on the family arms

BIRTHS
FROM THE TOWN RECORDS.
All events in Bethany unless otherwise stated

1852

Clark, Ann Eliza, dau of Stiles and Emma, b Nov 10
Ford,   , son of Clark and Thirza, Dec 28

1853

Russell, Grace Louisa, dau of Stiles A and and Susan, b Feb 22
Wheeler, Mary Maria, dau of Orrin and Mary, b Apr 24
Hotchkiss, Isa Annette, dau of Andrew T and Belinda C , b. Apr. 29
Baird, Sarah Maria, dau of Allen C and Abigail, b July 14
Johnson,   son of Andrew, b Aug 23
Basham, Hannah Rebecca, dau of William and Elizabeth, b Sept. 5
Moran,   son of John, b Oct 5
Bronson, Mary Jennett, dau of Jarvis F and Lovicy L , b Oct. 24
Hull, Foster Beecher, son of Morrison C and Eliza, b Nov 1

1854

Craw, Mary Agnes, dau of James and Martha L , b Jan 3
Mix,   son of Perry and Hannah, b Feb 1
Andrews, Frederick, son of Nehemiah and Nancy b Feb 1.
Perkins, Jay Willis, son of Henry W and Harriet, b March 2
Northrup, Fredie Allen, son of Allen and Jane, b April 21
Richards,   dau of Sylvester and Gratia
Perkins, Howard French, son of Wales and Maria, b April 23
Lounsbury, Mary Ann, dau of David A and Sylvia, b April 28
Northrop, Elmer Theodore, son of Charles and Adeline, b June 1
Shaffer, Hugh Gregory, son of Lewis and Mary, b Aug 18
Beecher, Harriet Elizabeth, dau of Hoel and Adeline, b July 30
Beach,   dau of Russell M and Eliza P , b Sept 17
Wheeler, Celia Ella, dau of Orrin and Mary, b Oct 14
Abbott, Jessie Letitia, dau of Samuel P and Margaret P , b Aug 20

1855.

Munson, Fannie Eva, dau of Lewis T and Lois, b Jan 23
Perkins, Edward Henry, son of Henry W and Harriet, b. Feb 20
Russell, Hattie Maria, dau of Daniel W and Henrietta, b. Apr 14.
Andrews, Charles Hubert, son of Nathan and Elizabeth, b May 16.
Northrop, Lucia Frances, dau of Allen and Jane, b. Aug 21
Wheeler, Margaret Beneccia, dau of Noyes and Charry S , b May —
Lounsbury, Eliza Duella, dau of Henry and Sarah, b. May 29
Bayley,   son of Allen and Susan P , b June 19
Basham, Mary Ann, dau of William and Elizabeth, b June 22.
Hubbell, Arthur Norton, son of Joseph O and Ann, b July 7
Braman,   son of John and Ellen, b July 29
Richards,   son of Sylvester and Gratia, b July 29
Gaylord, Hattie, dau of Lyman and Martha, b. Oct 2
Baird, Flora Grace, dau of Allen C and Abigail, b Nov 24
Sperry, Mary dau of Alonzo and Rebecca, b. Dec. 9
Peck, Frank Eser, son of Titus D. and Louisa E , b Feb 10.

1856

Warner, Adelaide, dau. of Frederick and Amanda, b Jan —
Perkins, Adna Todd, son of Isaac and Emily, b May 27
Russell, Mary Jane, dau. of Lucius and Elizabeth, b. May 7
Conoly, William Morris, son of William and Eliza, b May 28.
Perkins, Jane Rebecca, dau of Wales F and Maria, b June 23
Hull, Carrie, dau of Morrison C and Eliza, b July 17
Wheeler, Christiana Jane, dau of Orrin and Mary, b July 27
Perkins, Julia Maria, dau of Charles and Mary, b Aug 9
Peck, Mary Elizabeth, dau of Titus Dennis and Louisa E , b Oct. 2
Brown, Wilson Wilbur, son of Andrew P and Ruth Ann, b Oct 17.
Collins, James Buchanan, son of Jeremiah and Nora, b Dec 24
Collins, John Breckenridge, son of Jeremiah and Nora, b Dec 24.
Dorman, Frank, son of Philos and Eliza, b April 25
Northrop, Alvina Phinett, dau of Charles and Adelaide, b Aug 12
Watkins, Charles M , son of John and Emily A , b Aug 22.
Aspenwall, George C , son of George R and Eliza A , b Oct 2
Fitzgerald, Hannorah, dau of Michael and Bridget, b Oct 25
Bridge, Lillie Fremont, dau of Jesse F and Almira A , b May 26
Odholin, Frederick, son of Gustavus and Jane E , b Dec 5
Haley, Daniel, son of James and Mary, b June 25
Otsego,   of   , Aug 28

Clark, Sheldon, son of Charles F and Anna, b Sept 21

1857

Herwood, Thomas, son of Andrew and Daffany, b Jan 21
McDonald, Wm Henry, son of John and Mary Ann, b Jan 24
Bashan, Joseph Edward, son of Wm and Elizabeth, b Jan 30
Warner, Nelson, son of Eliza Warner, b Aug 16
French, Hattie Elizabeth, dau of David M and Sarah E, b Dec 28
Laittch, Charlie, son of Charlie and Theresa, b Dec 4
Pierce,   dau of Elijah S and Elizabeth S, June 11
Junius, Elizabeth, dau of Edward and Elizabeth, b June 11
Baehr, Oswald Charlie, son of Oswald and Julia, b Dec, 16
Keechwitz, Emeline, dau of Henry and Phippina, b June 7
Hackert, Julia, dau of Julius and Louisa, b Dec 1
Craw, Willis Eugene, son of James H and Martha L, b March 11
Hard, Ida Elizabeth, dau of Charles F and Polly E, b June 14
Abbott,   son of Smith and Julia B, b March –
Beecher, Frank Arthur, son of Frances A, b June 3
Hubbell, Josie Morton, son of Joseph O and Ann, b Jan —
Shaffer, Catharine Ann, dau of Lewis and Alice, b March 5
Allen, Frank, son of Julia, b July 8
Andrews, Noyes, son of Azariah and Sarah A, b April 7
Northrop,   , son of Allen and Jane, b Dec 4

1858

Wooding, Lilla, dau of John and Jennet, b Jan 3
Doolittle,   , son of Elizur B and Helen A, b Feb 26
Peck, Jane, dau of Titus D and Louisa E, b Sept 18
Goodyer, Cynthia, dau of George and Cynthia, b April 25
Foot, Sherman D, son of Samuel E and Clara J, b May 3
Dodd,   , dau of George, b Aug —
Downs,   , son of Elbert and Catharine A, b Nov —
Bronson, George, son of Allen C and Abigail, b July 17
Beard, William, son of Jarvis F and Lovicy P, b Sept 26
Todd, Ada Mariah, dau of Street B. and Sarah A, b Aug 4
French, Gertrude, dau of John C and Marietta, b March 23
Collins,   , dau of Jeremiah and Nora, b June
Shulz, Augusta, dau of Charles and Mary, b April 24
Bridge, Benjamin Herbert, son of Joseph M and Adelaide, b Sep 20
Schlisenza, Anna, dau of Augusta D and Jerusha, b Feb 2
Cunningham, Thomas, son of Thomas and Margaret, b Jan 16

Keening,   dau of   , b Oct —
Perkins,   , dau of Wales F and Maria, b March 8
Wheeler,   , dau of Orrin and Mary, b Dec. 5
Andrews, Fannie, dau of Azariah and Sarah A , b May 17
Johnson, Burton Frank, son of Andrew and Elizabeth, b March 2
Northrop, Willie Dwight, son of Charles and Adelaide, b May 5

                         1859
Billerwell, Elizabeth, dau of John and Susannah, b Jan 12.
Hotchkiss, Frank Lester, son of Lewis E and Elizabeth M , b Mar 2
Durand, Wm. Frederick, son of Wm and Ruth, b March 5
Earling, Julius, son of Charles and Julia, b April 7.
Clark, George Trumbull, son of Charles F. and Anna, b Nov 13
Stevens,   , dau of Charles E and Eliza, b Oct 13
Lounsbury,   , son of Henry and Sarah, b Sept 27
Hotchkiss,   , son of Andrew T and Belinda, b Nov 14
Boke,   , dau of John and Mary Ann, b Oct 9
Beecher,   , dau of Chauncey and Margaret, b May 22
Pritchard,   , son of George N and Laura Ann, b July 5
Hill,   , son of Smith D and Mary O , b July 10   .
Kotchwitz, Joseph Otto, son of Henry and Phippina, b May 19
Spencer, Margaret J , dau of John R and Mary, b Aug 5
Heublin, Clara G , dau of Frederick and Joanna, b Oct 28
Slasinger, Mary, dau of Augustus and Jerusha, b June 10
Joy, John, son of Michael and Mary, b April 15
Northrup, Rebecca L , dau of Allen and Jane E , b May 13
Russell,   , dau of Wm W and Henrietta, b Oct 25.
Allen,   , son of David and Emily, b July 12
Bush,   , son of Franklin K and Mary, b Aug —
                         1860
Atwater,   , dau of Franklin and Elizabeth, b Feb 19
Brown,   , dau of Andrew O and Ruth A , b Feb 24
Downs,   , dau of Albert and Catharine, b. July 13
Mansfield,   , son of Stephen and Amy, b July 21
Beecher,   , son of Chauncey T and Margaret, b Sept 15
French,   , son of Wales H and Mary S , b Nov 24
Peck,   , son of T Dennis and Lovisa E , b Dec 4
Cotter,   , dau. of James and Mary Jane, b Dec 27
French,   , dau of John and Marietta, b Aug 28
Earling,   , dau of Charles and Julia, b Nov —

Odholm, Emma, J , dau of Gustavus and Jane E , b Jan 23,
Luther,   , dau of James H and Mary, b Jan 18
Dibble,   , dau of Jacob and Teresa, b Oct 30
Huttman,   , dau of Frederick and Rosey, b Dec, 10
Coe,   , son of John and Mary, b Jan 27
Hard, Lydia Ann, dau of Charles F and Polly E , b Jan 24
Sackett,   , Emma M , dau of Wm W and Minerva, b Feb 12
Andrews, Mary E , dau of Azariah and Sarah, b Jan 21
Northrop, Hattie B , dau of Charles and Adaline, b April 17
Pielmoo,   , son of Frederick and Rosanna, b Oct 17
Northrop,   , dau of Allen and Jane, b May 26
Wood,   , dau of John W and Delia, b Aug 21
McClure,   , son of Wm and Hannah, b June 30
Johnson,   , son of Garry B and Huldah, b Dec 8
McClure,   , son of Catherine, b Feb   -
Daley,   , dau of Thomas and Bridget, b Sept 21

DEATHS

1852

White, John, b Derby, d Oct   , a 72
Perkins, David, farmer, d Nov 17, a 80
Atwater, Polly, b Bethany, d Dec 31, a 20

1853

Beecher, Jane, b Bethany, d Feb 11, a 13
Wooding, Uri, b Bethany, d Feb 16, a 58
Sanford, Cyrus, b Bethany, d Feb 28, a 84
Castle, Jehial, b Roxbury, physician d April 18, a 82
Russell, Stiles A , b Bethany, wagonmaker, d May 3, a 42
Wooding, Anna, b Woodbridge, d May 17, a 77
Sandford, Nancy, b Watertown, d July 5, a 76
Sperry, Samuel, b Woodbridge, d July 19, a 74, (pauper)
Sanford, Moses, b Bethany, d Aug 19, a 83
French, Harriet, b Derby, d Aug 26, a 62
Tolles, Nehemiah, b Bethany, d Sept 15 a 43
Sperry, Celia, b Bethany, d Oct 17, a 21
Wooding, Silas, shoemaker, b Bethany, d. Oct 29, a 50
Schaffer, Lewis,   , d Nov 30, a 2
Twitchell, Bennett, clothier, b Oxford, d Nov 4, a. 48

1854

Peck, Polly, b   , d Feb 21, a 72

THE CARRINGTON CEMETERY.

Carrington, Nehemiah, merchant, b. Bethany, d. March 26, a. 72.

Sanford, Lois, b. Hamden, d. April 11, a. 82.

Wheeler, Rhoda, b.   , d. May 6, a. 72.

Beecher, Lysias, b. Bethany, d. May 7, a. 76.

Pierpont, Grace, b. Bethany, d. July 25, a. 20.

Rosha, Elexis, joiner, b. Bethany, d. July 31, a. 55.

Brown, Emerett, b. Naugatuck, d. Aug. 6, a. 26.

Hotchkiss, Jared, b. Bethany, d. Aug. 24. a. 50.

Beecher, Lucy, b. Bethany, d. Aug. 26, a. 71.

Hitchcock, Abagail, b. Bethany, d. Sept. 9, a. 99.

Lines, Tempa, b. Woodbridge, d. Aug. 31, a. 67.

Driver, James, b. Bethany, d. Nov. 14, a. 76.

Sackett, Polly, b. Bethany, d. Sept. 11, a. 80.

Lines, Arma, b.   , d. Oct. 10, a. 96.

Hubbell, Josephine L., b. Bethany, d. Oct. 25, a. 1y., 2m., 19d.

Hubbell, Emma A., b. Bethany, d. Oct. 29, a. 3.

Andrews, Nehemiah, b. Bethany, d. Dec. 19, a. 3y. 10 months.

Northrop, Allen, b. Bethany, d. Nov. 17, a. 9 months, 20d.

THE CARRINGTON CEMETERY, LOOKING EAST.

Mix, infant son of Parry M., b. Bethany, d. Feb. 3, a. 3 days.
Richards, infant dau. of Sylvester, b. Bethany, d. April 23, a. —
Allen, Fredie, b. Bethany, d. Nov. 15, a. 7 months.

1855.

Scoville, Jane, b. Prospect, d. Feb. 26, a. 22.
Hotchkiss, Rhoda, b. Bethany, d. March 26, a. 55.
Perkins, Julia Ella, b. Bethany, d. April 15, a. 7.
Downs, Zephaniah, b. Bethany, d. April 17, a. 72.
Beecher, Herbert, b. Bethany, d. April 22, a. 6.
Perkins, Frances May, b. Bethany, d. May 1, a. 3.
Hotchkiss, Jane Ella, b. Bethany, d. May 22, a. 4.
Collyer, Henry, b.   , d. July 5, a. —
Peck, Titus, b. Bethany, d. July 27, a. 69.
Perkins, Howard F., b. Bethany, d. Aug. 24, a. 1 year, 4 mo. 1d.
Carrington, Henry A., b. Bethany, d. Sept. 8, a. 47.
Tuttle, Seymour, blacksmith, b. Bethany, d. Sept. 23, a. 71.
Sperry, Chillson, b.   , d. Nov. 19, a. 79.
Beecher, Dennis, teacher, b. Bethany, d. Nov. 22, a. 31.

Hitchcock, Mary, b.   , d Nov 22, a 73.
Lines, Thirza, b. Bethany, d Dec 6, a 66
Hotchkiss, Harvey, b. Woodbridge, d Dec 9, a 74
Beecher, Hoel, b Bethany, d. Dec. 22, a. 45.
Hotchkiss, Larchens, b. Bethany, d   , a. 78.
Coe, George Albert, b Bethany, d Oct 14, a 1y. and 2 months.
                         1856.
Lounsbury, Timothy, b Bethany, d. Jan 6, a 86
Russell, Polly, b Prospect, d Jan 9, a 57.
French, Miles, b. Bethany, d Feb 1, a 50.
Smith, Frank, b   , d April 3, a 5 months
Hoadley, Luman, b. Bethany, d June 4, a 59
Clark, Experience, b. Woodbridge, d. Aug 16, a. 80.
Sandford, Laura L , b Bethany, d Oct. 26, a. 14 y, 8mo.
Hotchkiss, Spencer, b Bethany, d Nov. 7, a 52
Sperry, Sally, b Bethany, d Dec 2, a 68.
Watkins,   , b   , d Sept 5, a 27
Conoly, William M , b Bethany, d. Aug. 17, a 27 y, 2 mo. 19 d
               , female, domestic, Oct 13, (no age given)
Otsego, Emily A , b Germany, d Sept 5, a 27
Otsego,   , infant of   , stillborn.
Haskert, Charlie, b Oxford, d Sept 19, a 8 months, 19 days.
Russell, Hattie M., b Bethany, d Oct 13, a 1 year, 6mo , 19d
                         1857
Bailey, Sheldon, b Chatham, d Feb 9, a 48
Bailey, Harriet, b Hamden, d Feb 22, a 12.
Deming, Lucy, b   , d March 7, a 51
Leavenworth, Polly S , b Huntington, d. April 30, a 63.
Sperry, Ella Jane, b. Bethany, d June 15, a 70
Sperry, Marcus, b Bethany, d July 12, a 45
Perkins, Ira, b Hamden, d May 15, a 68
Davis, Robert, b   , d Aug. 2, a 48.
Beecher, Sarah A., b. Bethany, d. Aug 14, a. 33 y , 3 mo
Conoly, Eliza, b Naugatuck d Oct 4, a 30
Judd, Dorcas, b Naugatuck, d Oct. 4, a. 93
Sanford, Betsey, b Prospect, d Sept. 28, a 63.
Todd, Bede, b North Haven, d Nov. Nov. 5, a 78.
Peck, Fanny, b. Bethany, d Nov. 7 a 76
Candy, Perus, shoemaker, b Waterbury, d Dec. 19, a 76

CEMETERY NEAR CENTER SCHOOL.

Allen, Fanny, b. Woodbridge, d. Jan. 25, a. 68.

Bradley, David H., tinner, b. Middlebury, d. July 4, a. 24.

      ,   , infant son of   , b. Bethany, d. Mar. 4, a. 1 d.

Bridge, Almira A., b.   , d. Aug. 26, a. 28.

Driver, Mary E., b. New Haven, d. Aug. 31, a. 1 year, 3 months.

Northrop, Finett, b. Bethany, d. May 12, a. 7.

1858.

Sackett, William, b. Bethany, d. Feb. 4, a. 83.

Hitchcock, Allen C., b Bethany, d. Feb. 19, a. 42.

Clark, Mrs. Emma, b. Middlebury, d. March 4, a. 33.

Hitchcock, Ebenezer, b. Bethany, d. March 4, a. 70.

Kingsley, Sarah, b. Cheshire, d. April 3, a. 83.

Barber, John C., laborer, b. England, d. May 4, a. 57.

Lounsbury, Mrs. Laura, b. Middlesbury, d. May 4, a. 64.

Hotchkiss, Philo, b. Bethany, d. July 16, a. 81.

Umberfield, Sally, b. Bethany, d. July 22, a. 67.

Sackett, Stern, b. Bethany, d. Sept. 5, a. 18.

Bagdin, Ester, b. Bethany, d. Oct. 4, a. 87.

Aspinwall, George C., b. Bethany, d. Oct 6, a 1 year, 11 mo 15d
Pierce, Emma, b Bethany, d Oct 9, a. 1 year, 3 months, 29 days
Bradley, Electa, b Bethany, d March 20, a 79
Beard, William, b. Bethany, d Nov 17, a. 79 years, 4 months
Truesdale, Lorenzo, b Seymour, r, Seymour, d April 7, (accident)

1859

Hotchkiss, Elizabeth, widow, b.   , d Jan. 6, a. 97
Perkins, Mrs Harriet C , b.   , d Jan 28, a 28.
Smith, Eliakim, b. Bethany, d March 9, a. 74.
Bradley, Joseph, b Woodbridge, d May 27, a. 77
Lounsbury, Mary, widow, b. Bethany, d. Jan 5, a. 88
Tuttle, Jeremiah, bookkeeper, b. Bethany, d. Sept. 29, a. 44.
Downs, Calvin, blacksmith, b New Haven, d. Nov. 17, a. 22.
Treat, Wallace L , b. New Haven, d Sept. 10, a 6 y, 24 d
Nettleton, Lydia, b. Middlebury, d April 19, a. 63.
Wilcox, Sarah, b Bethany, d. Dec. 30, a. 69.

1860

Griffin, Harmon, storekeeper, b Lime, d. Feb 20, a 59
Peck, George F., b Bethany, d March 25, a 78.
Hotchkiss, Harley, b Bethany, d March 26, a —
Lounsbury, Abraham, b. Bethany, d April 27, a. 61
French, Harry, b. Bethany, d. May 17, a. 78.
Russell, Grace, b Bethany, d June 28, a, 7
Judd, Leonard, b Bethany, d. July   , a.—
Munson, Lewis T , b Huntington, d Aug 2, a. 37
Deming, Delia, b. Hamden, d Sept. 6, a. 19
Beecher, Martha, b Derby, d Nov. 18, a. 2<.
Clement, John, laborer, b. England, d Dec. 14, a 51.
Hering, James, shoemaker, b Albany, d. April   , a 25
Earling, Charles, b Bethany, d May 9, a. 2.
Luther, Almira, b. Bethany, d March   , a. 7 weeks.
Fitzgerald, Bridget, b. York state, d. March 29, a 2
Hard, Joseph N , b New Haven, d. Sept 11, a 75
Joy, John, b Bethany, d May 1, a. 1.

A COLONIAL HALL IN THE WHEELER HOMESTEAD.

THE BEECHER—WHEELER HOMESTEAD.

Among the fine old mansions, large and roomy, with broad halls, well built and tastefully decorated in the style of the olden times, which dot the hills and in the valleys of Connecticut far from the hum of city life, is the Wheeler homestead, a few hundred feet north of the center, facing on the main road, looking southward toward where in the misty distance lies the city of New Haven, Long Island Sound and Long Island beyond.

Just south of the house, and at right angles to the main road, a road leads eastward, toward Mount Carmel, and in the other direction, past the residence of Deacon Horsfall, a road leads westerly to a parallel road on which may be seen the homes of Nathan Mansfield and B. M. Wellman, and what was recently the residence of Esquire Samuel R. Woodward, now occupied by his son, S. P. Woodward.

But to return to the Wheeler mansion. This house attracts the attention of the passerby by reason of the material and workmanship and the taste which speak well for the intellect and pocketbook of its long ago builder The underpinning is of fine cut sandstone, seldom to be found under houses built at the time Three large chimneys which project above the roof and together with the size of the structure tend to give it an air of superiority, with the many old fashioned windows which dot its sides

Looking closer one observes that the cornice, though not prominent nor imposing, but narrow and oldfashioned, shows taste and fine workmanship The portico is similarly ornamented, and should one chance to pass by when the front door is open on a summer afternoon, he would undoubtedly be surprised to see a large hall extending from the front of the main house, with handsome arches overhead The engraving above gives a fine view of the hall and bears out the assertion that this was worthy to be called an elegant residence

In view of the growing interest in historic residences further particulars of this remarkable house may not be amiss There are two front parlors, one on each side of the broad hall, each about fifteen feet square, with two fancy arched alcoves at the back, and a large fireplace and a handsome mantel between them

From floor to ceiling throughout the lower part of the house is a distance of over nine feet, and in several rooms the wall near the ceiling is ornamented by a handsome frieze There are at least eight large, light, airy rooms besides the main lower hall, the upper hall, and a dance hall some seventeen feet wide by thirtysix feet long There are no less than ten large fireplaces, furnaces and steam heaters not being in vogue when this house was built The dance hall has been used for holding church festivals, and for a time the regular town meetings The older people told of the socials and dances that they used to attend under its hospitable roof

What might be termed a curiosity is situated in the garret, and consists of a commodious brick smokehouse used for smoking hams or beef It is arranged to be connected by pipe with the kitchen stove and the chimney, thus enabling the accomplishment of curing the pork and beef for the larder without an extra fire, or the expenditure of unnecessary labor, an example of the idea expressed in the old adage, "Killing two birds with one stone "

We are told that the house was built by Darius Beecher, who was then quite wealthy, had two daughters and one son, went west with his family and lost his fortune The place was afterward occupied by Abram Beecher, who was, however, not related to the builder Later it was owned by Lewis Thomas, who occupied it with his family

It finally passed into the possession of Orrin Wheeler, who occupied it with his family till his death in 1874 His widow, son and unmarried daughters continued to occupy it until the death of Mrs Wheeler in 1898, and the death of the son in 1899 The Misses Mary and Christina Wheeler still cling to the associations which make the "Old Homestead" dear to them, and remain under the roof which has withstood the storms of the nineteenth century, and enters upon the twentieth still protecting a framework of massive oak, but little the worse for time and wear

A LEAF FROM THE OLD RECORDS

At a Lawfull Society meeting of the inhabitants of bethany held by adjurnment on the first wensday of desember 1765 it was then 1 voted that Timothy Ball Hezekiah Clark Jesse Bradley Deacon John White be the Commitey for this Society the year insewing

2 voted that a rate be laid at five pene on the pound to be paid on the twelf day of September next

3 voted that Neahemiah Toles Shall be the Colector of the above raight

4 voted that Valentine Willmott, Ben aj ' Peck and Stephen Sanford Shall time the psalm

5 voted that Caleb Tuttle Shall dig graves.

6 voted that this meeting be adjurned to the first wensday of desember next at four of the Clock in the afternoon at the Schoolhouse in bethany

At a Speshall Society meeting of the inhabitants of bethany held on the 11th day of november 1766 the inhabitants being Lawfully warned it was then

1 voted that Deacon Joel Hotchkiss Shall be moderator of the meeting

3 voted that we will apply to the honourabell County Court now Siting in new haven for a com" to cum to bethany to vew our Situation and Start a place for a meeting hous

4 voted that Deacon Joel Hotchkiss mr Daniel Toles mr Timothy Peck and mr Hezekiah Clark Shall be a commt to make applycation to the honourable County Court for the purpose afoursaid

5 voted that this meeting be adjourned without day

At a Lawfull Society meeting of the the inhabitants of bethany held by adjurnment on the first wensday of desember 1766 it was 1 voted that Isaac Beecher Deacon John White Timothy Ball Hezekiah Clark and Jesse Bradley Shall be a Comtt for this Society the year insewing

2 voted that a raight be Laid at two pene one farthing on the pound to be paid on the twelf day of September next

3 voted that Thomas Johnson Shall be the Colector of the above raight

4 voted that this meeting be adjurned to the first wensday of desember next at four of the Clock in the afternoon at the Schoolhous in bethany

At a Speshall Society meeting of the inhabitants of bethany held on the 15th day of January 1767 at the Sehoolhous in Sd bethany the inhabitants being Lawfully warned it was

1 voted that Deacon Joel Hotchkiss Shall be moderator of this meeting

2 voted that this Society will go the honurabell County Court now Siting in new haven to Establish the plais appointed by their Comtt for a meeting hous in Sd bethany

3 voted that mr Josiah Lounsbury mr Timothy Peck mr Daniel Toles mr Ebenezer Bishop mr John Perkins and mr Samuel Bisko Shall sit on the elders seat

4 voted that this meeting be adjurned without day

At a Lawfull Society meeting of the inhabitants of bethany held by adjurnment on the first wensday of Desember 1767 it was

10-9-07

1 voted that Isaac Beecher Timothy Ball John Lines Hezekiah Clark and Jesse Bradly Shall be a Comtt for this Society the year insewing

2 voted that a raight be Laid at three pene on the pound to be paid at the tenth day of September next

3 voted that Eliphalet Johnson Shall be the Colector of the above raight

4 voted that this meeting be adjurned to next wensday at two of the Clock in the afternoon at the schoolhous in bethany

At a Lawfull Society meeting of the inhabitants of bethany held by adjurnment on the Second wensday of December 1767 it was

1 voted that it is necesary for us to build a meeting house

2 voted that we will build a meeting hous fifty foot long and forty foot wide

3 voted that we will provide the boards Claboards Shingals nail and glas nesesory for building a meeting hous the year insewing

4 voted that Deacon Hotchkiss Timothy Peck Daniel Toles Isaac Beecher Hezekiah Toles Daniel Beecher Timothy Ball Deacon White Samuell Brisco and Israel Thomas Shall be a Comtt to provide the above Said articals for building a meeting hous

5 voted that a raight be Laid for building a meeting hous at four pene on the pound to be paid at the first day of october next

6 voted that half the above raight Shall be paid in flax seed or Sum other that will answer at newyork

7 voted that Benajah Peck Shall be the Colector of the above raight

8 voted that Short Shingals Shall be thurteen Shillings a thousand and Claboards five Shillings and Six pene pr hundred and boirds three Shillings and Six pence all delivered at the plais prefixed for a meeting hous.

9 voted that Isaac Beecher Daniel Toles and Deacon Hotchkiss Shall be a Comtt to go unto the propietors meeting to the broad street to help to purchis a plais for a meeting house in this Society

10 voted that this meeting be adjurned unto the first wensday of January next at five a Clock in the afternoon at the Schoolhous in bethany

THE SCHOOLS OF BETHANY,

BY WALLACE D. HUMISTON

In the geographies in common use fifty years ago it was said that Connecticut was famous for her excellent common schools. That our Puritan ancestors recognized the value of education is indicated by the early acts which were passed for the establishment of schools The "Code of 1650" required that "in order that learning may not be buried in the graves of our forefathers" that every town having fifty householders should maintain a school.

Soon after the settlement of New Haven, in 1638, a school was established which was taught by the noted Master Cheever. He was a worthy, well educated man. Many years elapsed after the time of his school before settlers had located in the upper valley of the West River in sufficient numbers to warrant the establishment of a school. Amity Parish, which included the present towns of Woodbridge and Bethany, was incorporated in 1737, and it is probable that there was a school in the parish previous to that date.

The first schoolhouse in Bethany was built in 1750, at the crossroads a few rods north of the residence of Judge E N. Clark. It was cared for by the Parish of Amity until 1762, when it passed under the control of the Bethany Ecclesiastical Society. The names of the teachers in this primitive school are not now available, but we may rest assured that they were worthy schoolmasters and and schoolmistresses In those times the schoolmaster was regarded with profound respect, and when he walked through the village, his head bowed in meditation upon some grave question or in solving a difficult problem, the boys in passing him doffed their caps respectfully. He was one of the few to receive the title of Mr , and he stood next to the minister in the minds of the people.

When the Bethany Parish was incorporated by an act of the General Assembly in 1762 the schoolhouse immediately became the center of ecclesiastical, educational and civil life. Here the sturdy children of the community came to solve hard "sums" and to con the lessons in the "New England Primer," which contained the Westminster catechism and an alphabet beginning with

> "In Adam's fall
> We sinned all."

and ending with

> ' Zacheus he
> Did climb the tree
> Our Lord to see "

Here on the Sabbath our ancestors met for public worship. Here they convened on the first Wednesday of each December, and on other "speshall" days, to discuss the civil questions of the parish.

At a meeting of this kind held in December, 1763, it was voted that "Timothy Peck, John White and Jesse Bradley be a commitey to take care of the school money of this society." Again Oct. 22, 1764, it was "Voted that the school money for this society shall be divided into three equall parts and to be laid out for Schooling in the most proper plaisses in this Society, it being left with the Committy to say where it shall be laid out." It seems evident that the three schools were organized in the South, North and East Districts, which correspond to the Centre, Gate and Downs Districts of the present day. As there were no schoolhouses in the last two districts, the schools were taught in private dwellings. During the year following the school money was expended in maintaining the above schools.

THE DOWNS STREET SCHOOLHOUSE.

In December, 1770, Daniel Beecher, Jesse Bradley, and Ezra Sperry were elected "to be a Com^tt for this Society to take care of the bank and School money the year insewing." It was "voted that the above Com^tt shall divide the School money into Destricts according to their discresion."

A schoolhouse was erected in the North District in 1781, at the junction of the Cheshire Road with the Straits Turnpike. One of the teachers was Isaac Judd, brother of Chauncey who was kidnapped during the Dayton Raid. This schoolhouse saw many years of service and was not replaced until 1880.

A schoolhouse was built in the East or Downs District before 1800 It stood nearly opposite the present edifice and was occupied for more than a hundred years It was demolished in 1900 Even the young people can remember this old, unpainted schoolhouse by the roadside

From the records we learn that the Beecher District, then called the Southeast, was established in 1789 A schoolhouse was soon built for the use of the district It was the first one of the three which have stood on the site of the present Beecher schoolhouse

The North-east or Smith district was established during the latter part of the eighteenth century The first schoolhouse was under the large chestnut near Mr J B Todd's A corner stone of the foundation can still be pointed out The furniture consisted of slab benches placed before a shelf which extended around three sides of the room. A fireplace was in one end For several years previous to the erection of Christ Church (1809) the services of the Episcopalians were held in this schoolhouse Among the teachers in this old-time school was Julia Bradley, who afterwards became Mrs. Leonard Todd. A Miss Sylvia Tuttle was also a teacher there The latter's sister, Miss Jennette Tuttle, taught later in this and other districts of the town She is now Bethany's oldest living teacher

More than a century ago a schoolhouse was standing on "Meeting House Hill," near Bethany Green It was in the Middle District The building was two stories in height, the upper part being the Masonic Hall. It was near the meeting house, and was heated each Sunday, in order that the congregation might repair hither between the services

In 1802 the South, West, and Middle Districts were consoli dated into the Union District, which was eventually called the Center When a new schoolhouse was built the old one was bought by Hezekiah Thomas. It was drawn across the valley to a site near the churches and served as a hall to a hotel built by Mr Thomas The hall was demolished about twentyfive years ago by the owner, Mr Perry

By virtue of her charter Connecticut claimed lands to the "South Sea," or Pacific Ocean These claims were ceded to the Federal Government with the exception of a tract called the Western Reserve This was sold in 1795 and the proceeds were set apart for a school fund which now amounts to more than two million dollars. From this fund an appropriation was granted to Bethany which gave a fresh impetus to school affairs. The school records, which had hitherto been mingled with the ecclesiastical records, were now written in a separate book. The first meeting of the School Society under the new conditions is thus recorded:—

"Oct. 31, 1796. A Lawful School Society meeting of the located Society of Bethany, holden at the meeting house in said Bethany, in the town of Woodbridge, for the purpose of forming a Society to take care of an appropriation the Interest of Monies arising from the Sale of Western Lands belonging to the State of Connecticut."

THE SMITH STREET SCHOOLHOUSE.

The parish districts had increased from three in 1764 to eight in 1797. The names of the districts and the committees in 1797 were:—

South (Center), Silas Hotchkiss.
West (Center) Eber Lines.
Middle (Center), Medad Hotchkiss.
(Northeast (Smith), Reuben Perkins.

North (Gate), Robert Russel
Southeast (Beecher), Joel Hotchkiss.
East (Downs), Eber Downs.
Southwest (annexed to Woodbridge 1806), William Andrews.

A school meeting was convened Dec. 27, 1811, in the Southeast District (Beecher), and it was "Voted that we build a schoolhouse on or about the same ground where the old house now stands, and fase it to the Est. Voted that Dennis Sperry, Chauncey Toles, Hezekiah Beecher, Isaac Sperry, Jr , be a committee to superintend in building said house. Voted that we cover sd house with good pine shingles and clapboards, clean stuff to the accep(t)ance of the Comittee Voted that we sell the old schoolhous at value due to be taken from this ground before the first of October next "

The vote regarding the material was rescinded at the next meeting, but the schoolhouse was built during 1812   January 19, 1813, it was "voted that we give the money to Mr. William Johnson that the book (tax levy) and old schoolhous raised over and above what the committee gave for building the new schoolhouse."

Other interesting records concerning this schoolhouse follow. "April 9, 1819,—Voted that the commity procure a teacher for the ensueing summer, to begin on the first Tuesday in May and continue five months or longer if wanted   October 27, 1820,—Voted the committee pay eight dollars per month for the ensueing winter   November 4, 1822,—Voted to have the school commence the first Monday in December and continue to the first of March.   November 19, 1827,—Voted Obadiah Lounsbury's shop be appointed for a place to set up notices for school meetings in addition to the schoolhouse for the year ensueing   April 9, 1832,—Voted that the committe employ Mrs Eliza Lines if possible at a rate not to exceed a dollar pr week   Voted that religious denominations be permitted to hold meetings at this house not to interfere with the school   March 21, 1833,—Voted that we tax ourselves to defray the expense of painting the schoolhouse and making all necessary repairs and to purchase the stove for the use of the school   March 31, 1837,— Resolved that the committee employ Mary Stevens to teach the summer school if she can be obtained for one dollar a week."

The old red school-house in the North or Gate District has been mentioned above   It was probably occupied for a century.

At a meeting convened in this place February 28, 1831, it was "voted that Julia Sperry teach the summer school."

The school year was then divided into two terms. The winter school began in December and continued three months. This term was invariably taught by a male teacher. A summer school was "set up" about the first of May and was in session four or five months. The wages for this term were usually one dollar per week. The teacher of the winter term received somewhat higher wages. It was the custom for the teacher "to board round the district," staying a week or two with each family.

THE BEECHER SCHOOLHOUSE.

The following are a few interesting items culled from the records of the Gate District:

March 29, 1831,—"Paid E J. Thompson, teacher of the North School, Bethany, the last season, the sum of $25.33." April 2, 1835,—"Voted that Mr. Russel Chatfield repair the fireplace and chimney sufficiently for the present and bring in his bill to the committee for the same." November 16, 1835,—"Voted that the committee procure a stove for the use of the school." March 20, 1843,—"Voted the teacher of the winter term, Mr. D.

Brooks, shall pay for the key he lost, if not deduct from his bill."
A district tax was levied in 1839 and the schoolhouse was thoroughly
repaired. Enos Perkins. Levi M. Marks, Harvey Hotchkiss and
A. A. Perkins were the committee for this work.

In 1832 a second school-house was built in the Northeast District on the site of the present building. Plans were discussed in
regard to the erection of this structure as early as 1826. The
present structure was built in 1876.

THE CENTER SCHOOLHOUSE.

The Center schoolhouse was built about 1834 and is the oldest
one in the town. It is situated near the roadside a short distance
south of the churches. It has been thoroughly repaired several
times and is now in good condition. A few years ago a porch and
cupola, for a large bell, were added. Hezekiah Thomas was one
of the first teachers in this schoolhouse. Miss Jane French, afterward Mrs. Peck, also taught here.

The Southeast District is now known as the Beecher District,
deriving its name from the many families of that name who have

lived in the district. The schoolhouse now standing there was built in 1870, and is the third erected on that site. It was enlarged in 1899. A porch and large bell were also added. The schoolhouse is located in the highway a few rods south of the "four-corners" at the residence of Mrs. Allen.

The Smith District provided for the erection of a schoolhouse in 1876, on the site of the former one. D. B. Hoadley was the builder. It was ready for occupancy early in 1877. Mrs. Justine C. Coe was the first teacher in the new schoolhouse. It is very pleasantly located on a hillside which slopes to West River. There are abundant shade trees near the edifice.

THE GATE SCHOOLHOUSE.

The Straits Turnpike was built a century ago, and a tollgate was maintained near the Major Lounsbury house, now the residence of Cleveland Doolittle. The locality was designated as the "Gate." The tollgate disappeared long ago, but the name clung to the hamlet, and finally, about 1880, it was applied to the school district. The schoolhouse in this district having fallen into a condition unfit for school purposes, the school board threatened to withhold the appropriation for its maintenance, and after considerable deliberation it was decided to build a new schoolhouse. Wales H. French, Allen Lounsbury and Arthur Lacey were elected a building committee. A knoll a short distance south of the old schoolhouse, called "The Sandhill," was chosen for the site of the new building, and it was completed in 1880

The most recently built schoolhouse is found in the Downs District. It was erected in 1897–8, with a thoroughness very creditable to its builders. The structure is located on elevated ground on Downs Street, nearly opposite the site of the old building. An extensive and pleasing view, reaching terough the "Gap" of West Rock Ridge, may be enjoyed from the schoolhouse door.

The district system of school management was abolished in 1901, and the local school affairs have since been controlled by a town school committee. Under tne new management the schools have been kept in good condition, and compare favorably with those in other towns.

> " When care and time our memories blot,
> When years our measure fill,
> We'll think sometimes of the dear old spot,
> The schoolhouse 'neath the hill "

OLD CEMETERY, NEAR THE RESIDENCE OF ALLEN G. SPERRY.

"There scattered, oft the earliest of the year,
By hands unseen are showers of violets found;
The redbreast loves to build and warble there,
And little footsteps lightly print the ground."

REPRESENTATIVES TO THE GENERAL ASSEMBLY

1883-4, David Beecher
1835-6, Andrew Beecher
1836-7, Harry French
1838, Leverett Thomas
1839, John Russell
1840, Anthony F Stoddard
1841, Job Andrew
1842, Abel Prince
1843, Burton Sperry
1844, Guy Perkins
1845, Joseph N Stoddard
1846, Miles Hitchcock
1847-8, Miles French
1849-50, Charles French
1851-2, Edwin Pardee
1853, Miles Hitchcock
1854-5, Robert Clark
1856, Wiles F Perkins
1857, Ezra S Sperry
1858, Adna Hotchkiss
1859-60, Dwight N Clark,
1861, George Hotchkiss
1862, Ezra S Sperry
1863-4, Andrew Beecher
1865-6, W B Dickerman
1867-8, Andrew T Hotchkiss

1869-70, Asa C Woodward
1871, Buel Buckingham
1872, Miles Hitchcock
1873-4, Garry B Johnson
1875, Allen Lounsbury
1876, Samuel G Davidson
1877, George W Woodward
1878, Henry E Lounsbury
1879, Edward Beecher
1880, Street B Todd
1881, Denzel B Hoadley
1882, Samuel R Woodward
1883, Charles C Perkins
1884, Evelyn O Pardee
1885, Dwight L Johnson
1886, David F Smith
1887, Theron E Allen
1889, Andrew J Doolittle
1891-3, Ransom Chatfield
1895, Harry F Peck
1897, Dwight L Humiston
1899, Arthur H Doolittle
1901, George I Babcock
1903, Noyes D Clark
1905, Jerome A Downs
1907, Noyes Andrew

THE DOWNS FAMILY

John Downs came from Cornwall, England, to New Haven before 1616
His children were

John. b Mar 5, 1658 9
Samuel, b Oct 28, 1662, d Dec 23, 1711, bu in Cong'l cem , West Haven.
Mary, b Jan 28, 1664, m Reuben Hinman
Ebenezer, b April 3, 1667, d Mar 20, 1711, bu West Haven
Deliverance b April 19, 1669
Elizabeth b April 19, 1669
Hannah, b June 19, 1670
John, b Nov 25, 1672
Daniel, b Aug 29, 1674
Nathaniel, b Dec 27, 1676
Ruth, b July 5, 1679

SAMUEL, son of John Downs, m July 1, 1692, Christian Pinion   Children
Elizabeth, b Aug 28, 1693
Samuel, b July 23, 1696
Thomas, b June 7, 1699
Nathaniel, b July 17 1702
Abigail, b Nov 4, 1704

EBENEZER, son of John Downs, m Nov 28, 1694, Mary Umphreville
Children
Esther, b Sept 5, 1695
Hope, b March 11, 1696
Ebenezer, b June 9, 1700
Mary b Jan 22, 1701
Seth, b Aug 16, 1704
Ebenezer, b March 28, 1707
Mehitabel, b Aug 23, 1709

SAMUEL, son of Samuel and Christian Downs, m Oct 29, 1717, Mary Blakeslee Tradition is that he was one of the earliest settlers of Bethany, coming
here about 1717, and settling on a large tract of land which comprised the en
tire valley at the base of Mad Mare s Hill   The road which led past his home is
still called " Downs street "   Children
Mary, b June 5, 1718
Jonathan, b April 26 1723
Samuel, b June 1, 1720
Daniel, b July 18 1726

THOMAS, son of Samuel and Christian Downs, m (1) Dec 20 1722, Mehitabel
Clark, who died Oct 25 1723 a 22, and was buried in West Haven, (2) Dec 16,
1725 Elizabeth Bristol   Children
Mehitabel, b Oct 4, 1723
Elizabeth, b Aug 31, 1726, d soon

Elizabeth, b Nov 17, 1727, d Oct 1729

Abigail, b May 1, 1730

Thomas, b Nov 2, 1732, d Sept 5, 1751

Benjamin, b March 23, 1734-5

Elizabeth, b May 30, 1737, d Oct 19, 1751

Sarah, b May 7, 1739

Thankful, b June 2, 1742, d Dec 10, 1743

Daniel, Feb 13, 1746 7

NATHANIEL, son of Samuel and Christiana Downs m , ——— had two children

Nathaniel, b Oct 28, 1731, m Sarah Ives served in Rev War

Obedience, b Sept 21, 1733

SETH, son of Ebenezer and Mary Downs, m June 8, 1727 Mary Sperry Children

Mary, b May 6 1728

Seth, b March 13, 1730 1

Joseph, b Feb 22, 1732-3

Marcia, b Sept 16 1737

Ebenezer, b Nov 14 1741, m Sarah Sperry, Nov 28, 1763

JONATHAN son of Samuel and Mary Downs, m ——— Children

Jonathan b April 11 1745

Sarah, b March 11 1747

SAMUEL son of Samuel and Mary Downs. m Dec 10 1746 Sarah Humphrey ville He inherited the paternal acres and lived in the house built by his father on Downs street, Bethany This old dwelling was demolished in 1871, and at that time was probably the oldest house in the town He was a respected citizen of the parish and was several times elected to various church offices He died Feb 7 1801, and was buried in the "old cemetery" Children

Sarah b Nov 29 1747

Eber, b Sept 30, 1749, d Feb 17 1810

Samuel, b April 1752 d May 29 1819

Jarib, b 1755 d Feb 26, 1802

Felix b 1759, d Feb 3 1848, aged 89 years

Zeri, b 1769, d in Bethlehem May 3 1810

EBER son of Samuel and Sarah Downs, m Anna Hitchcock Resided in Bethany Children

Isaac

Polly m Ben Beecher

Calvin, m ——— Dorman

Abner

SAMUEL son of Samuel and Sarah Downs married Rachel ——— who died May 6, 1819 They lived in Bethany They had one child

Merritt, b 1780 d June 13 1805

JARIB son of Samuel and Sarah Downs, m Candace Downs Children

Lyman, ——- ——- d Oct 14, 1851 aged 72

Laban

Lucena

Electa

Alma, m William Clark

Anna

FELIX, son of Samuel and Sarah Downs, married Phebe Downs who died Feb 9 1844, aged 79   He was a prosperous farmer, and built a commodious house on Downs st, Bethany   Children

Leveritt, d in 1852

Samuel Lewis, d in Oxford August 28, 1874, aged 69

Sidney d in Derby, Sept 2, 1883 aged 81 years

Harriet, m Elias Lounsbury

Nancy

LYMAN, son of Jacob and Candace Downs, m Amy, dau of Job Sperry a Revolutionary soldier   Lyman lived on the old homestead in Bethany   His wife was b July 9, 1787, and d Feb 20 1871   Children

Polly, m Orange Race, res Plainville

Charles b May 2 1822, d in Bethany Feb 27, 1902

Elbert b June 18 1830, d Oct 22 1900

Rebecca, res Bethany

Julianna m S Lewis Downs

LABAN son of Jacob and Candace Downs m Harriet—— Children

Mary Ann

Ransom

Mark

George

Willis

John

Henry

LEVERITT, son of Felix and Phebe Downs m Anna Atwater   Moved to Oxford Ct, in 1836, lived on the northly slope of Chestnut Tree Hill   Children

Laura

Robert, enlisted in Co H, 15th C V, Aug 18th, 1862 for three years, and was honorably discharged June 27 1865

Mary Ann

Clarissa

Jeanie res Boston

SAMUEL LEWIS son of Felix and Phebe Downs, m Julianna Downs dau of Lyman Downs who died July 16 1882 aged 72   They lived on the Chestnut Tree Hill road Oxford, north of the schoolhouse, Children

Sarah, b Feb 6, 1839 m William Buley

Mary

Eldredge lives in Oxford, on the Chestnut Tree Hill road

Alonzo

Frank, William A, m Nancy A Smith

SIDNEY son of Felix and Phebe Downs m 1st Emily Sanford who d Oct 9, 1855, aged 26   He m 2d Mrs Ruth Alling   Residence Bethany   Children

Harriet m Clark Hotchkiss

Julia m Eber Carpenter

Emma m Elwin Bardick

ZERI son of Samuel and Sarah Downs, m in Westville, Rachel, dau of Elihu and Sybil (Dickerman) Sanford, who died May 22, 1861, aged 92   Late in life Zeri removed from Bethany to Bethlehem   He was a tailor   Children

Wealthy, m ——— Cowles, resided Bethlehem, Ct

Anna, m 1st, ———— Kimberly , 2d Shelton Brown, res Bethlehem

Willis, b Dec 26, 1788 , m Millicent Guernsey, of Watertown, March 13, 1833, residence Woodbury, occupation miller, d June 2 1860

Lucretia, m Frederick Luddington, res Bethlehem, d July 14, 1843

Betsey, b 1804, residence Bethlehem, d Jan 11, 1849, unmarried

Lewis, machinist, res Derby, m Louisa Buel

Albert Zeri, b 1806, m Sarah Cook Pritchard, d in Westville June 19, 1834

Frederick, farmer, residence Bethlehem, m Phebe Hawley

Bantha, residence Groton, m William Cash

Henry, b 1817, cabinet maker, res New Haven, m Fannie Gabriel, d April 30, 1872

WILLIS son of Zeri and Rachael Downs m Millicent Guernsey   He located in Woodbury, Conn , where he was engaged in the grist and sawmill business

ALBERT Z , son of Zeri and Rachel Downs, m in Waterbury, Oct 12, 1830, Sarah Pritchard, occupation, cabinet maker   Residence, Woodbury and New Haven   Children

Francis Henry, b Waterbury, May 17, 1832 now living in Oklahoma

James Isaac, b Dec 16, 1833, in Waterbury, engineer d in Westville Sept 3, 1889

Frederick Augustus, b Woodbury Nov 22, 1835, farmer, res Lyndon, Kas , m Amanda Bales, of Des Moines, Iowa, Feb , 1867

Albert Z , b in Woodbury Dec 31, 1838, m Emily Evarts

Edward Sanford,* b Feb 15, 1841, m Hattie Umberfield, d Sept 18 1880

Sarah Louisa, b in Woodbury Apr 21, 1843, m Smith Abbott of Derby July 4 1887

William Pritchard, b Woodbury Sept 16, 1845, machinist, res Westville, m Emma Boardman Sept 16 1877

Maria Elizabeth b Oct 31, 1847, m Thomas Robertson

Ella Cornelia b Oct 18, 1850, m Alfred Cooper Oct , 1897, res Branford

Helen Augusta, b April 21 1853 m S Hart Culver of Seymour, Aug 10, 1873 dau., Helena A , b May 18, 1875, m Oliver M Williams

Clara Jennie, b in Bethlehem, May 12, 1855, d in Westville, Feb 5, 1860

*Enlisted in Co F, 6th C V , Sept 8, 1961, re-enlisted in 1863, was promoted sergeant June 26, 1865, and served until the close of the war, m Harriet E Umberfield in Seymour Mar 20, 1867, d Sept 10, 1880, aged 39

ALBERT ZERI, son of Zeri and Sarah Downs, m Emily A Evarts, May 1, 1867, in New Haven   Residence Westville   Occupation machinist   Children

Linna Emily

James Evarts

Edytha Alma

Alberta Mabel

WILLIAM HENRY, son of Charles and Sarah Downs. m. Nov. 28, 1880, Laverna, dau. of Frederick and Rhoda (Austin) Tuttle, Resides in Bethany. Child: John Samuel, b. Sept. 26, 1882; m. Oct 9, 1907, Blanch E. Harrington of Naugatuck. Residence Bethany.

ORIGINAL DOWNS HOMESTEAD, DOWNS STREET, BETHANY.

ELBERT, son of Lyman and Amy Downs, m. Feb. 26, 1858, Catherine, dau. of Selden and Susan (Dorman) Bailey. Resided on the old home farm, Downs street, Bethany. Children:

    Theodore, b. Dec. 14, 1878, m. Minnie McClure June 15, 1904, res. Downs st., Bethany.

    Lillian, b. July 13, 1860.

    Katie. b. Oct. 21, 1862, m. Dwight L. Humiston Nov. 27, 1879, res. Bethany.

    William, b. July 18, 1864.

    Theodora, b. Feb. 10, 1876, d. April, 8, 1876.

    Elbert S., b. Feb. 6, 1878. Res. Bethany.

LONSO, son of Lewis and Julianna Downs, m. Nancy Smith. Resides in Southford, Ct. Children:

    Rosa.

    Fanny.

    William.

    Harriet.

    Lewis.

ISAAC, son of Eber and Anna Downs, m. Mabel Perkins of Bethany. He lived in Wolcott, Conn.   Children :
    Kneeland, b. 1809, d. Sept 30, 1864.
    Harley, m. Leonora Norton lived in Wolcott; had dau. Esther, who m.
    Elizabeth, m. ———Camp.   [James Huff.
    Harriet.
    Esther, m. ———Woodruff.
    Ambrose Ives, had a son Isaac.

KNEELAND, son of Isaac and Mabel Downs, m. Ann Andrew, who d. Aug. 6, 1889, aged 85.   He was one of the foremost in promoting the interests of the Methodist church of Bethany, and aided materially in its construction in 1840. Children:
    Sarah A., b. March 26, 1832, m. John T. Beach.
    Jerome Andrew, b. June 2, 1838.
    Mary Esther, b. July, 1844, m. John J. Warner.

JEROME A., son of Kneeland and Ann Downs, m. 1st, Eliza D. Tolles, 2d, Dec. 2, 1868, Alta H. Porter. He enlisted in Co. K., 10th C. V., Sept. 26, 1861, and served three years in the Civil War, receiving an honorable discharge at the expiration of the term for which he had enlisted.   He was one of Bethany's most respected citizens, a trustee and steward of the Methodist church, and had been elected to various offices in the gift of his townsmen.   He died March 8, 1904.   Children:
    Clifton T., residence, New Haven.
    Jerome A., b. Sept. 10, 1869, residence, Bethany.
    Alta H., b. Nov. 2, 1870, d. Jan. 6, 1871.

JEROME A. DOWNS.
1838-1904.

CHARLES. son of Lyman and Amy Downs, m. Sarah Durant.   Children:
    William Henry, b. April 13, 1848.
    Leander, b. June, 1854, lives in Hamden, (West Woods.)
    Josephine, b. Oct. 1856.
    Augustus Thomas.
    Zina, m. Elizabeth Thomas.   Res. New Haven.   Children: Ella, Charles.
    Samuel B., b. Mar. 25, 1859, m. Addie Warner Oct. 25, 1898; res. Bethany.

JEROME ANDREW DOWNS, son of Jerome A. and Alta H. Downs, m. 1st, Nov. 6, 1890, Florence A. Rathburn ; who d. Feb. 3, 1894 : 2d, Jan. 6, 1897, Josephine Nettleton. He has been first selectman of Bethany for several years and represented the town in the Connecticut legislature in 1905. He has been a member of the Order of Patrons of Husbandry for twentytwo years, and Master of Beacon Valley Grange, No. 103, for four years. He was a member of the Governor's Guard for twelve years and was on the Major's Staff for six years with rank of Lieutenant. He is a charter member of Croswell Lodge, No. 39, of the I. O. O. F., of New Haven, and has been a member of the Young Men's Republican Club for sixteen years. Children :

JEROME A. DOWNS, 2D.

Jerome Andrew, b. July 11, 1892.
Florence Faith, b. Jan. 16, 1894.
Josephine Emogene, b. Feb. 21, 1898.
Alta Sarah, b. Nov. 12, 1899.
Kneeland Porter, b July 6, 1902.
Dwight Baldwin, b. July 6, 1902.
Stanley Hotchkiss, b. July 12, 1906.

FRANK, son of Lewis and Julianna Downs, m. Charlotte Smith. Children : Elizabeth.
Frederick, m Nellie Bunnell.
Elliot, m. Mary Donahue. Nelson.

LEANDER, son of Charles and Sarah Downs, m. Julia Sanford. Residence, Hamden. Children :
Burton. Jessie. Irving Tuttle.

SAMUEL B., son of Charles and Sarah Downs, m. Oct. 25, 189-, Addie Warner. Residence, Bethany. Child:
Samuel A., b. Aug. 25, 1899.

THEODORE, son of Elbert and Catherine Downs, m. June 15, 1904, Minnie McClurre. Residence, Bethany.

WILLIAM B., son of Elbert and Catherine Downs, b. in Hamden July 18, 1864; m. Jan. 2, 1888, Etta Blakeslee. Residence, Downs street, Bethany. Children : Ralph, b. Dec. 12, 1891.   Isabel, b. July 29, 1993.

CLIFTON, son of Jerome and Eliza D. Downs, m.————. He is an engineer, residence, New Haven. Children :
Rollin.
Warren.

ROBERT DOWNS, of Oxford, son of Leverett and Anna Downs, was born in Bethany Mar. 10, 1835, his parents moving to the Red Oak district, on the Chestnut Tree Hill road, Oxford. in 1836. He enlisted Aug. 18, 1862, for three years. in Co. H. 15th C. V., and was in the battle of Fredericksburg, the siege of Suffolk, and the battle of Kinston, N. C., Mar. 8, 1865, where he was taken prisoner and taken to Richmond, but was paroled after three days, and after a furlough was again in the service. At the close of the war he returned to the old homestead in Oxford which he occupied until his death in 1906. He was a member of the Methodist church in Naugatuck and was one of Oxford's most respected citizens.

THE CARRINGTON FAMILY.

This has been one of the most respected families of the town of Bethany and in fact of New Haven County. The "Commemorative Biographical Record" of the county says—"Few names in the history of New Haven have been more potent and influential," and refers to the late John B. Carrington, for many years the publisher of the New Haven Journal and Courier, who was born in Bethany in 1811. He was the son of Alling and Nancy (Atwood) Carrington. The family history has been so well written up that only more recent names and events need be given here.

ABRAM E. CARRINGTON, whose portrait is here given, was the son of David and Rachel A. Carrington of Bethany. He m. 1st, April 8, 1857, Sarah E., daughter of Jabez E. and Lucretia Pritchard of Seymour, who died Dec. 19, 1874; 2d, Mary J., daughter of Henry and Malenia Patterson of Naugatuck, May 19, 1875. He was one of Bethany's most respected citizens, a devoted husband and a kind father. He died Jan. 24, 1908, aged 78 years, leaving an honored name and an example of good citizenship. He had enjoyed a long and successful life, and his end was as peaceful as his life had been. Children:

Mary E., b. Aug. 26, 1859; d Jan. 28, 1864.
Willie E., b. July 22, 1862; d. Jan. 23, 1864.
IDA M., b. Feb. 6. 1865; m. Wm. H. Lowell of New Haven Oct. 15, 1896; dau: Marion Pauline, b. Oct. 18, 1897.

Charles P., b. Dec. 12, 1867; res. Brooklyn, N. Y.
Ella S , b. Jan. 16, 1870; m. Burton W. Holbrook of Seymour. June 23, 1892. Children:
    Gladys Carrington, b. July 20, 1897.
    Helen Isabel, b Aug. 15, 1903.

Otis E , b Feb 24, 1876, m Charlotte Clark June 20, 1901   res   Bethany
Children
  Bernice Ruth, b Mar 22 1902
  Beatrice May, b Aug 6, 1904
  Alfred Otis b July 9 1907
Burton A., b June 12, 1877, m Cora E Loomis Mar 11, 1903
Henry P , b July 30 1880
Rachel M b April 9, 1882, m Sherman P Woodward Oct 25, 1905, res
  Bethany
Hiram D , b Jan 3, 1886
Ralph W , b April 8, 1888
Ruth E b Sept 27, 1891

DANIEL CARRINGTON. son of David and Thankful Carrington, m Rachel
A Dorman June 30, 1820   Residence on Skokorat   Children
  David, b July 14 1821, m Elizabeth Robinson, d Dec 27, 1859
  Eliza A , b April 17, 1824, m Smith Terrill of Seymour
  Albert D , b May 14, 1826
  Abram E , b Oct 31,1832, m Howard Chatfield of Seymour, d Nov 12,1906
  Emily G , b Feb 16, 1838, m Howard Chatfield

ALBERT D CARRINGTON son of Daniel and Rachel A , m 1st, Dec 24, 1851,
Lucretia Wheeler of Oxford, who died July 21, 1872, 2d, Sarah F Buckingham
Dec 3, 1872 Children
  Daniel, b Sept 25, 1852, m Cornelia T Hubbell Oct 19, 1871   Res
    Beacon Falls
  Wheeler, b April 6 1865
  Lulu. b Oct 12, 1873
  Jessie b Sept 8, 1876, m Caleb S Fuller of Torrington Nov 28, 1891
  Milton, b Nov 10, 1879

THE ANDREW FAMILY

WILLIAM ANDREW was at Cambridge, Mass , in 1634   He was constable in
1635 and 1640 and selectman in 1635   Mary, his wife, died Jan 19, 1639-40
He m 2d widow Reana James, of Watertown, Mass , about Aug 1640   He died
1652   He had a son—
  Samuel b in England about 1621, d in June, 1701
SAMUEL ANDREW, son of William and Mary, m Elizabeth White Sept 22,
1652   Children
  Samuel, b Jan 29 1655 6 d Jan 24, 1738
  William, b June 7, 1658
  John b March 2, 1660, d May 30, 1693
  Elizabeth b April 5 1663, m William Gedney
  Thomas, b May 13 1665, d Feb 24 1666 7
  Mary, b Dec 28, 1666, d June 20, 1667

Thomas, b March 23, 1667
Mary, b Feb 22, 1671, d Feb 29, 1671
Jonathan, b 1698, d May 9 1700

SAMUEL ANDREW, son of Samuel and Elizabeth, was a graduate at Harvard 1675 and removed from Cambridge to Milford Conn , where he was ordained pastor of the church Nov 10, 1685 He worked with Pierpont and others in the founding of Yale College, was a member of the first board of trustees, was president of the college from 1707 to 1719 an instructor in the college for several years and a member of the corporation until his death   He was a clergyman for 52 years   He married Abigail, dau of Governor Robert and Jane Treat of Milford   Children

Abigail, bapt Jan 16 1687, m Jonathan Law Aug 1, 1706
Samuel bapt Oct 11 1688, d April 26, 1728
Elizabeth bapt June 1690, m Timothy Cutler
William, bapt May 8 1692, d May 2, 1712
John, bapt July 22 1694, d Dec 25, 1714
Jane, bapt Jan 7 1696 d Feb 1, 1696
Mary, bapt Jan 7, 1696
Jane, bapt April, 1699, m Andrew Durand
Jonathan, bapt Aug 24 1701, d 1740
Hannah, bapt Nov 19, 1704

JONATHAN ANDREW son of Rev Samuel and Abigail, m Elizabeth, dau of Walter Smith, of Milford, Jan 5 1727   Children

Elizabeth, bapt Sept , 1728,
Jonathan, bapt Oct 1730
Abigail, bapt March, 1732
William, bapt June 1731, d Aug 28, 1796
Mary bapt June, 1734
Samuel, bapt June, 173—

WILLIAM ANDREW, son of Jonathan and Elizabeth, m 1st Esther dau of Samuel Merchant, 2d Margaret Merwin, of Oyster River   Children

William, b 1764, d Dec 7 1831
Mary, m Stephen Prindle
Elias, m Huldah ————
Esther, m Thaddeus Bryan
Roxana, m Jeremiah Peck,
Merwin, m Susan Platt

WILLIAM ANDREW, son of William and Esther m Mary, dau of Phineas Terrel Res Bethany Children

Mary, b 1792, m Clark Hitchcock
William, b Aug 3, 1794, d Nov 22, 1856
Job b Aug 19, 1796 d Aug 18, 1868
Samuel, b 1800, m Salmah Smith
Esther, b 1803, m Amos Hine
Nehemiah b June 5, 1805, m Phinette Sperry, d Feb 16, 1889
Ann, m Kneeland Downs

WILLIAM ANDREW, son of William and Mary, m Temperance, dau of Silas Hotchkiss, of Bethany   Children

  Mary, b Sept. 15, 1813, m Samuel Bassett
  Hiram, m Grace Tyrell
  Susan, m Stiles Russell
  William Wooster
  Harriet, b 1818, m Joseph G Reynolds
  Ann, m Jackson Johnson
  Theodore Read, m Mary Sperry

JOB ANDREW, son of William and Mary, served in war of 1812, and represented the town of Bethany in the legislature in 1841   He m Jan 4, 1815, Lois Prince, who d M y 9, 1874, aged 97   Children

  Maria, b April 5, 1817, m Sheldon Alling of Orange
  Jeremiah, b Feb 15, 1819, d Mar 12, 1888
  Azariah, b June 29 1821, d Feb 23 1898
  Nathan, b Aug 26, 1823, d Dec 13, 1872
  Eliza Ann b Sept 19, 1833, m William Smith of Seymour

JEREMIAH ANDREWS son of Job and Lois m in 1841 Hannah Cooper, who d Apr 11, 1888, aged 72   Res Seymour, 3rd house south of the Bungay schoolhouse   He was for many years a prominent and efficient member of the Great Hill M E Church   Children

  Grace Adelaide, b Nov 20, 1842 m Wm Leroy Williamson Mar 17, 1866
  Hannah C, b Dec 8, 18—, m Edward N Childs July 31, 1869 Res Seymour
  George W, b May 31 1855   Res Seymour

AZARIAH ANDREW, son of Job and Lois, m June 29, 1856, Sarah A Pardee of Orange, who died Jan 11, 1901   Res Bethany   Children

  Noyes, b April 7, 1857
  Fannie P, b May 17, 1858, m John Earley of Seymour, d June 19, 1894
  Mary E, b Jan 21, 1860, m Manson S Burgess of Derby
  John D, b June 9, 1861

NATHAN ANDREW, son of Job and Lois, m Elizabeth Nettleton, who d Dec 28, 1870 aged 45   Occupation, sawyer   Res Bethany   Children

  Celia E, b Oct 1 1846
  Jerome b Feb 18, 1848
  Llewellyn b Nov 18, 1850, m Teresa E Washburn May 1, 1872   Res Oxford   Occupation, miller
  Jeremiah, b Oct 5, 1852, m Hattie E Sackett
  Charles Hubert b May 16, 1855
  Eliza Ann, b ———, d 1871
  Nelson, b Mar 1861

JEROME ANDREW, son of Nathan and Elizabeth, m Martha E Osborn Mar 26, 1873   Res Beacon Falls   Ch

  Fred Lucius b June 8 1877, m Mabel Kate Lacey Apr 9, 1901

JEREMIAH ANDREW son of Nathan and Elizabeth Andrew, m Hattie Sackett Dec 9, 1874   Res Seymour   Children

  Walter J, b June 6 1878
  Jennie E, b Dec 10, 1881

THE HOTCHKISS FAMILY

SAMUEL HOTCHKISS, (probably from Essex, England, and traditional brother of John of Guilford Conn ,) was in New Haven as early as 1641 In August, 1642, he married Elizabeth Cleverly, and d Dec 28, 1663   Children

    John, b 1643
    Samuel, b 1645
    James, b 1647
    Joshua, b Sept 16, 1651
    Thomas, b Dec , 1654
    Daniel, b June 8, 1657

ENS JOSHUA HOTCHKISS, son of Samuel, m Mary Hotchkiss   Children

    Mary, b April 30, 1679
    Dea Stephen b Aug 12, 1681
    Martha, b Dec 14, 1683
    Priscilla, b 1688
    Abraham
    Desire, d in 1702
    Isaac, b 1701
    Jacob, b Feb 7, 1704

ABRAHAM HOTCHKISS, son of Joshua, settled in Bethany, and had three daughters

ISAAC HOTCHKISS, son of Joshua, settled in Bethany   Children

    Abraham
    Isaac
    Jacob
    Jabez
    Joseph, and others

JABEZ HOTCHKISS, son of Isaac, was a lifelong resident of Bethany Children.

    Stephen, b Oct 31, 1761, d Nov 5, 1847
    Mary, b June 3, 1762
    Timothy, b Jan 22, 1766
    Lydia, b Apr 1, 1768, d 1773
    Eleazor, b June 4, 1770
    Lydia, b June 7, 1774

STEPHEN HOTCHKISS, son of Jabez, m Hannah Brown   Children

    Harriet
    Harley, b Sept 12, 1791, d Mar 29, 1860
    Rebecca m Minott Collins
    Wealthy, died young
    Eber
    Stephen, m Abigail Hotchkiss of Prospect, Sept 10, 1847
    Hannah, m John Russell
    Jared, m Amy French   He died Aug 25, 1851 aged 50
    Jesse, m Caroline Sperry
    George, m Laura Sperry

HARLEY HOTCHKISS, son of Stephen, m Harriet, dau of Benjamin Collins, who died in 1862 Res Bethany, near the Beacon Falls line Children

Wealthy Ann, m Thomas Gilyard

Andrew T, d in Bethany in 1877

Harris, died young

Charles T, b July 9, 1834

EBER HOTCHKISS, son of Stephen, m Thirza Driver Children

Dilazon

Gracia

Samantha

Jane　.

Samuel

Hooker

JARED HOTCHKISS, son of Stephen, m Amy French of Prospect, Sept 13 1840 Children

Henry Hooker, bapt Mar 24, 1842, died young

Caroline Lucina, bap Dec 1844

GEORGE HOTCHKISS, son of Stephen, m Laura Sperry, April 4, 1841 Res Bethany Children

Erban Evander, bap Aug 13, 1843, m Elizabeth Crabtree

——(dau)

——(dau)

ANDREW T HOTCHKISS, son of Harley, m Belinda Buckingham Children

Ernest Z

Isa Annette, b Apr 29, 1853

Harley D

Andrew T

CHARLES T HOTCHKISS, son of Harley, m in 1861 Emma V Watson He is a school teacher, res Cheshire, Conn Children

Mary Claribel, m Warren Andrews

Clarence H, d at 6½ yrs

Harriet I, m Everett Pardee

DAVID HOTCHKISS came from Woodbridge and settled in Bethany

HARVEY HOTCHKISS, son of David, m Sarah Alling He built the house near the southern bank of Lebanon Swamp

JARIUS B HOTCHKISS, m Eunice Russell Jan 13, 1839 Res. Bethany Children

Philo Delos b Dec 7, 1839

Edward Lester, b Dec 11, 1840

Juliet Christina, b Aug 21, 1843

Jane D, b Sept 5, 1845

HARPIN H HOTCHKISS, m Charlotte E Alling Feb 15, 1852 Res Bethany Children

Katie Irene

Ida Estella

Adelia May, bap Dec 7, 1872

HARVEY HOTCHKISS son of ———— b 1781, d Dec 9, 1855, m 1805 Sarah, dau of Gideon Alling of Milford   Res Bethany   She died Sept 21, 1862   Children

>Sheldon Alling, b Apr 22, 1808

>Eliza Samantha b Sept 18, 1810, d Feb 14, 1876

>Solomon b Jan 18 1813, m Charlotte Hemingway, d Jan 7 1886

>Beecher Delos, b Feb 11, 1815, m Betsey Perkins, d Oct 30, 1866

>Julius Leonard, b June 17, 1817, m Saphronia ————, d Feb 17, 1879

>Theodore Nelson, b Dec 20, 1819, m Lucia Sperry, d Feb 27, 1888

>Sarah Finette, b Oct 29, 1822, m De Witt Clinton Castle of Seymour Mar 5, 1848, d Jan 15, 1878

>Orlando Thomas, b Aug 8, 1825 d Dec 11, 1828

>Harvey Harpin, b Feb 16, 1828

>Margaret Dianthe, b June 16, 1730, m Matthew Trewhella of Cheshire, d Feb 14, 1872

HARPIN HARVEY HOTCHKISS, son of Harvey and Sarah, m Feb 15, 1852, Charlotte Eliza Alling   Res Prospect   Children

>Adella M, b Dec 13, 1852, d Jan 3, 1873

>Orson B, b July 8, 1854, m Sept 12, 1892, Lillian Alling

>Katie I, b Dec 17, 1859, m June 29, 1881, Herbert E Doolittle

>Ida E, b May 6, 1861, m Nov 29, 1882, Geo R Doolittle

>Etta I, b Feb 1, 1868, d Sept 17, 1881

CLARK HOTCHKISS, son of Isaac and Elizabeth, m Caroline A Sperry, dau of Chillon Sperry   He was for many years both deacon and chorister of the Congregational church, Bethany   He lived in the house now occupied by Clifton Rosha   Children

>Mary, m 1st, Elizur Hicock 2d, Thomas Cochran

>Isaac m Mary Reed

>Sarah

>Isaac G, res Brent Creek, Mich

>Fanny, 2d wife of Adrian Rosha

>Julia, m Thomas Higgins of Ansonia

>Anna Gertrude m in 1868 Adrian C Rosha

>Arthur m Eugenia Sperry

>Martha, m Lyman Gaylord of Bethany, now of Moundsville, Marquette Co, Wis

BEECHER D HOTCHKISS m Betsy Perkins, dau of Guy Perkins, who d Oct, 3, 1863, aged 42   He had a blacksmith shop across the road from his house, and a sawmill near, and was known as a man of varied mechanical genius   He d Oct 31, 1866, aged 62

THE LOUNSBURY FAMILY

RICHARD LOUNSBURY came from England, and his son John, of Rye N Y, had a son —

JOSIAH LOUNSBURY, 1st, who came from Rye, Westchester Co, N Y, to New Haven, and m Ruth Lines May 7, 1721 removed to Bethany   Children

    John, b Jan 18, 1724 5
    Jacob, b March 6, 1726
    Mary b Feb 12, 1727-8
    Josiah b Aug 5, 1729
    Samuel b 1731   served in the Revolutionary War
    Ruth b 1733, m Nehemiah Tolles, Sept 20, 1759
    Daniel, b 1735
    Stephen, b 1736, m Hannah Sperry Oct 26, 1761
    Esther, b 1738   Timothy, b 1740, d 1821

JOSIAH LOUNSPURY 2d, son of Josiah and Ruth, m Martha Hotchkiss of Woodbridge, Oct. 26, 1749   Children

    Hester, b 1750   Linus, b Jan 3, 1752
    Josiah, b 1754   Obadiah, b 1759

LINUS LOUNSBURY, son of Josiah and Ruth, m Prudence Scott of Oxford in 1783   He was a soldier in the war of the Revolution, enlisting in Gen Wooster's regiment in April, 1775 at the first call for troops by the legislature   In 1776 he was in Wadsworth's Brigade which was sent to reinforce Washington's army at New York   His name appears in the list of pensioners in 1832   Children

    Josiah, b 1785   Lyman, b 1791
    Calvin, b 1786   Esther, b 1793, m Edmund Mallory
    Amelia, b 1788, m Daniel Davis Martha, b 1795, m Titus Smith
    Ansel, b 1790

JOSIAH LOUNSBURY, 3d, son of Linus and Prudence, m Sarah, dau of Erastus Lines of Bethany, in 1815   Res Bethany   Children

    Harriet, b 1817, m Willis Umberfield, res Seymour
    Caroline, b 1821, m Jessie Hotchkiss
    Ransom, b Jan 30 1828, m Mary Joyce of Trumbull Aug 25, 1847

JAIRUS LOUNSBURY, son of John and Ruth m Amelia Chapman, removed to Vermont, and after some years returned to New Haven   He was a soldier of the Revolution   Children

    Collins b July 19, 1783, lived in Vermont, d 1863
    Clarissa b Feb 11, 1791, m John Gamsby
    Betsey, b Aug 11, 1794, m Harvey Finch
    Victory, b Sept 8, 1795, d Nov 25, 1868
    Sally b April 13 1800, m Russell Moulton
    Crownage, b May 20, 1803
    David b Aug 15 1805, d April 1, 1877

TIMOTHY LOUNSBURY, son of Josiah and Ruth, m 1st, Hannah Smith, 2d, Sally——   Res Bethany   Children

    Lucy, m James Hotchkiss

Hannah F , b ——— , m Robert R Russell

Timothy, b ———

Eri, b ——— , m Sarah ———

Eunice, b ——— , m Truman Prince,

———(son) b ———

TIMOTHY LOUNSBURY, son of Timothy and Hannah, m Hannah, dau of David and Lois French of Bethany Res Bethany He was a man of excellent judgment and was regarded as one of the most thorough and thrifty farmers in the town He lived for a long time in a little house much too small for the convenience of his eleven children, but, in 1811, before his twelfth child was born, he built what was then the largest and the most costly house in the town He at one time owned fourteen hundred acres of land in Bethany and in New York state On what was then his farm, a few rods from the old homestead is the Lounsbury cemetery, which was set apart by Timothy and enclosed with a neat and strong iron fence Children

Dorcas, b July, 1798 m Jabez Wilcox

Timothy b March 25, 1791, m Mary Ann Clark

Lewis b 1793, m Charity, dau of Amos Clark of Nyumphs

Daniel, b 1795, m Sarah dau of David Wooding of Bethany

Jesse, b Dec , 1796, m Bede, dau of Jesse Bradley of Bethany

Hannah, b 1799, m Herschel Sanford of Prospect

Smith, b ———, m Jennette Tomlinson Feb 11, 1824

Allen, b 1803, m Maria, dau of Elam Cook of Cheshire Res Bethany

Eunice, b Jan 14 1805, m 1st, Vincent Brown, 2d, McDonald Fisher

Mary b Mar 14, 1807, m Burritt Hitchcock son of Timothy

John, b Aug 16, 1809, m Mary Church, d April 6, 1895

George, b Nov 23, 1812, m Mary Austin of Prospect

Eri, m Sarah Carrington

ERI LOUNSBURY son of Timothy and Hannah, m Sarah Carrington Res Lounsbury street, Bethany Children

Abram	Sally, m Lyman Wheeler
Isaac, m ——— Lodemann	Harriet, m William Todd
Polly, m Miles Horton	Lucy, d unmarried
Rebecca, m Asa Bradley	William H , b Dec 30, 1815
Lucretia, m Selden Hoadley	

ABRAM LOUNSBURY, son of Eri and Sarah, m Emily dau of David and Lolly (Todd) Perkins, Sept 12, 1824 Res Bethany Children

Sarah, b May 2, 1826, m Nathan Clark, Sept 6, 1843

David A , b Mar 11, 1831

John Wesley, b Aug 10, 1838

ISAAC LOUNSBURY, son of Eri and Sarah, m Lodema ——— Children

Isaac   Obed, located in Meriden

WILLIAM H LOUNSBURY, son of Eri and Sarah, m 1st, Charity Buckingham, 2d, Sept 8 1873, Susan Beard Children

Irvin, b July 9 1843, d Sept 23, 1861

Elford, b Oct 17, 1845

Celia b Sept 26, 1848, m Charles D Allen of Hamden Dec 23, 1872

Delia, b Sept 29, 1848
Etta, b June 6, 1874
William, b June, 1876, d May, 1877
William, b Oct 3, 1879

DAVID A LOUNSBURY, son of Abram and Emily, m 1st, May 6, 1852 Susan M Doolittle of Hamden, m 2d Nov 18 1854 Nancy A Hopkins m 3d, May 16, 1878, Margaret Billetwell Res Bethany, until 1906, when he removed to Bridgeport Children

Mary Etta, m Albert Beardsley
Ives, b April 21, 1861
John Clarence, b June 6, 1879
Bertha, b Nov 23, 1881
Clara b April 22 1886, d 1886
Dorothe b Aug 19, 1893

DR JOHN LOUNSBURY, son of Timothy and Hannah, studied at Wilbraham Mass, and then at Yale graduating from the medical department with the class of 1837 He settled in Oxford and practiced there for many years He married Mary, dau of William and Lois (Pitcher) Church, of Oxford Children

Emma, b June 25, 1845 Res Oxford
Tully, b March 8, 1847

CROWNAGE LOUNSBURY, son of Janus, m Eliza Samantha Hotchkiss of Woodbridge, Feb 14, 1831 Children

William H, b July 25, 1833, m Julia Ladue, who d Dec 29, 1892, m 2d,
    Fanny M Hunter Res Westville
Mark, b Aug 11, 1835, m Ann Webster June 14, 1857, res Seymour
Sarah S, b May 4, 1839, m S Chauncey Hooker, res Willimantic

REV ELFORD LOUNSBURY, son of William and Charity, m Adella Seaman He is a Methodist clergyman of New York City and has served as a missionary in Bulgaria Children

Ethel and Irvin, died in Bulgaria   Erma
Elfreda   Floyd

ELIAS LOUNSBURY, son of Stephen, m 1st Appahna Judd, 2d Mary Perkins Children

Elias
Major
Newel m Jennette Hungerford of Bethany Feb 12, 1837
Marlin
Belus
Ursula

MAJOR LOUNSBURY, son of Elias and Mary, m Hannah Beecher, who d Mar 7, 1876 aged 77 Res Bethany Children

Henry E, b Feb 9, 1829, m Mary F Dickerman April 1, 1866

RANSOM LOUNSBURY, son of Josiah and Sarah, m Mary Joyce of Trumbull, Aug 25 1847 Res Beacon Falls Children

Charles H, b Sept 18, 1848
Eliza, b July 19 1851, m Herbert Beers
Ella b July 23, 1864 m 1st, Frederick Colwell, 2d, Charles D Roberts

CHARLES H LOUNSBURY, son of Ransom and Mary, m Jennie, dau of John Titley of Beacon Falls He represented the town of Beacon Falls in the legislature of 1877 and later removed to Seymour where he has for many years been a successful merchant He was the first selectman for a number of years, has since been chairman of the Board of Assessors, and is now president of the Business Men's Association Children

    Jessie May, b June 19, 1879, d Aug 15, 1881
    Mary E , b Sept 12, 1881
    Charles H , b Nov 1, 1883, m Minnie E Simmonds April 16, 1907
    John Titley, b Nov 15, 1890

THE DOOLITTLE FAMILY

This family has included many citizens of sterling worth in this grand old town, men whose influence has also been felt far beyond its limits, and men who in the earlier years did their full share in the formative period of our free institutions The family is descended from Abraham Doolittle, one of the earliest settlers of New Haven, owning a house there as early as 1642, and was prominent in the affairs of the then new settlement He died Aug 11, 1690, aged 69, and his wife, nee Abigail Moss, Nov 5, 1710

ISAAC DOOLITTLE of Bethany, son ot Reuben and grandson of Caleb of Hamden, m Ursula, dau of Ami Hoadley Children
    Andrew J , b ———, 1842
    Ellen S , m George Dorman
    Mary J , m Hezekiah Lindsley
    Luther, enlisted in the 10th C V and was killed at the battle of
        Kingston, N C
ANDREW J DOOLITTLE, son of Isaac and Ursula, served in the war of the Rebellion in Co H, 23d C V He is a member of Admiral Foote Post, G A R , of New Haven He was elected representative to the General Assembly in 1888, and has been selectman and assessor He m in 1870 Josephine, dau of Benjamin Bishop of Woodbridge They have one son
    ARTHUR H DOOLITTLE, b Aug 12, 1871 He represented the town of Bethany in the legislature in 1899, and has filled various positions of responsibility and trust He is a member of Olive Branch Lodge F & A M , and Crosswell Lodge, I O O F , and was for two years master of Woodbridge Grange
DENNIS W DOOLITTLE son of Bennet and Minerva Doolittle and grandson of Reuben, kept a grocery store at Mt Carmel for a short time and in New Haven for about fifteen years and was engaged in the wood and coal business there for several years In 1834 he settled in Bethany and in 1836 opened a grocery store there He m 1st, in 1867, Evelina I , dau of Philos Dorman, 2d, in 1878, Rosa N Dorman, sister of his first wife Children
        Cleveland B , b in 1884
        Warren P , b in 1885

BETHANY

SKETCHES AND RECORDS

PART 2.

BETHANY

SKETCHES AND RECORDS,

PART 2.

PUBLISHED BY

W C. SHARPE. SEYMOUR. CONN.

RECORD PRINT SEYMOUR
1913

INDEX.

ILLUSTRATIONS

PORTRAITS.

PINE GROVE, ON THE BORDER OF BETHANY LAKE.

Bethany Hills, Bethany Vales and Bethany Lakes are worthy representatives
of New England scenery.

THE CONGREGATIONAL CHURCH.

THE CENTENNIAL CELEBRATION, OCT. 12, 1863.

(From the Connecticut Herald and Journal, New Haven, Nov. 1, 1863.)

On the twelfth of October the people of Bethany celebrated the one hundredth anniversary of the first organization of a church there, and the settlement of the first pastor, Rev. Stephen Hawley. At 10 o'clock they assembled around his grave where a handsome stone bears the inscription. "Erected on the Centennial, October 12, 1863," and sung "One Hundred Years Ago," united in prayer, and listened to an address by Rev. J. L. Willard, of Westville. They then passed to the field in which Mr. Hawley was ordained in the open air, and sung "One Hundred Years to Come," and were addressed by Rev. E. W. Robinson, of Bethany, and Rev. D. M. Elwood, of Woodbridge.

In the afternoon an address was delivered in the Congregational church by Rev. S. C. Brace, the pastor, from the historical portions of which we are permitted to publish the following extract:

In 1739 one hundred and one years after the settlement of New Haven, the parish of Amity was set off, containing territory from the townships of New Haven and Milford. In 1742, Rev Benjamin Woodbridge was settled as the pastor.

In 1762, upon the memorial of Joel Hotchkiss and others, it was enacted by the general assembly, that the inhabitants of the Parish of Amity, "living north of an east and west line drawn from the south end of the Widow Hannah Sperry's dwelling house," should be a distinct Ecclesiastical society to be named Bethany.

The first meeting of this society was held November 13, 1762, at the school house in Bethany, probably that which stood near the present residence of Mr John Kline. Deacon Joel Hotchkiss was chosen moderator, and James Sherman, clerk, who was sworn by Samuel Sherman, Esq.

A society's committee was then chosen, viz Timothy Peck, John White, Isaac Beecher, Daniel Tolles and Joel Hotchkiss.

It was voted that meetings shall begin on the second Sabbath in December and hold until the last in April. A rate, or tax, was laid at a penny half-penny on the pound, for defraying the charges of preaching for the year ensuing. Gershom Thomas was chosen collector. This meeting is described in the records as a lawful society meeting of the inhabitants of Bethany in New Haven and Milford. It is to be presumed that public worship was instituted in accordance with the vote, but where it was held and who officiated as the preacher, are not known.

At a society meeting held in March, 1763, it was voted that meetings shall begin in this place on the second Sabbath in November next, and at a meeting in April, Deacon Joel Hotchkiss and Mr Timothy Peck were appointed a committee to apply unto the Reverend Association, at their next convention for their advice to a candidate to preach in said society upon probation, in order to settle among them.

The association held its meeting at Waterbury, May 31, and the minute on this subject, as recorded by Rev Warham Williams, contains these words "We, having maturely considered the matter, unanimously advise said society to Mr Stephen Hawley, as a suitable person, highly approving of him for that purpose."

In June, Mr Isaac Beecher and Mr Samuel Downs were appointed "to apply unto Mr Hawley" and it was voted "that the time of probation shall be for the space of three months."

In August, the society invited Mr Hawley to become the pastor, offering him "two hundred pounds settlement, and proposing to give him fifty-five pounds salary the first year and then rise with the list to seventy pounds a year, and there stop." Mr Hawley's reply was dated Bethany, Sept 12, 1763.

At a society meeting in September, it was voted that the ordination take place on the second Wednesday in October, and that on the first Wednesday a fast preparatory to the ordination should be observed. It was also resolved "to apply unto the Rev Mr Woodbridge, of Amity, the Rev Mr Trumbull, of North Haven, and the Rev Mr Waterman, of Wallingford, to attend the above said fast."

At the same meeting, it was voted that Deacon Joel Hotchkiss, Mr Daniel Tolles, Mr Timothy Ball, Mr Samuel Biscoe and Mr John White, be a committee "to apply unto the Rev Moderator of the Consociation of New Haven county, in order to settle the Church of Christ in Bethany, according unto the established ecclesiastical constitution of this colony, and to transact all the affairs of the society that are necessary in carrying on said ordination."

The tradition is that the ordination services were performed in the open air, in a field near the fork of the roads below the residence of Mrs Mary Brad ley It is believed that there was in that field a small rude building which was used as a house of worship, until the church edifice was erected, six years after the ordination of Mr Hawley The society meetings were always held in the school house, during these six years In December, 1763, it was voted "that the society's committee take care and provide some person to sweep the school house and take care of the door " This provision we should hardly expect for society meetings alone, and it might be inferred that the school house was the place of worship But in 1767, it was voted "that Mr Timothy Peck, Mr Daniel Tolles, Mr Ebenezer Bishop, Mr John Perkins and Mr Samuel Biscoe sit on the fore seat " This vote seems hardly applicable to a school house Besides in Mr Hawley's New Year s discourse for 1769, it is said of those who died during the year—"their places are empty in this house of God " From this language we should infer that they then worshipped in an edifice set apart for that purpose

The ordination sermon was delivered by that eminent Divine, Dr Bellamy, of Bethlehem, from I Corinthians 11, 2 Mr Hawley was a native of New Milford and was graduated at Yale college in 1759, in the same class with Dr Trumbull, of North Haven At the time of his ordination, he was 26 years of age It is probable that he studied theology with Dr Bellamy Before coming to Bethany he had resided for a time in Stratford, where his eldest child was born

Three years after Mr Hawley s ordination, i e, in November, 1766, the society adopted a resolution "that it is necessary for us to build a meeting-house" A committee was appointed to apply to the county court to fix the place Difficulties seem to have arisen, a second application to the court was made in 1768, a third in 1769, and at length in May, 1769 it was voted "that we are willing to build a meeting house at the last stake set by the Honorable County Court s Committee" On this question there were 29 in the affirmative and 10 in the negative A committee, consisting of Isaac Beecher, "Ensign" Clark, and Israel Thomas, were appointed to purchase the land from Isaac Hotchkiss

The edifice was erected in the latter part of 1769 on the summit of the hill south of the churches now standing, near the present residence of Mr Edward Buckingham In December of that year, a committee was appointed "to seat the three first seats in the meeting house "

During this period of delay, the society passed some votes which amuse us at this day In December, 1767, it was voted "that we will provide the boards, clapboards, shingles nails and glass, necessary for building a meeting house the year ensuing " A tax was laid and it was decided that one-half might be paid in "flax seed, or some other species that will answer in New York " The society fixed the price to be paid for different kinds of lumber The building was to be fifty-five feet long and forty feet wide

In December, 1768, a vote was passed 'that we get the timber this winter and set up the meeting house as fast as we can " It was ordered "that those that score timber for the meeting house shall have two shillings sixpence per day and those that hew shall have three shillings and sixpence per day' Deacon White and Deacon Hotchkiss were appointed 'to cull the clapboards and shingles for the meeting house"

In March, 1769, it was voted 'that this Society give free liberty for a belfry to be built on the meeting house,' but this liberty was not then used

In January, 1770, the Society meeting was held for the first time, in the meeting house When edifice was dedicated is not known

It was customary to appoint particular persons "to tune the psalm" In 1765, the choristers were Valentine Wilmot, Benajah Peck, and Stephen Sanford In 1770, on entering the new church, a larger number received this appointment, viz Isaac Baldwin, Joel Hotchkiss, Thomas Beecher, Anav Ives, Lazarus Tolles, Timothy Lounsbury, Nathaniel Tuttle, and Nehemiah Tolles At this time it was voted that the choristers sit together near the foot of the pulpit stairs

The sacred edifice was still what we should esteem uncomfortable In 1771 a committee was appointed "to give liberty to people to build pews in the meeting house where they see cause"

In 1773 a tax was laid to color the meeting house, and case the windows, and to provide boards for the inside of the house

In 1774 a vote was passed "that the meeting house be colored blue, and the windows white," but soon a special meeting was called and it was decided to color it white

In December 1776 it was voted "to finish the lower part of the meeting-house, and in front of the galleries"

In 1777 Nathaniel Tuttle, Isaac Baldwin, Daniel Tolles and Joel Hine were chosen "to tune the psalm, and sit in the fore seat in the front gallery"

In 1778 it was voted "that the Society shall pay Mr Hawley's salary in provisions, labor and other species, according to the first stating of provision by the General Assembly—wheat at six shillings, and other things in proportion, and those that do not pay in the aforesaid species of provision, &c, shall pay money equivalent"

At the same meeting a committee was appointed to seat the meeting-house, viz Deacon Peck, Capt Ball and Ensign Jacob Hotchkiss, and it was ordered that "the committee shall have regard to age and what each one has paid to the building of the said house, and according to their discretion with all"

In December, 1779, a vote was passed "that the Committee shall lay out the over-plus money of finishing the meeting-house, on the steps and other ways as they think best"

Thus at the end of ten years from its raising the house seems to have been considered as in a manner finished In 1791 the Society voted "to take up three seats in the square body and to build pews on each side of the broad alley" In 1792 it was resolved, "That the Society may build a steeple to the meeting house, if they can get money enough signed to build said steeple" But the steeple and bell were not added until 1803

Going back in the history we find in 1783 a committee appointed "to assist the church of England committee to find a place for them to set a church on"

In 1779 the society began "to confer with Amity about being made a town" This subject was one of much discussion and negotiations, and of some strife in regard to a place for a town house The town was set off in 1784 and named Woodbridge in honor of the first minister of Amity The separation of Bethany as a town began to be agitated in 1803 but was not accomplished until 1832

Other names of those who acted in society business before 1800, are (placing them in order of time), Jesse Bradley, William Wooding, Deacon Isaac Johnson, Josiah Lounsbury, Deacon Peter Perkins, John Lines, Timothy Hitchcock, Ephraim Turner, Abraham Carrington, Ezra Sperry, Daniel Beecher, Jonathan Andrew, Reuben Sperry, Amos Hitchcock, Jonathan Tuttle, Deacon James Wheeler, Jacob Hotchkiss, Jared Sherman, Edward Perkins, Jesse Beecher, David French, Raymond Sanford, David Thomas Lamberton Tolles, Roger Peck, John Russell, Medad Hotchkiss, John

Thomas, Hezekiah Thomas, Caleb Andrews, Elihu Sanford, Jr, Reuben Perkins, Hezekiah Johnson, Lucas Lines, Jared Tolles, John Wooding, Darius Beecher, Deacon Hezekiah Beecher Jared Beecher

Two men are still living who were members of the Ecclesiastical society in Mr Hawleys time—Eden Johnson and Joel Andrews

Mr Hawley became so infirm at about 60 as to be unable to preach constantly, especially in the winter months But he continued to officiate more or less until 1803, the year before his death Some now living remember him as a trembling old man, with white locks He was often led to the church, and assisted into the pulpit and was sometimes able to deliver only a part of his discourse It is remembered that on one occasion he fell in the pulpit, and was carried home He was tall and very spare, and his appearance made a deep impression on the young

In the Connecticut Journal, (New Haven), of July 26th, 1804, the following obituary notice of Mr Hawley appeared —

Woodbridge, July 23

On the evening of Tuesday, the 17th inst after a long and tedious illness, departed this life in hope of a blessed immortality, the Rev Stephen Hawley, Senior Pastor of the church in Bethany, in Woodbridge, in the 67th year of his age

This worthy and good man, after having received a liberal education in Yale college, where he was graduated in 1759, was afterwards settled in the ministry at Bethany There he labored, to good acceptance, for a number of years, until by the Providence of God he was disabled from his work The Rev Mr Jones was, in June last, ordained a colleague pastor with him

The funeral was attended on Thursday last The corpse was borne to the meeting house by a number of respect-able citizens A solemn and well adapted sermon was delivered before a deeply affected audience by the Rev John Foote, of Cheshire from Job XIV-4—'If a man die, shall he live again?' All the days of my appointed time will I wait, till my change come' After Divine service the interment was performed with decency and solemnity

Such was this Christian minister He was very useful to his people during his ministry and was sincerely beloved by his flock who in his visitations, as well as in his ministrations in the sanctuary, "he held his face as it had been the face of an angel for he was conversant among them with gravity, prudence, modesty, humility, candor, wisdom and benevolence"

———

Mr Hawley's first wife was Mary Bellamy, of Hamden She had three children The second wife was Mehetable Hotchkiss, daughter of Deacon Joel Hotchkiss She removed to New Haven in 1806, with her three children, and resided there until her death in 1827

Two of Mr Hawley's New Year sermons were printed—those of 1769 and 1771 They give the reader a most favorable impression in regard to his activity of intellect, and his solemnity and earnestness as a preacher They are certainly the productions of a man above mediocrity They show that he himself was deeply serious, and that he possessed uncommon ability to set forth his thoughts in an impressive manner There is a remarkable vividness of style and even something of imaginative brilliancy, but all is deeply solemn The statements of evangelical truth are clear and Scriptural and the appeals to the hearers are forcible and affecting

A few months before his death Mr Hawley selected out some of his sermons for the use of his family, and the widow was in the habit of read-

ing them to her children   The remainder, written chiefly in shorthand,
(as in part were those which were
preserved) he destroyed   His pen-
manship when he wrote with care, was
beautiful

It is gratifying to have, in the two
printed sermons, so strong a portrait-
ure of Mr Hawley's mind and heart—
glimpses of the preacher as he was, in
thought, feeling, and expression   Thus
he 'being dead, yet speaketh"

CHRONOLOGICAL DATA

1730—First place of public worship erected
   Used also for a schoolhouse and always so
   mentioned in the records

1735—Winter parish privileges granted by the
   General Assembly

1762—Bethany incorporated an ecclesiastical an
   civil society similar to other parishes in
   Connecticut

1763, Oct 12—The Church of Christ organized
   and the Rev Stephen Hawley ordained and
   installed first pastor

1763-1773 —The meetinghouse erected

1784— Town privileges granted to the parishes of
   Amity and Bethany

1803—Steeple and bell added to the meetinghouse

1804 June 6—The Rev Isaac Jones ordained
   and installed second pastor of the church,

1804 July 17—Death of the Rev. Stephen Hawley

1806—Trial and deposition of the Rev Isaac
   Jones

1808—Close of a controversy which resulted in
   the withdrawal of sixty one members

1809—The endowment fund increased by subscription

1810 August 22—The Rev Nathaniel G Huntington ordained and installed third pastor
   of the church

1823—Dismission of the Rev Mr Huntington on
   account of ill health

1826—Court decision obtained that church funds
   should be exempt from taxation in Connecticut

1829 Jan 17—General Conference convened in
   this parish which resulted in the addition
   of thirty two members to the church

1831 Oct 13—Dedication of present house of
   worship

1832—Incorporation of the town of Bethany
   with the same geographical limits as the
   parish

1832- The Rev Jarius Wilcox installed pastor

1834—Installation of the Rev John B Kendall

1851—Old parsonage sold and the house oppo-
   posite present house of worship purchased

1855—Installation of the Rev E W Robinson
   as pastor

1863 Oct 12—Celebration of the one hundredth
   anniversary of the church   Erection of
   monument at the grave of the Rev. Stephen
   Hawley

1866 -Meetinghouse extensively repaired and
   altered by lowering galleries removing
   pews and enclosing porch

1876 April 5—Ordination and installation of
   the Rev W S Woodruff who was dismissed
   two years later

1890—Death of Deacon Clark Hotchkiss who
   served the church in this capacity sixty two
   years

1897 Nov 3—Ordination of the Rev Chas S
   MacFarland

1903—Church edifice repaired

1913—One hundred fiftieth anniversary of the
   organization of the church

THE MINISTRY OF THE CHURCH

In all the New England settlements the first public organization was the church. The first public building was the meeting house. The first public officer provided for was the minister. As an old writer says: "In the first settlement of New England, when the people judged their number competent to obtain a minister, they then severally seated themselves but not before, it being as unnatural for a New England man to live without a minister as for a smith to work his force without a fire."

The first minister of the Church of Christ in Bethany was the Rev. Stephen Hawley. His pastorate was the largest in the history of the church, and worthy perhaps of the most extended notice, but a good sketch of Mr. Hawley's life written fifty years ago by the Rev. S. C. Brace, having appeared in a recent issue of the Record, is it considered advisable to omit in this article.

Rev. Isaac Jones, son of Isaac Jones, was born in New Haven Feb. 16, 1775, and graduated from Yale college in 1792. He came to Bethany to preach June, 1803. Jan. 26, 1804, the society voted to call Mr. Jones. Daniel Tolles Col. Joel Hine and John Thomas were appointed a committee "for that purpose." Mr. Jones' license had expired and had not been renewed. He brought a paper from certain ministers in Georgia. An advisory council was called April 17, 1804, but contrary to their advice, the consociation was invited to ordain him without a renewal of license.

Mr. Jones made the following reply to the call:

"To the Church and Congregation of Bethany in Woodbridge.

"Gentlemen—I have officially received from you a paper containing your desire, as expressed in a vote, that I should engage to settle with you in the important work of the evangelical ministry, for which you will be pleased to accept my sincere gratitude.

"The object for which you have called me is certainly noble and important. It is of immense magnitude both as it respects yourselves, and the rising generation among you, and it may be observed that the societies are doubtless at liberty to make choice of a minister whose example they would make the pattern of their morals, and whose powers they judge will be the most persuasive to righteousness. The minister whom you have therefore chosen, is to be your spiritual teacher in holy things, to preach the word, to be instant in season and out of season, to reprove, rebuke and exhort with all long-suffering and doctrine.

"I have considered my inability without the strength of the Divine Immanuel, and although I have been sustained through some trials uncommon to the morning of ministerial life, by a very kind and blessed Providence yet my ardor and delight in the sacred ministry is not lessened.

"I have therefore considered your vote with that attention that it merited, and accordingly I do now signify my acceptance of your call to the work of the gospel ministry.

"I am, with gratitude and esteem, yours,

'ISAAC JONES, Jun'r
"Woodbridge Feb. 24, 1804."

April 18, 1804, the Ecclesiastical society voted—"To concur with a vote passed by the church to call the Western consociation to ordain Mr. Jones." "Voted—The 6th day of June next at 11 o'clock, be the time for ordination, and the council meet the day before at 10 o'clock in the forenoon"

The Consociation met at the house of Rev Stephen Hawley, June 5 1804 Dr Benjamin Trumbull, of North Haven, moderator, and Rev Ira Hart, of Middlebury, scribe Rev Mr Hawley expressed a desire that the consociation would proceed to ordain Mr Jones The council held in April had declared—'That to admit the license which Mr Jones received from certain ministers in Georgia would be to relinquish very necessary and useful regulations and stipulations, and that it is unhappy that the church and society proceeded to improve and make choice of Mr Jones, and that he accepted their choice, when the recommendation of the association which introduced him as a candidate for the ministry had expired and was not renewed ' The consociation, quoting these words, concurred in this declaration, but in consideration of concessions made by Mr Jones to the council in April, and promises to abide by the usages and order of the Consociation—signed by him—and in order to adjust matters peaceably, the Consociation voted to ordain Mr Jones, but adding the solemn protest against all such irregularities

The appointments for the religious service were

Rev Daniel Bronson, .
                    Introductory Prayer
Rev James Dana, D D
                    Ordination Sermon
Rev Benj Trumbull, D D
                    Consecrating Prayer
Rev Messrs Williston, Trumbull, Alling Smith   To Impose Hands
Rev Noah Williston   Charge
Rev Abraham Alling
                    Right Hand of Fellowship
Rev Bezaleel Pinneo
                    Concluding Prayer

The sermon delivered by Mr Jones on the Sabbath after his ordination, as his inaugural sermon was printed A number of copies of this sermon are still to be found in Bethany homes

At a church meeting holden on the 16th day of October, 1806

"Voted—That Isaac Jones, Jr, be the clerk, pro tempore This church taking into consideration their peculiar situation as a Consociated church, occasioned by the extraordinary and unprecedented proceedings of the association now in session on certain charges exhibited by Mr Timothy Hitchcock (through the procurement of Mr Medad Hotchkiss, who is not a church member,) against the Rev Isaac Jones, pastor of this church, and, for the reasons this day detailed by our worthy pastor, in his remonstrance to be handed in to said association, as well as for other reasons,

"Voted—That this church do now withdraw from all connection with the Consociated churches in the Western district in New Haven county, and do hereby declare and make it known that in future this church will be and remain an independent church Passed in church meeting unanimously, (thirteen members present)"

Attest Isaac Jones, Jr, Moderator and Clerk pro tem

There were present at the Consociation, November 18, Benjamin Trumbull, D D, and Rev Messrs Abner Smith, Oliver Hitchcock, Bezaleel Pinneo, Abraham Alling, Howard Weeks, Ira Hart, John Hyde and delegates Rev Dr Trumbull retired from the Consociation

In regard to the whole result of the association, the Consociation, on review, ratified and established it 1, pronounced a sentence of exclusion from all ministerial and Christian fellowship upon Mr Jones and declared that he had no longer authority from the Consociation to preach or administer the gospel ordinances

A communication was sent to Mr Jones by the Consociation containing a statement of their doings This Mr

Jones refused to accept, declaring that he would receive no communication from this body. Advice being asked: "The Consociation advise the church that in case Mr. Jones and the seceding brethren propose in a constitutional way to call the Eastern Consociation in New Haven, to sit with this body and hear the allegations against Mr. Jones, they consent to the same." April 21, 1807. The two Consociations met, and were in session three days. It was decided that Mr. Jones might be restored on making suitable confession. A confession was prepared and Mr. Jones publicly assented thereto. But November 3, 1807 the New Haven West Consociation assembled at Woodbridge, declared that Mr. Jones had not complied with the advice of the united Consociations and was pursuing a course subversive of ecclesiastical order; and therefore that the decision of November, 1806, was in full force, and Mr. Jones was without ministerial authority. His farewell sermon was preached in the hall of the Wheeler house, December 11, 1808. His text was from Jeremiah 12:10-11: "Many pastors have destroyed my vineyard, etc." The address was printed. Mr. Jones became an Episcopalian with many of his congregation. On November 6, 1809, the newly formed Episcopal society voted Isaac Jones "a person worthy and well qualified for the gospel ministry." He was admitted as a candidate for orders, later becoming a deacon and a priest, in regular succession. He was the first rector of Christ church and remained here for about two years. He was stationed in Litchfield, 1811-1826; in Huntington, 1831-1834; Hitchcockville, 1837-1839; Bethany, 1841-1842; Milton, 1845-1847, and then for years chaplain in the Litchfield county prison. He died in Litchfield, March 17, 1850. He had a son and a daughter. The son died a year after the father, the daughter the next year and the mother the next.

Rev. Nathaniel Gilbert Huntington, son of Deacon Josiah and Abigail (Gilbert) Huntington, was born in Rocky Hill, Connecticut, Oct. 30, 1785. He was fitted for college under Rev. Dr. Nathan Perkins of West Hartford. He was graduated from Yale College 1806. June 6, 1809 the Hartford North Association licensed him to preach and he came to Bethany, the following October. June 6, 1810 the Ecclesiastical society voted, This meeting does concur with the vote of the church in this place this day to give Mr. Nathaniel G. Huntington a call to settle with us in the work of the "Gospel Ministry." The consociation met at the house of Elihu Sanford Aug. 21, 1810; and the ordination took place on the following day:

SERVICES.

Rev. Caleb Pitkin ....
.... Introductory Prayer
Rev. Nathan Perkins, D. D ..Sermon
Rev. Benj. Trumbull, D. D. ......
.... Consecrating Prayer
Trumbull, Smith and Pinneo ....
.... Impose hands
Rev. B. Pinneo .... Charge
Rev. Jason Allen ....Right hand
Rev. Abraham Alling ....
.... Concluding Prayer

There were fifteen ministers present at the ordination of Mr. Huntington.

About two years after his ordination Mr. H. had a hemmorhage—he took a year's rest. During the remaining years of his pastorate his health was poor. The state of his health is indicated by a number of communications which he made to the society, and it became worse as the years went on so that he asked to be dismissed. His dismission occurred in March 1823. He remained in Bethany, then removed to Oxford, where he was a farmer fourteen years, supplying the pulpit sometimes at Salem (Naugatuck); and he preached three or four Sabbaths in Oxford His health became worse and he removed to Orange, lived nine years there in tolerable health and died Feb 10, 1848 His wife was Betsey Tucker, of Bethany, a native of Derby, whom he married in 1821 Her father was Zephemah Tucker She was the mother of four children Mr Huntington issued two geographies published in Hartford He wrote for the Christian Spectator

After Mr Huntington's dismission the pulpit was supplied, for four years, chiefly by Rev Abraham Alling of Hamden From March 1826 to March 1827, Rev Samuel Tillotson Babbit preached half the time, alternating with Mr A Abraham Alling was born in Stamford, Dutchess county, N Y He came to Hamden and at 16 or 18 joined the North Church in New Haven He became a farmer At 44 he was ordained and installed pastor of the church in Whitneyville (Oct 19, 1797-Oct 22 1822) After the close of h s pastorate there he became act ng pastor of the church in Bethany He died on h s farm in Hamden July 22, 1827 Aged 83 Samuel Tillotson Babbitt, born in Huntington Mar 30, 1809 was graduated from the Yale Theological Seminary in the class of 1826 He was ordained at New Haven, Nov 7, 1827 He preached in the new settlements of Western New York fo nearly th rty years Mr Babbitt never had a pastoral charge

Rev Ephraim G Swift preached here from Jan 1828 to Jan 1831 He was the son of the Rev Seth Swift of Williamstown, Mass He had been a colleague with Dr West, in Stockbridge, Mass and had preached in Oxford He was in Killingworth 1843-50, afterwards at Chester He died while on a visit in the state of New York, Aug 28 1858

In 1830 S C Baldwin and Geo Goodyear preached here

The Rev Nathaniel Taylor, D D of Yale supplied the pulpit much in 1831, 1832 He preached the dedication sermon of the present house of worship, Oct 13, 1831 There were several other ministers present on the same occasion Dr Taylor died Mar 12 1858

Jairus Wilcox was born in Cromwell, Conn (Upper Middletown) Mar 8, 1802 He studied for a time at Bangor Theological Seminary and then at Yale Theological Seminary (two years) class of 1830 The consociation met at the house of Lewis Thomas (Wheeler house) Nov 6 Present Rev Stephen W Stebbins Zephanah Zwift, Leonard Bacon Chas Thompson, Abraham Browne Jason Atwater Corresponding members, E T Fitch D D J B Richardson, Henry Herrick

Introductory Prayer   C Thompson
Sermon   E T Fitch D D
Ordaining p'ayer   S W Stebbins
Swift and Stebbins   Impose hands
Charge   Sw ft
Right hand   Browne
Address to people   Atwater
Concluding prayer   Herr ck

1834, June 17, Consociation met to dismiss Rev J Wilcox, who was dismissed w th testimony to his abil ity and fru tfulness

1834, July 23 Rev John B Kendall was called by this church and society and installed Aug 12, 13 1834 He was d smissed June 7, 1836

From 1836 to 1840 the pulp t was supplied by many different preachers Rev Erastus Colton came in 1836 and was succeeded by Rev I D Moore In 1838 Rev W lliam H Adams, Rev Josiah Abbott and Rev Geo Taylor supplied In 1839 Rev Eli B Clark, Rev Irvin and Rev J Curtiss

In March 1840 Rev Saul Clark was hired and remained until March, 1842 He came to Bethany from South Egremont, Mass While here he taught a high school in addition to his pastoral duties

In 1842 the pulpit was supplied by Rev Cyrus Brewster, Rev Geo Thatcher and others

The services of Rev Daniel B Butts were engaged in May 1843 Mr Butts was born in Rome N Y During the years he lived in Bethany he occupied the Congregational parsonage, which stood on the cross-road west of Chas Booth's After it was sold the house was known as the Parson Butts place It was burned several years ago Two of Rev Mr Butts children were baptized in Bethany, Eugene and Edwin. Eugene died Jan 24 1846 and is buried in the Congregational cemetery Mr Butts remained in Bethany five years, until 1848

Rev W W Belden preached here in 1848 and was invited to settle as pastor but declined In 1848 Rev Augustus Smith, and Rev Ira H Smith were supplies

Rev Fosdick Harrison was engaged in March, 1849 and remained until December 1851

He began to preach in Bethany on the second Sabbath in March 1849 He lived while in Bethany in the Lyman Beecher house, now occupied by Mr Murphy

While in Bethany, he officiated at the funeral of George Peck, who was the first one buried in the Methodist cemetery Mr Harrison was the author of the interesting epitaph which Peck's gravestone bears

The Rev Fosdick Harrison, who is pastor of the Southington Congregational church is a grandson of the Bethany minister

In December, 1851, Rev Alexander Leadbetter was hired as supply, and remained until Sept 1854

Rev Ebenezer W Robinson came from Hanover, Conn, (a village in the town of Sprague,) October, 1854, and was installed Pastor May 2, 1855 The services were as follows

Prayer and Reading of Scriptures, . Rev C S Sherman
Sermon Rev Mr Hazen
Installing Prayer Rev S Topliff
Charge Rev Cleaveland
Right Hand Rev Putnam
Address to the People Rev Beebe
Concluding Prayer Rev Thayer

Rev Mr Robinson lived in the parsonage which the society had purchased in 1851, where Mrs Celia Perry now lives He was dismissed August 15, 1860, but continued to reside in Bethany until about 1865, when he was dismissed by letter to the Congregational church in Washington, D C In 1863 he was one of the speakers at the Centennial

Rev Seth C Brace, son of the famous Rev Joab Brace, was ordained and installed pastor of this church June 26, 1861 The services were as follows

Prayer and Reading of Scripture Rev W W Atwater
Sermon Rev John Todd, D D
Ordaining and installing prayer Rev E L Cleaveland, D D
Charge Rev Jonathan Brace, D D
Right Hand Rev Austin Putnam
Concluding Prayer Rev A C Raymond

A few of the older members of the church remember Mr Brace

He prepared a historical address for the Centennial celebration, and after that event collected a large amount of matter which has never been published Much of the data in this article is obtained from this source Mr Brace resigned the pastoral charge April 17, 1864 In his communication to the society, he wrote "I wish to be considered as making this proposition not only without complaint, but with grateful acknowledgement of your forbearance and kindness, and most earnest wishes for the prosperity of this church and society" The consociation assembled May 18th and resolved "That in assenting to the dismissal of Rev S C Brace, from the pastoral charge of the church in Bethany, this council desires to express its high estimate of the Christian and ministerial character of the retiring "pastor of his fidelity and zeal in discharging the duties of his pastorate * * * and of his scholarly and ministerial ability" He lived in New Haven until 1871 and after that date in Philadelphia until his death January 25, 1897, aged 85

Rev D M C Elwood, M D, of Woodbridge, was the acting pastor of the church for a number of years, until 1867 We regret that we have few facts in regard to Mr Elwood

S W Barnum was stated supply in 1869 and 1870

The church voted December 12, 1875, to extend a call to Rev William Louis Woodruff He was ordained and installed pastor of the church April 5, 1876 He lived in the house nearly opposite the church, which had formerly been the parsonage He conducted a school for boys which became popular Perry's hall was built for the gymnasium for his academy and after the school was closed it was called Gymnasium hall for many years Mr Woodruff was a man of great intellectual ability He presented, December 12, 1876, his resignation, to take effect in three months as previously agreed, and June 9, 1877 the church voted to unite with Mr Woodruff in calling a council for his dismission The council failed to convene Another invitation was extended and a council, consisting of ministers and delegates from neighboring churches, convened and the pastoral relation was dissolved July 7, 1878

Mr Woodruff went from Bethany to Hamden and was master of the Everest school, in Centerville, for a time

Since Mr Woodruff's time the pulpit has been supplied by ministers studying at the Yale Divinity school The high reputation of Yale attracts many ordained ministers, who have graduated from some other theological seminary, but who desire to obtain a degree from Yale Thus the church has been able often to secure men of marked ability who have maintained a higher standard of preaching than would have been the case if a resident minister had been maintained with the salary which this church can offer On the whole this has been the most satisfactory plan, circumstances considered, although the system has its serious drawbacks The chief of these, nonresidence of the minister, has been partly offset by the fact that many of the ministers have spent the long summer vacation in Bethany

George Boothwell supplied the pulpit from March, 1880, to March, 1881

William G Roberts, March 20, 1881, to March 20, 1882

J C Mitchell was acting pastor from March, 1882, to March, 1884

C B Whitcomb, April, 1886, to April 1887

R J Thomson, May, 1892, to December, 1892

J O Jones, March, 1893, to October 1894

J Deane, November, 1894

H W Johnson, September, 1895, to September, 1896 Mr Johnson wrote a history of the church which was printed in the Seymour Record He was eventually ordained to the Congregational ministry, which was not the denomination to which he had previously adhered

Rev Charles F MacFarland began his work in Bethany in October 1896 He expressed a desire to be ordained here, and a council was called for that purpose, which met on Wednesday Nov 3 1897 The order of service was

Invocation Rev Frederick Lynch
Anthem, Choir
Reading of Scripture, Rev B M Wright
Hymn 339 Congregation
Sermon, Rev Professor L O Brastow

Prayer of ordination, Rev Professor E I Curtiss

Anthem, Choir

Charge to the candidate, Rev Professor G B Stevens

Right hand of fellowship, Rev John C Wilson

Hymn, 1,019, Congregation

Prayer, Rev S P Marvin

Benediction

Rev C F MacFarland was the seventh minister to be ordained by this church. He remained in Bethany until 1899. In the summer of 1898 he was in Europe and during his absence the pulpit was supplied by E G Zellars, of Yale. Mr MacFarland has risen high in the ministerial ranks, is the author of many religious books, and is at the present time executive secretary of the Federal Council of the Churches of Christ in America. He lives in New York city.

Rev Philip J Phelps preached here during 1899. He now resides at Bakersfield, Cal, without pastoral charge. He was ordained in 1901.

The church was closed for about a year, being reopened Nov 1, 1901 with Rev Shirley J Case for its minister. Mr Case was an interesting speaker. He remained here until December, 1903, when he received a call to the United church Beacon Falls.

In December, 1903, Rev J F Johnston, M A (Yale) Ph D began to preach in Bethany. He went from Bethany to Seymour Congregational church in June, 1904.

Rev Van Lubken preached here from June, 1904, until June 1905.

Rev Otto W Burtner, ordained in 1901, began here in June 1905. Mr Burtner, as well as several succeeding ministers officiated at the Methodist church, Bethany, in the afternoon. He was called to the First Congregational church of Ansonia in September, 1906, where he is still pastor.

Rev Dr Roop officiated here for a few months following, from September to December, 1906.

In December 1906, Rev G Douglass Milbury of New Brunswick, Canada, began his labors in this church. Five members were added during his ministrations. He took a great interest in the people of the community and succeeded in increasing the size of his congregations. He also preached at the Methodist church. Upon finishing his course in the Yale Divinity school he returned to New Brunswick, in June 1908, preaching his farewell sermon here on the 14th.

Rev Elmer Edwin Burtner, brother of the Rev Otto W Burtner, preached here beginning June 21, 1908. His home was in Hinton, Virginia. He was a very popular young minister and the church regretted to have him leave in January, 1909, for the First Congregational church Derby, where he was ordained Oct 12, 1909.

It seems a noteworthy fact that from Bethany ministers have accepted calls to Beacon Falls, Seymour, Ansonia and Derby in regular order. Mr Burtner remained in Derby to 1910, accepting at that date a call to the First Congregational church of Missoula, Montana.

Rev Herman Henry Lindeman of Nebraska, supplied the pulpit from January 1909 to May 22 1910 a longer period than most of the recent ministers have spent here. He was ordained in 1910 and the same year became pastor of the church at Red Lodge Montana.

Rev Howard Grant Parsons gave his first sermon in Bethany, May 23, 1912. He gained the respect and esteem of the people of Bethany. His last Sunday here was Dec 18th 1910.

The next minister was Paul L Kirby who remained here until June 1911 then, after finishing his course in the Divinity school he accepted a pastorate in Maine.

Rev Homer L Scott came next and preached during the summer. His home is in Concord, N C Rev Everett E Bachelder, of Pittsfield, N H, a graduate of Dartmouth college, was here from Sept, 1911, to June 2, 1912 The Sunday school was re-organized while he was the minister He accepted a call to the church at Stanwich, Conn, where he was ordained Oct 5, 1912

Rev James W Newton, of London, England, began his ministerial labors in Bethany in June, 1912, and continued to officiate here until May, 1913

He took a very keen interest in the affairs of the church and sought in every way to promote its interests He now has charge of a church in North Madison

The present minister is Rev John W Wright, of Pylesville, Md He graduated from the Western Maryland college in 1911 Mr Wright's sermons are preached without reference to notes and they are so helpful and instructive that he holds the close attention of his audience

THE HOADLEY FALLS.

THE MEMBERS OF THE CHURCH.

A most important phase of the history of a church is its membership. The members indeed, make the history. They represent the highest and best type of society in the community in which they live and they set a standard for morality. If some fall short of high ideals and, in the words of a member of long ago, have thereby "wounded the cause of Christ and the brethren and sisters of this branch of His church," it is not just for us to condemn the whole church for the sins of a few.

That the names of those who, during the last hundred and fifty years have

been connected with the First Church of Christ, in Bethany, may be made accessible and convenient for reference, the following list has been prepared:

There is now no record of members of the church from its organization until 1814, a period of just about fifty years, although the early records are complete in most other respects. Rev. Seth Brace stated fifty years ago that the earliest lists were lost, and it seems improbable that they will ever be recovered. To overcome this deficiency the names of those who labored in the cause of Christ during the long and prosperous ministry of the Rev. Stephen

Hawley, have been compiled in alpha-
betical order The list contains the
names of all who worshipped in his
congregation before 1800, as far as the
records show   Here again we find unfortunately that the names of few women have been preserved Most of the
persons mentioned were probably com-
municants   All were inhabitants of
Bethany before 1800, and many of them
were the first settlers   A few of the
first comers had died before the incorporation of the parish

Alling, Lemuel

Alling, Noah

Andrew, Jonathan, the son of Jonathan 4, Rev Samuel 3, Samuel, 2, William 1, lived in the 'Milford Side" of
the parish

Andrew, William, son of Jonathan
above, married, first, Esther March-
ant, second, Margaret Merwin   He
was baptized June, 1734, and died
August 28, 1796

Andrews or Andrus, Caleb, was early
appointed to dig graves

Andrews, Ebenezer

Andrews, Widow Sarah

Atwater, Amos, son of Jonathan and
Sarah (Beach) Atwater, married
Hannah Ives, of Cheshire

Atwater, David, son of Jonathan and
Sarah Atwater, lived near the Anan
Atwater house, (now occupied by D
L Humiston) He was the father of
Anan Atwater

Atwater, Jesse, brother of David Atwater

Atwater, Jonathan, a descendant of
David Atwater, the first settler, lived
on the corner south of the Smith
school He married Sarah Beach He
died February 24, 1795, aged 75

Atwater, Moses, son of Jonathan
above

Baldwin, Isaac

Baldwin, Matthew

Ball, Timothy, died June 7, 1786, aged
78   His son Timothy, moved to Waterbury about 1815   Descendants live
in Oakville

Ball, Widow Mary

Barnes, Jacob

Beecher, Beri, son of Deacon Hezekiah
Beecher, married Polly, daughter of
Isaac Downs He lived where Wallace Saxton now lives One of his
sons was Beri, Jr

Beecher, Calvin, lived on the Krell
farm He died May 11, 1806, aged 35
and his widow married a Kimberly

Beecher, Daniel Lieut, died November
5, 1796, aged 67

Beecher, Darius, was a man of wealth
He built the fine house later occupied by Lewis Thomas and Orrin
Wheeler He moved to the West and
lost his fortune, it is said

Beecher, Widow Hannah, probably the
widow of Samuel Beecher, who died
in 1760

Beecher, Deacon Hezekiah, the son of
Isaac and Mabel (Hotchkiss) Beecher, was born April 6, 1738

Beecher, Isaac, son of Samuel and Hannah Beecher, was born in 1717 He
died October 28, 1801 Married Mabel
Hotchkiss, who died February 19, 1798,
aged 79 Samuel Beecher, his father,
was a son of Isaac 3, Isaac 2, John 1,
the first settler

Beecher, Jared

Beecher, Jesse, son of Isaac and Mabel
(Hotchkiss) Beecher, was born April
20, 1741 and died April 7, 1813 His
son, Jesse, was an itinerant Methodist minister Hoel Beecher was a
son of the latter

Beecher, Justus

Beecher, Lyman, "Bethany and its
Hills," states that the Beechers in
Bethany claim relationship with Lyman Beecher, the noted Litchfield
minister

Beecher, Lycias, built the house at the
center, north of churches

Beecher, Thomas

Beecher, Wheeler

Beers, David

Beers, Nathan, lived north of the
Smith school He died May 9, 1837,
aged 74 Mary, his wife, died August

RESIDENCE OF NATHAN F. MANSFIELD.

9, 1845, aged 74.

Bishop, Ebenezer, became an Episcopalian and was a warden. He died January 2, 1794, of smallpox.

Bishop, Joseph, died February 27, 1819, aged 62. Olive, his wife, died November 20, 1842, aged 79.

Bradley, Jesse.

Bradley, Jason, son of Joseph and Miriam (Gilbert) Bradley, was born January 1, 1741. Joseph was the son of Joseph 3, Joseph 2, William 1.

Bradley, Reuben.

Briscoe, Samuel.

Briscoe, Widow Mary.

Briscoe, Widow Sarah.

Bronson, Timothy.

Brown, Timothy.

Buckingham, Abijah.

Buckingham, Oliver, father of Buel Buckingham, of Beacon Falls.

Carrington, Abraham, lived in "Milford Side" and his barn is still standing.

His estate was settled June 5, 1799. Father of Alling Carrington.

Castle, Jehiel, Dr., came from Waterbury just before 1800 and succeeded Hooker as the parish doctor. Father of Dr. Andrew Castle. One of the latter's daughters married Orrin Wheeler, another John W. Weed.

Clark, Aaron.

Clark, Lazarus, Jr.

Clark, David.

Clark, D. E.

Collins, Benjamin.

Collins, Joe.

Collins, Joseph.

Downs, David, son of Eber and Anna (Hitchcock) Downs, was baptized in Bethany, June 29, 1783 by Rev. Bela Hubbard, of Trinity church, New Haven. He lived on Downs street.

Downs, Felix, son of Samuel and Sarah (Humphreyville) Downs. He married Phebe Downs, who died Feb-

ruary 9, 1844, aged 79 He built a large
house on Downs street, which was
torn down about fifteen years ago
He died February 3, 1848, aged 89

Downs, Isaac, son of Eber Downs, was
baptized June 29, 1783 He married
Mabel Perkins and moved to Wolcott,
Conn Father of Kneeland Downs

Downs, Joseph, son of Seth and Mary
(Sperry) Downs, was born February
22, 1732-3

Downs, Samuel, son of Samuel 3,
Samuel 2, John 1, married Sarah
Humphreyville He died Feb 7,
1801, aged 81

Downs, Widow Sarah

Downs, Zeri, son of Samuel and Sarah
Downs, moved to Bethlehem, Conn.
and died there May 3, 1840

Driver, James

Foot, Isaac

Ford, Amos

French, Esq David, son of Israel and
Sarah (Loveland) French, was born
Jan 30, 1742 Married Lois Lines He
died Aug 4, 1821 Jane French,
daughter of Harry, the son of David
French, married Justin Peck, of
Cheshire Harry F Peck, their son
lives near the old homestead

Hine, Capt Joel, one of the leaders in
the Isaac Jones controversy, is
buried in rear of Episcopal church

Hitchcock, Amos, Capt, son of John 3,
Nathaniel 2, Matthias, was born in
1724 and died in 1791 He married
Dorcas Foot, of Br ford

Hitchcock, Amos, son of the above,
was born 1762 and married Sarah
Sperry of Bethany Lived in the
valley just north of where Sergent's
brook crosses the road

Hitchcock, Ebenezer, son of Capt
Amos and Dorcas (Foot) Hitchcock,
was born in 1751

Hitchcock, Eli, son, Capt Amos and
Dorcas (Foot) Hitchcock, lived in
Bethany, where Albert Hosley lives,
the farm is still owned by a descen-
dant He had two sons, Grant and
Miles He died Sept 27, 1846, aged

78 Abigail, his wife, died Nov 8,
1808, aged 36

Hitchcock, Joseph, son of Ebenezer
and Anna (Perkins) Hitchcock Ebenezer was son of Nathaniel, son of
Matthias

Hitchcock, Rebeckah, daughter of
Ebenezer and Rebekah (Thomas)
Hitchcock

Hitchcock, Timothy, son of Ebenezer
and Anna (Perkins) Hitchcock, was
born 1713

Hitchcock, William

Hooker, Dr Hezekiah, lived in a
"mansion" on the north side of the
old Bethany Green The celar place
is still visible He died in 1799

Hoadley, Ami, lived at Hoadley Mills
The house (torn down and moved to
Prospect a few yea s ago) and mills
were built by him His children
were Ursula married Isaac Doolittle,
Harriet married William Burnham,
and Garry married Lucy Doolittle
and remained at the homestead

Hotchkiss, Aaron

Hotchkiss, Abraham, son of Ensign
Joshua and Mary Hotchkiss, was
one of the first of the name to locate
here

Hotchkiss, Benjamin

Hotchkiss, David E sha, lived north
of the Smith school

Hotchkiss, Elias

Hotchkiss, Ezekiel

Hotchkiss, Jabez, son of Isaac, born
June, 1701, who was son of Ensign
Joshua and Mary Hotchkiss

Hotchkiss, Jacob, son of Isaac 3,
Joshua 2, Samuel 1

Hotchkiss, Joseph, son of Isaac

Hotchkiss, Capt Joel He was one of
the first deacons of the church He
died Feb 3, 1819, aged 73

Hotchkiss, Joel, Jr, son of t e above

Hotchkiss, Medad, Lieut

Hotchkiss, Samuel

Hotchkiss, Solomon

Hotchkiss, Stephen, son of Jabez
Hotchkiss

Hotchkiss, Silas

THE LAMBERT WOODING HOMESTEAD.

Hotchkiss, Zedekiah.

Ives, Anan.

Ives, Abel.

Johnson, Eden—Lived in a house east of Frank Warner's residence. He and Joel Andrews were the only two members of the ecclesiastical society of Mr. Hawley's time who were living at the time of the centennial.

Johnson, Eliphalet.

Johnson, Gideon.

Johnson, Hezekiah, died March 6, 1818, aged 70.

Judd, Asi (?) Built the house where William Keefe lives.

Kimball, Thomas, son of Thomas and Mary Kimball, died Sept. 6, 1830, aged 91.

Lines, Abel.

Lines, Ebenezer.

Lines, Eber.

Lines, John

Lines, Lucas. He was a tory and was known as Luke Lines.

Lounsbury, Elias.

Lounsbury, Eri, son of Timothy and Hannah (French) Lounsbury, married Sarah Carrington. Two of his sons were Abram and W.lliam H. The latter was born Dec. 30, 1815. His son, also William, lives at the old homestead at the present date.

Lounsbury, Josiah, son of Josiah and Ruth (Lines) Lounsbury was born Aug. 5, 1729. He married Martha Hotchkiss.

Lounsbury, Linus, son of Josiah and Martha, was born Jan. 3, 1752.

Lounsbury, Stephen, son of Josiah and Ruth (Lines) Lounsbury was born 1736 and married Hannah Sperry, Oct. 26, 176..

Lounsbury, Timothy, son of Josiah and Ruth was born 1740, died 1821. He married first Hannah, daughter of David French He built the fine old mansion on Lounsbury street in 1811

Martin, Samuel

Nelson, Silas

Nettleton, Eli, lived in North Bethany, where his lineal descendant, Harry Nettleton now lives

Nettleton, John

Nettleton, Widow Sarah

Payne, Abraham

Payne, Isaac

Parker, Ebenezer

Peck, Benajah Deacon

Peck, Lydia

Peck, Samuel, son of Timothy Peck

Peck, Timothy, was the first of the name to settle in Bethany He was a prominent man and was influential in obtaining winter parish privileges in 1755 He was the son of Samuel 3, Joseph 2, Henry 1

Perkins, Archibald, son of Azariah and Anne (Johnson) Perkins, (Azariah 4, John 3, John 2, Edward 1) He kept the old Perkins Tavern after the death of Edward Perkins He married Sarah Nettleton

Perkins, David, son of Reuben Perkins

Perkins, Edward, probably the first proprietor of Perkins Tavern, was born Oct 25, 1743 He was the son of Peter and Mary (Peck) Perkins, son of Peter and Hanah (Lord) Perkins, son of Edward and Elizabeth (Butcher) Perkins Edward married first Mary Thomas, second, Rosanna Judd, sister of Chauncey Judd, the stolen boy

Perkins, Isreal, son of Edward Perkins above, was born Dec 30, 1767 He married Milly Judd, sister of Chauncey Judd He died Sept 8, 1846, aged 79 Rev Israel Perkins Warren was a grandson

Perkins, Joel

Perkins, John

Perkins, Deacon Peter, son of Peter Perkins, was often entrusted with various ecclesiastical duties He died Nov 23, 1790, aged 58 Elizabeth, his

wife, died April 7, 1798, aged 58

Perkins, Reuben, lived north of the David Perkins place The cellar and well are still descernible No public road crosses in at vicinity at present He married Thankful Smith He died in Hamden about 1800, aged 64 His widow died in Bethany, Sept 6, 1831, aged 85

Russell, Widow Anne The statement, "Mrs Anna Russell was the first person born in Bethany," probably refers to the above

Russell, Elmore

Russell, Enoch

Russell, John His wife, Abigail, died June 1, 1813, aged 61

Russell, Robert

Sackitt, Jonathan Sarah, wife of "John" Sackitt, died Jan 12, 1794, aged 20

Sanford, Cyrus

Sanford, David

Sanford, Col Elihu, lived in the Ebenezer Dayton house, east side of the meeting-house green "He was the father of Elihu and Harvey Sanford, esquires, long known as among the most respectable citizens of New Haven" He donated the land for the Congregational cemetery

Sanford, Jonathan

Sanford, Mehitable

Sherman, James

Sherman, Samuel

Smith, Ezekial

Smith, Jonathan

Smith, Samuel

Sperry, Demas, son of Reuben, lived on the farm now owned by D L Johnson He was the father of Col Alvin Sperry who built the house now standing He died June 27, 1833, aged 68 His wife, Elizabeth, died December, 1849, aged 81

Sperry, Elam, was a member of the church

Sperry, Ezra Lived in the house which stood on the corner diagonally from the Wheeler house He was the

THE HOADLEY MILL, TORN DOWN ABOUT 1904.

father of Ezra Stiles Sperry. Capt. Ezra Sperry died Nov. 10, 1803, aged 73. His wife, Ruth, died July 2, 1815, aged 82.

Sperry, Elijah, Capt.

Sperry, Hannah. It was south of her house, probably, that the parish line extended.

Sperry, Hezekiah.

Sperry, Isaac, built the Henry Sanford house. Father of Enos Sperry. He died Feb. 7, 1844, aged 84. His wife Mary, died Oct. 28, 1835, aged 71.

Sperry, Medad.

Sperry, Reuben, father of Demas above, and others probably. He died May, 1795, aged 62. His wife, Eunice, died Dec. 6, 1820, aged 83.

Sperry, Uri.

Sperry, Zeri.

Talmadge, John Alsop.

Terrel, Widow Phebe. Widow of Phineas Terrel, son of Samuel, of Milford.

Terrel, Ebenezer.

Terrel, John.

Terrel, Deacon Phineas, son of Phineas and Phebe Terrel.

Thomas, Gershom Ensign, (Israel 3, Daniel 2, John 1), was born March 17, 1725, and died before May 7, 1792. He married April 26, 1749, Mabel Dorman, widow of Joel Perkins. She died March 19, 1787, aged 66.

Thomas, David, was baptized May 3, 1752. Was a leader in the Jones

controversy, to whom he was opposed He was son of Israel 4,
Israel 2, Daniel 2, John 1

Thomas, E Downs

Thomas, Elizabeth

Thomas, Hezekiah, brother of David
Thomas, was the first town clerk
He was proprietor of the Hezekiah
Thomas hotel which later became
the Congregational parsonage He
married Chloe Beecher Their
daughter, Tabitha, married Isaac
Jones

Thomas, Israel (Israel 3, Daniel 2,
John 1), born June 5, 1720, died
1784 He married June 24, 1746,
Martha, daughter of Ambrose Hine

Thomas, Esquire John (John 4, John
3, John 2, John 1), born April 16,
1755 Lived on Lebanon Hill He
inherited considerable wealth and
was probably the richest man in the
parish His wife, Lydia, died July
13, 1815, aged 50 He died April
21, 1839

Thomas, John Jr, lived on Lebanon
Hill

Thomas, Noah, son of Gershom and
Mabel Thomas, married Sept 9,
1781, Mary Tolles, daughter of
Daniel and Thankful (Smith)
Tolles On Oct 26, 1818, his widow
Mary and Aner Thomas became ad-
ministrators of his estate which was
divided between the widow Mary
and Aner Thomas, Laura Robinson
and Leverett, Ransom and Charles
Thomas Noah died Sept 16, 1818,
aged 62 His wife died Sept 10,
1842, aged 87

Todd, Charles, son of Jonah Todd
Lived in North Bethany He married Lydia Ives

Tolles, Abraham, son of Daniel, mar-
ried Elizabeth ——— He died
May 20, 1793, aged 38 She died
Feb 14, 1788, aged 22

Tolles, Chauncey, lived in the southern part of the town, where his son
Lewis built the house where

Elizur Doolittle lived Chauncey
died April 1, 1824, aged 46 His
wife Eunice died Nov 23, 1865,
aged 91

Tolles, Daniel, son of Henry and
Dorothy (Thomas) Tolles, married
Thankful Smith He died Jan 20,
1782, aged 77 His wife died June
28, 1769, aged 58

Tolles, Daniel, Jr, married Mary
Hine

Tolles, Jared, was a soldier in the
Revolution

Tolles, Lamberton, married Abigail,
daughter of Samuel and Ruth
Briscoe

Tolles, Lazarus, married Sibyl Bellamy

Tolles, Lyman

Tolles, Nehemiah

Tuttle, Amasa, son of Uri and Thankful (Tuttle) Married Esther
Tolles

Tuttle, Jonathan

Tuttle, Nathaniel, brother of Uri
Tuttle, Sr He died Feb 20, 1802,
aged 59 Elizabeth his wife, died
April 4, 1819, aged 72

Tuttle, Thankful Widow of Uri Tuttle, daughter of Jonathan Ives

Tuttle, Uri, Jr, son of Uri and
Thankful Married Electa Perkins,
daughter of Edward

Tyrrel, Deacon Jesse

Warren, Edward

Warren, Nathaniel

Wheeler, Deacon James, (record elsewhere)

Wheeler, Joel

White, Deacon John, son of Capt
John and Susannah (Alling) White,
was born May 19, 1722 He married Mary, daughter of Isaac and
Mary (Atwater) Dickerman, Dec
27, 1744 He was appointed a deacon of the Church of Christ in
Bethany as soon as its organization was effected He died in New
Haven, Nov 24, 1797

Wilmot, Valentine, (record given

RESIDENCE OF MRS. A. H. DOWNS, EAST BETHANY.

elsewhere),

Wilmot, David.

Wilmot, Walter.

Wolcott, Joseph.

Wooding, David. Keeper of the Smith Tavern previous to Theophilus Smith.

Wooding, John.

Wooding, John Jr.

Wooding, William, lived near Hoadley's Mills, house later owned by the Roswells.

It was during the period closely following 1800 that the greatest religious controversy that this town and few other towns in Connecticut have ever known. It was waged at fearful cost to the church. We learn that the congregation dwindled from one hundred and sixty-four families in 1799 to eighty in 1811, as shown by seats assigned to heads of families in the seating plans, still in existence. During this period but few new names were added to the parishioners but we give them so far as the records show: Allen, Richard; Beecher, Timothy; Benworth, Orange; Clark, Isaac; Dudley, Caleb; Hotchkiss, Harvey; Hotchkiss, Seymour, Hotchkiss, Sheldon; Hotchkiss, Zaccheus, Prince, Nathan; Robinson, Elihu; Sanford, Tubal; Sperry, Alvan; Sperry, Chilion; Stone, Richard; White, John; Wilmot, Amos; Wilmot, John.

From various sources it is ascertained that the men mentioned below were members of the church, previous to 1814 Joseph Collins, Eden Johnson, Jesse Beecher, Phineas Tyrrell (Deacon), Hezekiah Beecher (Deacon), Daniel Tolles, Moses Clark, Joel Hine, Bezaleel Peck and Joel Andrews and wife

List of church members January 1, 1814 This is the earliest complete list of members extant

Andrew, Mary (Tyrrell), wife of William Andrew, daughter of Deacon Phineas Tyrrell Wlliam A was born 1764 and died December 7, 1834 She died March 10, 1836, aged 67

Driver, Lydia (Hitchcock), wife of Samuel Driver, daughter of Timothy and Abigail Hitchcock She was sister of Elizabeth wife of Darius Driver Albert Driver was a son of Samuel and Lydia Driver

Hitchcock, Timothy, son of Ebenezer and Rebecca (Thomas) Hitchcock, was born Nov 8, 1747-8, died August 5, 1820

Hitchcock, Abigail (Clark) wife of Timothy H, daughter of Hez Clark One of her sisters, Elizabeth, was the mother of Deacon Clark Hotchkiss, another was the wife of Deacon Jas Wheeler Abigail H, was born January 2, 1755, died September 9, 1854

Hitchcock, Sarah (Sperry) wife of Amos Hitchcock She died August 27, 1842, aged 69 He died May 21, 1849 aged 87 Grandparents of Ransom Hitchcock, of Bethany Center

Hitchcock, Amos, son of Benjamin Hotchkiss, was born 1778 He married Lois Todd, sister of Mrs David Perkins His father, Benjamin H, died March, 1809

Hotchkiss, Lois (Todd), wife of last In 1828 the church withdrew "watch and care" from Amos Hotchkiss and wife

Hotchkiss, Eunice (Atwater), wife of Elias Hotchkiss, daughter of Jonathan and Sarah (Beach) Atwater She died in New Haven

Hotchkiss, Elizabeth (Clark), wife of Isaac Hotchkiss, daughter of Hezekiah Clark She was born May 9, 1762 Mother of Deacon Clark Hotchkiss

Hotchkiss, Deacon Jacob, son of Isaac Hotchkiss, married Mary Perkins He died June 26, 1825, aged 89 Grandfather of Spencer Hotchkiss, who lived on the Street Todd farm

Hotchkiss, Mary (Perkins), wife of Deacon Jacob Hotchkiss

Hotchkiss, Susannah (Peck), wife of Silas Hotchkiss, mother of Mrs Andrew, grandmother of Mrs Susan Russell She died February 20, 1839 aged 67 He died February 21, 1849, aged 83

Lanes, Ruth (Sperry), sister of E S Sperry's father She died March 27, 1837, aged 77

Lounsbury, Hannah (Sperry), widow of Stephen Lounsbury, whom she married October 26, 1761 Grandmother of Newell Lounsbury and Major Lounsbury

Nettleton, Comfort (Hine), wife of John Nettleton She died January 31, 1841 He outlived her

Perkins, Thankful, widow of Deacon Peter Perkins Grandmother of Anson Perkins

Perkins, David, son of Reuben and Thankful (Smith) Perkins, married, 1797, Lola Todd He was a member in Mr Hawley's time Lived on the old road which intersects the turnpike north of the home of Mrs Jane Perkins (his grand-daughter) He died November 16, 1865, aged 80

Perkins, Lola (Todd), born 1772, died March 13, 1811, aged 38

Prince, Lois (Hotchkiss), wife of Nathan Prince, died Jan 9, 1823, aged 63 Mr Prince died January 25, 1824, aged 74

Sackett, Mary (Wheeler), daughter of Deacon James Wheeler, wife of John Sackett Her first husband, Briscoe

Sanford, Widow Hannah

Sanford, Damaris Widow

Sanford, Elihu Col, Married Sarah

HOME OF MRS. M. B. MC CLURE.

Thorp. He died October 9, 1839, aged 81, and was buried in the Congregational cemetery, a few months after donating the land for that purpose.

Sanford, Sarah (Thorp), wife of Col. Elihu Sanford died July 14, 1837, aged 75.

Sperry, Elam, removed to Ohio.

Sperry, Anna (Smith), wife of Elam Sperry, sister of Olive M. Bishop. In 1828 the church w . drew "watch and care" from her and her husband.

Sperry, Elizabeth (Perkins), wife of Demas Sperry, daughter of Deacon Peter Perkins. She died December 1, 1849, aged 81. Husband died June 27, 1833, aged 67.

Tyrrell, Deacon Jesse, died March 15, 1814, aged 70. He married first Mabel ——, who died September 23, 1786, aged 40. His second wife was Thankful Merwin. "As an expression of his regard to the prosperity of Zion of the Church and Society of which he was a member, he bequeathed the chief of his estate to the support of a Preached Gospel." Tombstone inscription.

Tyrrell, Thankful (Merwin), second wife of Deacon Jesse Tyrrell, buried at her request in the new burying ground.

Tyrrell, Mrs. Mary (Curtiss), widow of John Tyrrell, who hanged himself. Married in Colebrook second husband named Oatman. She removed to Pennsylvania and died there.

Thomas, David, brother of Hezekiah Thomas. His first wife was the mother of Mrs. Zaccheus Hotchkiss. Thomas, Sarah (Perkins), wife of E. Downs Thomas, sister of Mrs. Demas Sperry.

Umberfield, Matty (Hotchkiss), wife of John Umberfield, daughter of Captain Joel Hotchkiss. Died in New Haven, October, 1856.

Wilmot, Mrs. Comfort, wife of Amos ot. First husband was Eli Nettleton. She died April, 1844. er of Isaac Nettleton.

Wilmot, wife of Valentine Wilmot. Her

maiden name was Fenn Mother of
John Wilmot, who married Asenath
Clark Their son, Noyes Wilmot,
lives in Naugatuck
Wooding, John, ancestor of all of the
name in Bethany

1814

Perkins, Eli, admitted March 6, married Ann Wheeler, daughter of Deacon James Wheeler In 1828 the
church withdrew "watch and care"
from him

1815

Atwater, Lydia (Shepard), wife of
David Atwater Restored August 31
She died February 10, 1850, aged 88
Anan Atwater was one of their sons
Bradley, Abiah (Hotchkiss) daughter
of Joel Hotchkiss Admitted May
14
Hotchkiss, Mehitabel, sister of the
last Admitted May 14
Tolles, Eunice (Bradley) wife of
Chauncey Tolles She was born
August 6, 1774, admitted May 14,
died Nov 23, 1865 Mr Tolles died
April 1, 1824 aged 46
Wilmot, Valentine (restored May 22)
Hotchkiss, Capt Joel (July 2) He
died Feb 3, 1819, aged 73 His wife
died Nov 13, 1831, aged 81
Hotchkiss, Martha (Peck) (July 2)
wife of Capt Joel Hotchkiss, daughter of Deacon Timothy Peck
Hitchcock, Jabez Deacon (July 2) a
grandson of Capt Amos and Dorcas
(Toot) Hitchcock, died Feb 19, 1842,
aged 77 His wife, Experience
Bishop, (sister of James Bishop),
was a pious woman though not a
church member She died Mar 30,
1843, aged 84
Sperry, Hannah (July 2) sister of E
S Sperry's father, died March 6,
1843, aged 78
Platt, Sybil wid (Sept 3, letter from
Milford) First husband Nettleton,
mother of John Nettleton
Perkins, Sarah, (Nov 6 letter from
Woodbridge) second wife of David
Perkins She was the sister of

Enoch Sperry Her first husband
was named Merwin She died Feb.
1861 in Woodbridge, aged 85
Peck, Sybil (Nettleton) (letter from
North Milford,) sister of Isaac Nettleton

1816

Nettleton, Betsy (Nettleton) daughter
of Eli Nettleton, sister of the last
She was admitted by letter from
North Milford March 3. Married
Isaac Bradley, and died in Prospect.
Hotchkiss, Clarissa (Sperry) (July 4)
wife of Sheldon Hotchkiss and
daughter of Isaac Sperry Husband
was son of Elias Hotchkiss Died in
New Haven
Hotchkiss, Eunice (Beecher) July 4,
wife of Seymour Hotchkiss, mother
of Mrs Alonzo Sperry, sister of Andrew Beecher He died Oct 28, 1822,
aged 41
Hotchkiss, Content, July 4, daughter
of Joel Hotchkiss, unmarried
Platt, Sarah, Aug 29, wife of Ebenezer, sister of Deacon Theophilus
Smith, died in Orange
Hotchkiss Mary (Sperry) Aug 29, wife
of Joel Hotchkiss, daughter of Isaac
Sperry Moved to Readsville, Penn
where they died
Hitchcock, Elizabeth, (Oct 27) sister of
Timothy Hitchcock, unmarried

1817

Sanford, Lois (Dickerman) Jan 5
wife of Cyrus Sanford She died
April 11, 1854, aged 82 He died
Feb 28, 1853 aged 84
Platt, Ebenezer, March 23, letter from
Bethlehem He died in Orange May
20, 1864, aged 83
Wilmot, Asenath (Clark) July 6, wife
of John Wilmot, who was a son of
Valentine Wilmot Moved to Naugatuck April 1830 She was the
daughter of Andrew and Annie
Clark of Milford She was born
April 29, 1789 and died Feb 1, 1887
John W was born 1779, died 1837
Perkins, Ann (Wheeler) May 4, wife
of Eli Perkins Letter from Oxford
She died deranged

THE CAPT. DAYTON PLACE.
Recently the Home of the Late James Cotter.

White, Martha (Hotchkiss) Sept. 7 sister of Deacon Clark Hotchkiss, married John White, a grandson of Deacon John White, first deacon of the church.

Peck, Lauren (Oct. 5) letter from Amity. He and his wife removed to East Bennington, Vermont. In March 1839, probably some years after their removal there, they asked for a letter.

Peck, Sally E. (Baldwin) wife of Lauren Peck.

Hotchkiss, Isaac, (Nov. 2) father of Deacon Clark Hotchkiss, died May 11, 1828, aged 70.

White, John, (Nov. 2), son of Lieut. John and Anna (Bostwick) White, son of Deacon John and Mary (Dickerman) White, married Feb. 9, 1802

Martha, daughter of Isaac and Elizabeth Hotchkiss. He was a carpenter and millwright. He was born Dec. 29, 1780 and died Nov. 7, 1852.

Robinson, Elihu, (Nov. 2) died June 10, 1849, aged 64.

Baldwin, widow, Sarah, (Nov. 23) mother of Mrs. Sally Peck.

Hitchcock, Lady, (Nov. 23) sister of Miles Hitchcock. She married in Prospect, I. Smith.

1818.

Atwater, David, (March 1) son of Jonathan and Sarah (Beach) Atwater, married Lydia Shepard. He was the father of Anan Atwater. He died June 15, 1829, aged 67.

Atwater, Jesse, (March 1) brother of David Atwater.

Bradley, Electa, (March 1) wife of Jason Bradley, daughter of Lamberton Tolles She died March 20, 1858, aged 79

Thomas, Allen, lived where Abner Warner now resides 'Ie died April 11, 1849, aged 49

Bradley, Deacon Jesse, (March 1) lived just south of the corner south of D L Johnson's on the opposite side of road He died Oct 25, 1839, aged 65

Hitchcock, Samuel, (March 1)

Bradley Beda, (March 1) daughter of Deacon Jesse Bradley, married Jesse Lounsbury

Hotchkiss, Hiram, (March 1) lived at Bethany Center in house now owned by Charles Booth He was a son of Silas Hotchkiss He died Jan 22, 1850

Atwater, Polly (Brockett) July 5, wife of Jesse Atwater, had been of Dr Trumbull's congregation in North Haven Married Mitchell Peck

Bradley, Mary, (July 5) wife of Deacon Jesse Bradley, was born Jan 28, 1779, died about 1865

Sanford Polly (Newton), July 5, wife of Tubal Sanford Tubal Sanford was born Oct 20, 1783, died April 14, 1874 His second wife Lucinda Barns was born Sept 13, 1806, died July 5, 1882

Andrew, Job, (July 5) son of William and Mary (Tyrrell) Andrew was born Aug 19, 1796, died Aug 18, 1868 He married Lois Prince, born Jan 15, 1797, died May 7, 1874

Atwater, Eunice, July 5, daughter of David Atwater, married Uri Woodling They lived in the valley east of home of Jerome A Downs, Jr She died March 23, 1861 He died Feb 16, 1853, aged 58

1820

Thomas, Naomi (Hotchkiss) wife of John Thomas, first husband was named Johnson She brought letter from Amity and was dismissed to Naugatuck May 25, 1845 where she died

1822

Perkins, Mary, (May 26) wife of Benoni Perkins, daughter of Eli Nettleton

1823

Nettleton, Oliver, (March) letter from Watertown, died at Westville, Jan 31, 1864

Nettleton, Mrs Oliver, (March) letter from Watertown

Thomas, John, (March)

Sanford, Cyrus, (March) died Feb 28, 1853, aged 84

1824

Hotchkiss, Martha, (May 2) wife of Zaccheus Hotchkiss, daughter of David Thomas She died Feb 18, 1856, aged 82 He died Nov 30, 1855, aged 79

Thomas, Mary, (May 2) daughter of David Thomas, died unmarried

1827

Theophilus Smith (Jan 7, letter from Milford) He kept the tavern on the Straits Turnpike It was the custom when the pulpit was supplied by ministers from New Haven for them to come out to his tavern in the stage Saturday and return Monday He died Nov 5, 1873

Silas Hotchkiss (March 2) son of Joseph Hotchkiss He died Feb 21, 1849, aged 83

May 4, 1828

Andrew, Lois, wife of Job Andrew, died May 7, 1874

Bradley, Miles, son of Deacon Jesse Bradley, moved to Westville where he was a merchant

Bradley, Mary (Morgan) wife of Miles Bradley Her sons were named Dwight and Theodore

Bradley, Isaac, son of Jason Bradley, died Feb 26, 1830, aged 25

Bradley, Jason Willis, son of Jason and Electa (Tolles) Bradley, married Oct 23, 1834 Elizabeth Sperry He was born Jan 10, 1809, died Oct 12, 1888

Bradley, Electa, daughter of Jason, married Bazil Smith of Woodbridge

THE ARCHIBALD PERKINS HOUSE, NORTH BETHANY.

Hine, Lewis, died Aug. 2, 1863, aged 62.

Hine, Martha, wife of Lewis, daughter of Silas Hotchkiss.

Hotchkiss, Philo, son of Isaac Hotchkiss. He died Jan. 16, 1837, aged 54

Hotchkiss, Betsy (Thomas) wife of Philo Hotchkiss, daughter of Elijah Thomas, died May 13, 1838, aged 48.

Hotchkiss, Rebecca, wife of Hiram, sister of Deacon Clark Hotchkiss. She died Sept. 28, 1849, aged 52.

Hotchkiss, Clark, son of Isaac Hotchkiss, married Caroline, daughter of Chilion Sperry. He was deacon of the church for over sixty years. He died July 1890.

Kimball, Miranda, married Charles Thomas. She died Oct. 14, 1864, aged 64. He died Oct. 27, 1863, aged 62.

Sanford, Austin.

Smith, Betsy, second wife of Theophilus Smith, daughter of Lysias Beecher. She died March 7, 1830, aged 31.

Sperry, Caroline, daughter of Chilion Sperry, married Deacon Clark Hotchkiss. She died Dec 30, 1891.

Russell, Harriet, sister of Lovisa, wife of Jarvis Bronson. She married John Bradley.

Russell, Nancy, sister of the above, died unmarried Jan. 16, 1889, aged 79.

Thomas, Lewis, lived in the Wheeler house Bethany Center. The ministers were often entertained at his house. He was born 1798 and died 1840.

Thomas, Louisa, wife of Lewis Thomas, daughter of Phineas Peck. Married second Sheldon Hotchkiss.

She was born 1799, died 1876

Thomas, Mary (Gilbert) wife of Allen Thomas Removed 1855 Dismissed to church in Galesbury, Ohio, Oct 12, 1862

Thomas, Harriet Emily, daughter of John Thomas, married Dr F Spencer He lived on Lebanon Hill Their house burned and he and two young sons perished in the flames She was dismissed soon after the tragic event to Naugatuck, May 25, 1845

Tolles, Lewis, son of Chauncey, married Eliza Sanford He died 1880, aged 75 years

Tolles, Eliza, wife of Lewis Tolles, daughter of Tubal Sanford

Tolles, Elizabeth, married William Peck of Woodbridge

(July 6)

Lounsbury, Abram, son of Eri and Sarah (Carrington) Lounsbury, married Emily, daughter of David and Lola (Todd) Perkins He died April 27, 1860, aged 61

Lounsbury, Emily, (Perkins) wife of Abram Lounsbury, died June 20, 1881, aged 78

Perkins, Alvin, son of David and Lola (Todd) Perkins, married Lucretia, daughter of Henry Sanford Moved to Westville

Hotchkiss, Rhoda, wife of Spence• Hotchkiss, daughter of Zedekiah Hotchkiss Restored to membership Feb 28, 1844, died March 5, 1856

Thomas, Mary Ann, daughter of Allen Thomas, married John Bassett and removed to Illinois

(Sept 7)

Lounsbury, Jesse

1833

Hitchcock, Abby L (Judson) wife of Amos Hitchcock, received by letter from Humphreyville March 3 She died Aug 22, 1862

Lounsbury, Isaac, (March 3) son of Eri Lounsbury, married Lodema ——— Located in Meriden, Conn

Hotchkiss, Pennina, (March 3) daughter of Elias Hotchkiss Died about 1863

Platt, Susan Ann, (March 3) married Bushnell and lived in New Haven

Platt, Sarah L., (March 3) married a Clark of West Haven

Platt, Harriet, (March 3) married Boardman, Orange, died 1878

Hotchkiss, Jane, (March 3) married Thomas Sanford of Woodbridge

Hitchcock, Sarah (May 5) daughter of Amos and Sarah (Sperry) Hitchcock, died unmarried Oct 1883 in Watertown

Bishop, Olive M (Smith) (May 5) wife of Joseph Bishop She died Nov 20, 1842, aged 79

Hotchkiss, Harriet, (May 5) daughter of Silliman Hotchkiss, married a Wooding of Prospect

Hitchcock, Grant, (May 5) son of Eli Hitchcock, lived at the old Hitchcock homestead, now occupied by a granddaughter, Mrs Florence Beecher He died March 23, 1861, aged 61

Hitchcock, Anna (Doolittle) (May 5) wife of Grant Hitchcock She died July 10, 1877, aged 72

Bradley, Jesse Geo, (May 5) son of Deacon Jesse Bradley, became well-known as a maker of whip-lashes

Hotchkiss, Eliza Ann, (May 5) was daughter of Hiram Hotchkiss She was dismissed to Monroe and married there, later returned and married, second, Henry Sanford

1833

Platt, Jonah, (Nov 3) dismissed to Milford, Nov 17, 1834

Wilcox, Marietta, wife of Rev J Wilcox, by letter from Stockbridge, Mass

1834

Perkins, Lucretia (Sanford) (May 4) wife of Alvin Perkins Received by letter

Porter, Sally, widow, (May 4 by letter) Removed to Naugatuck and died there.

RESIDENCE OF SAMUEL B. DOWNS.

Warren, Israel Perkins, (May 4 by letter) became a Congregational minister. He was born in Bethany April 8, 1814; and died in Portland, Maine, Oct. 9, 1892.

1837.

Hitchcock, Amos, Jr., (July 16) son of Amos and Sarah (Sperry) Hitchcock married Abby L. Judson. He died April 27, 1888.

Nettleton, Orril, (July 16) daughter of Oliver Nettleton, married Farnum of Westville.

Purdy, Eunice (Newton) (July 16) wife of William Purdy, lived a half-mile east of the old red school house in the Gate District. Removed to Plymouth and died there.

Thomas, Frances, (July 16) daughter of Allen Thomas, Married Day and removed to Illinois. Dismissed May 4, 1845.

Thomas, Harriet L., (July 16) daughter of Lewis, married Bachelor in New Haven.

Thomas, Nancy, (July 16) daughter of Allen Thomas, married Adams and removed to Illinois.

Warren, Leonora, (July 16) wife of Isaac Warren, daughter of Israel Perkins. Mother of Rev. I. P. Warren. Removed to Goshen, Ct.

Warren, Susan Harriet, (July 16) daughter of the last.

Thomas, Caroline, (April 5) daughter of Allen, married in Oxford Fanning. Dismissed to Patchogue, L. I., March 3, 1844.

Bishop, Maria, (July 13) was cut off. (Joined Mormons.)

1840.

Clark, Amy, (June) wife of Rev. Saul Clark, by letter from S. Egremont, Mass.

Clark, Marietta Smith, (June) daughter of the Rev. Saul Clark.

1843.

Butts, Julia, (July 2) wife of Rev. D. B. Butts, by letter from Stanwich, Conn.

Clark, Esther (Treat), September 3, wife of Isaac Clark. She died March 21, 1862.

Hotchkiss, Andrew P., September 3, son of Hiram Hotchkiss, removed to New Haven.

Hotchkiss, Wales, September 3, son of
Hiram Hotchkiss, was a portrait
painter in New Haven, many years.

Kingsley, Eunice, September 3, unmarried, died December 14, 1863, aged 84

Thomas, Eliza E, September 3, daughter of Charles Thomas, married William Conolly, an Irishman She died
a Catholic, October 4, 1857.

Warner, Martha, September 3, wife of
Miles Warner

Peck, Justus, Nov. 5, letter from
Cheshire. Married Jane French He
died February 3, 1885, aged 75 His
first wife, Marietta Moss, died August 23, 1835, aged 33.

1844

Sharp, Eliza A, March 3, daughter of
Hiram Hotchkiss Married second
Henry Sanford. She died about 1865

1845.

Beard, Allen C, May 4, by letter from
Milford His daughter, Mrs Kate
Lacey, lived at the old homestead

Beard, Abigail, May 4, wife of Allen
Beard She died January 20, 1870

1850

French, Truman, January 6, Dismissed
December, 1851 Removed to New
Haven

French, Susan Lee, January 6, widow
of Truman; daughter of Rev C G
Lee Dismissed December, 1851

Francis, Mrs Charlotte W, January 6
Died in Welton

Harrison, Caroline F, July 5, letter
from Bethlehem, daughter of Rev. F.
Harrison Married Samuel Bird, of
Bethlehem.

Harrison, Fanny, July 5, letter from
Bethlehem, daughter of Rev. F. H
Died at Bridgewater.

Peck, Mrs Jane French, January 6,
wife of Justus Peck, daughter of
Harry French She died November
16, 1894, aged 81

Smith, Elizabeth B, January 6, daughter of Theophilus Smith She married Rev Edmund Peck, a Methodist
minister, was dismissed to M. E
church in West Haven, and later restored to membership in this church.
Lives in Waterbury.

1851.

Sperry, Lucina S, September, letter
from Plymouth Hollow, Ct, wife of
Marcus Sperry

1855

Robinson, Rev E W, July 3, letter
from Hanover, Ct, died in Washington, D C.

Robinson, Sarah B (Adams), July 3,
wife of last

Robinson, N Emmons, July 3, son of
Rev E. W. R.

1857.

Ward, Willis Edwin, a colored man,
was baptized and admitted to the
church on his sick bed in the presence of several members of the
church, November 27 On the 29th the
church formally ratified the admis-
sion. On the 2d of December the
Lord's Supper was administered to
him, a number of the members of
the church being present. He died
December 14, aged 35.

1858

Sarah L Clark, December 6, wife of
Nathan Clark, daughter of Abram
Lounsbury She died Dec 21, 1893,
aged 67. Her husband, Nathan Clark,
son of Isaac, died September 21, 1893,
aged 69

Russell, Mary E, December 6, daughter of Stiles and Susan (Andrew)
Russell She married Ransom Hitchcock and was for many years the
postmistress of Bethany. She was
born April 6, 1839, died August 22,
1904.

Robinson, James A, December 6, son
of Rev. E W Robinson He died
August 21, 1863, in Ohio. He was in
the army, U S. volunteers

1861

French, John C, July 14, lived on the
road to Beacon Falls, in a locality
which later became a part of that
town

French, Marietta (Hotchkiss), July 14,
wife of John French

A BETHANY CHARCOAL PIT.

1863.

Driver, Mrs. Eliza, May 3, letter from M. E. church in New Haven, wife of George Driver. Relation removed to M. E. church, New Haven, in 1874.

1864.

Scranton, George B., March 6, letter from Whitneyville. Lived on Chatfield Hill, in house which was burned in 1912. He died January 20, 1872

Scranton, Hannah, March 6, letter; wife of George Scranton. Hanged herself May 14, 1875.

1865

Peck, Marietta, dismissed Sept. 2, 1877, to Congregational church in Wallingford.

Russell, Ellen, daughter of Stiles Russell, a wheelwright. She married Nathanial Newell, and was dismissed to the First Congregational church of Branford.

Russell, Annie E., daughter of Stiles and Susan (Andrew) Russell, married H. D. Seldon, was dismissed April, 1886, to church in Chester.

McClure, Hannah, daughter of William McClure. She has been a member of the church for the longest continuous period of any one now living.

Beard, Susan, daughter of Allen and Abigail Beard, married first William H. Lounsbury, September 8, 1873; second, Mr. Noble She was dismissed September 2, 1877 to the M. E. church, Bethany.

Beard, Andrew, son of Allen and Abigail Beard, was a school teacher in Bethany. He was dismissed in 1883 to the Congregational church, Aspen, Colo. Died recently

Beard, Cecelia, daughter of Allen Beard, married Dennis Smith Dismissed to First Church, of Milford

Munson, Mrs Betsey A. (Hitchcock), wife of Alva Keep Munson, daughter of Grant and Anna (Doolittle) Hitchcock She died November 14, 1901, aged 72 A K Munson, born March 27, 1827, died May 1, 1908

Robinson, Sarah M , April 9, daughter of Rev E W. Robinson Dismissed October, 1865, to First Congregational church, Washington, D C.

Robinson, Mary L , April 9, same record as above

Robinson, Emily E , as above.

Driver, Laura E , dismissed to St Johns church, New Haven, Oct 17, 1869 She was a sister of George Driver

Scranton, Eliza, daughter of George and Hannah Scranton, died May 22, 1876

Scranton, Elizabeth, sister of the last.

1866

White, May, daughter of William White, and a descendant of Deacon John White

Hotchkiss, Fanny E , daughter of Deacon Clark and Caroline (Sperry) Hotchkiss, married Adrian Rosha Dismissed to church in Westville, but later in 1894 returned to Bethany and is an active member

Sperry, Ann, wife of John Sperry Letter from Seymour She died April 1883

Andrew, Sarah (Pardee), wife of Azariah, son of Job and Lois (Prince) Andrew She died January 10, 1901, aged 77 Azariah Andrew was born June 29, 1821, died February 23, 1898 Their son Noyes, lives at the old homestead

Clark, Emma, daughter of Nathan Clark, married Pearl Sperry

Sanford, Mary, daughter of Henry Sanford, died July 27, 1892

Sperry, Mary, wife of Sidney Sperry.

1869

Smith, Eliza (Sperry), July 11, wife of Theophilus Smith She died September 27, 1884.

1870

Lounsbury, David A , March 6, son of Abram and Emily (Perkins) Lounsbury, was born March 11, 1831, and was the first child baptized in the present church edifice He lives in Bridgeport

Scranton, Andrew, March 6, son of George Scranton, died 1902

Lounsbury, Nancy A (Hopkins), July 3, second wife of David A Lounsbury She died February 24, 1877, aged 49.

1874.

Lounsbury, Julia Ann (Ladue), November 1, first wife of William H , son Crownage Lounsbury Letter from Presbyterian church, New York. She died December 29, 1892

Sperry, Eugene S , November 1, son of Sidney Sperry. He lives in Florida.

1876.

Woodruff, William Louis, March 19, cut off by vote of church, November

1877.

Woodruff, Julia B , March 19, wife of the Rev William L Woodruff. Became an Episcopalian, 1877

Osgood, Lucy M , (March 19) Letter from Plainsville Congr church. Dismissed by letter.

Forbes, Katie M , (March 19) Letter from Plainsville Cong church Married Chester A Bailey Dismissed by letter.

1878

Beard, Grace, daughter of Allen Beard, (Jan 20) Dismissed to Pres church, Aspen, Colo.

Clark, Edwin, (Sept 8) son of Nathan and Sarah (Lounsbury) Clark, was organist of the church for many years He moved to Seymour in 1913.

Clark, Hannah (Basham), (Sept. 8) wife of Edwin N Clark.

Lounsbury, Ives D , (Sept 8) son of David and Nancy (Hopkins) Lounsbury Lives in Woodbridge.

Burnet, Frank, (Sept 8) Dismissed to church in West Haven, April, 1879.

THE GATE SCHOOL.

Robbins, Lucretia S., (Sept. 8) Lives in Hamden.

Davis, Martha A., (Sept. 8.) Dismissed to Park street church, Bridgeport, Nov. 4, 1883.

Lounsbury, Margaret (Billerwell), (Sept. 8) third wife of David A. Lounsbury. Lives in Bridgeport.

Cutler, Francis B., (Sept. 8.) Letter from M. E. church, Bethany. Dismissed to M. E. church, Orangeville, Ohio, Feb. 1879.

Philips, Mrs. Emily J., (Aug.) yetter from Cheshire Cong. church.

1881.

Hitchcock, Ransom, (Jan. 2) son of Amos and Abby Louise (Judson) Hitchcock. He married Mary Russell. He was born Jan. 6. 1835; died March 5, 1905.

Lacey, Arthur J., (Jan. 2) married Kate S. Beard, daughter of Allen Beard.

Johnson, Harriet A. (Wellman), (March 6) wife of Dwight L. Johnson.

Peck, Lydia Ann, (March 6) wife of Harry F. Peck.

Wellman, Urania B., (May) Letter from 2nd Cong. church, of Watertown. She died Feb. 10, 1887.

Barnard, Andrew J., (July 17) Letter from 2nd Cong. church, of Watertown.

1883.

Peck, Harry F., (March 4) son of Justus and Jane (French) Peck.

Megin, James Lee, (April 1) son of Hugh and Marietta (Dorman) Megin. Was soldier in the Civil war.

Megin, Orrie Jane (Hotchkiss), (April 1) wife of James L. Megin.

Megin, Lucia Charlotte, (Apr. 1) daughter of James and Orrie Jane (Hotchkiss) Megin. She married William Haskell and lives in Chicopee, Mass.

Horsfall, Thomas, (April 1.) Letter from 3rd Cong. church of New Haven. He has been a deacon of the church since April 1, 1883.

Horsfall, Elvira Virginia, (April 1) wife of Deacon Thomas Horsfall, daughter of Stiles and Susan (Andrew) Russell She died Aug 24, 1891

McClure, Minnie Rebecca, (May 6) married Theodore Downs, son of Elbert and Catharine (Bailey) Downs.

1886

Hitchcock, Mary Alice, (March 21) daughter of Ransom and Mary (Russell) Hitchcock She married M Goldsmith. Resides in Portland, Oregon

Hitchcock, Carolyn Louise, (March 21) daughter of Ransom and Mary (Russell) Hitchcock Married John E Hinman

Sperry, Isabel Emily, (March 21) daughter of Pearl and Emma (Clark) Sperry.

Sperry, Isadora Sarah, (March 21) daughter of Pearl and Emma (Clark) Sperry Removed to Ansonia, Conn.

Peck, Mary Elizabeth, (March 21) daughter of Rev. Edmund and Elizabeth (Smith) Peck. She lost her life in the fire that destroyed their home, Jan 4, 1902, aged 38 The Rev. Edmund perished also, aged 84

Munson, Florence Betsy, (March 21) daughter of Alva Keep and Betsy (Hitchcock) Munson Married Elson E Beecher

Rosha, Clifton DeWitt, (March 21) son of Adrian and Fanny (Hotchkiss) Rosha He has been a deacon of the church since Aug, 1895

Peck, Henry Bigelow, (March 21) son of Harry and Lydia Peck. He died March 12, 1898

1894.

Wellman, Burton M, (May 13) lives on the Darius Driver farm, Bethany.

Wellman, Lucy, (May 13) wife of Burton M Wellman

Johnson, Walter B, (May 13) son of Dwight and Harriet Johnson Married and lives in Seymour

Hitchcock, Annie S, (May 13) daughter of Ransom and Mary (Russell) Hitchcock.

Moddell, Frederick W., (May 13) dismissed to Cong church, Bridgeport.

Moddell, Mary J, (May 13) dismissed to Cong church, Bridgeport

Lacey, Mabel, (July 15) daughter of Arthur and Kate (Beard) Lacey Married April 9, 1901 to Fred Lucius Andrew of Beacon Falls.

Lacey, Ethel, (July 15) daughter of Arthur and Kate (Beard) Lacey. Was graduated from Northfield Seminary, and intended to become a missionary. She married— Died in Syracuse, N. Y, Nov, 1907.

Stahnke, Emma, (July 15) daughter of Frank and Emma (Engle) Stahnke, who were born in Germany. She married Francis Ferdinandus and lives in New Haven Dismissed to the Dwight Place church, New Haven, April 19, 1896.

1897.

Sperry, Harold C, (June 27) son of Pearl P. Sperry

1899.

Clark, Lena B, (Oct 22) daughter of Edwin and Hannah (Basham) Clark. Married.

Lounsbury, Bertha E, (Oct 22) daughter of David and Margaret (Billerwell) Lounsbury Married July 1, 1908, Alton Parker Christain Lives in Bridgeport, Conn.

Lepper, Hanry, (Oct 22) lives in Naugatuck, Conn Was blinded in an accident a few years ago

Lepper, Mrs Henry, (Oct 22).

1902

Peck, Nelson Justus, (June) son of Harry and Lydia Peck.

Peck, May, (June) wife of Nelson Peck.

Wellman, Harriet, (May 10) daughter of Burton and Lucy Wellman. She married Carl, son of Frank and Emma (Engle) Stahnke.

Johnson, Carrie, wife of Frank Johnson.

1906

Burtner, Rev Otto W, (June) dismissed to First Cong church, Ansonia, Dec. 2, 1906.

Photo by F. H. Simonds, New Haven.

PERRY'S HALL,

As Prepared for the Dinner at the Time of the 150th Anniversary.

Burtner, Mrs. O. W., (June) dismissed.

1908.

Carrington, Ralph W., (May 3) son of Abram and Mary Carrington.

Carrington, Auth E., (May 31) daughter of Abram and Mary Carrington.

Clark, Walter E., (May 3) son of Edwin and Hannah (Clark). Married Bessie Botsford. Lives in Seymour. Dismissed to Cong. church.

Lacey, Abigail, (May 3) daughter of Arthur and Kate (Beard) Lacey.

Humiston, Wallace D., (May 24) son of Dwight and Katie (Downs) Humiston.

1909.

Booth, Mary Stillson, (Sept. 5) wife of Charles Booth.

Booth, Frances, (Sept. 5) daughter of Charles and Mary Booth.

Lindemann, Rev. Herman H., (Sept. 5) dismissed.

BAPTISMS IN THE CHURCH

May 4, 1828.
Lewis Thomas (adult)
Betsey Hotchkiss (adult).
Mary Bradley (adult)
Caroline Sperry (adult)
Harriet Emily Thomas (adult).
Miranda Kimball (adult)
Harr.et Russell (adult).
Nancy Russell (adult)

May 25, 1828
Phineas Peck Thomas (son of Lewis)
Harriet Lydia Thomas (daughter of Lewis).

Aug 10, 1828
Sarah Lola Lounsbury (daughter of Abraham).

July 26, 1828
Abraham Lounsbury.
Rhoda Hotchkiss

Oct 31, 1829
Elizabeth Hotchkiss (daughter of Philo)
Jarus Buret Hotchkiss (son of Philo)
Aaron Thomas Hotchkiss (son of Philo).
Rebecca Hotchkiss (daughter of Philo)
David Lounsbury.

Nov. 1832
Hart Hotchkiss (son of Hiram).
Sarah Hotchkiss (daughter of Clark)

March 3, 1833
Isaac Lounsbury (adult)
Penina Hotchkiss (adult)
Susan Ann Platt (adult)
Sarah L Platt (adult)

May 5, 1833
Jane Hotchkiss (adult)

July 23, 1833
John Thomas (son of Allen).

Sept 15, 1833
Mary Hale Tolles (daughter of Lewis).

Feb 16, 1834
Noyes Sylader Wilmot.

June 1, 1834
Watson Henry Wilcox (son of Rev. Jairus)

July 16, 1837
Susan Harriet Warren

June 30, 1843
Eugene Daniel Butts (son of Rev Daniel).

Sept 5, 1845
Edwin White Butts (son of Rev Daniel)
Edgar Giles Smith (infant).
Marion Cecel.a Beard (infant)

Nov 1, 1845
Lucien Hitchcock (infant).
Ellen Hannah Hitchcock (infant)

Jan. 6, 1850
Jane French (wife of Justus)

July 20, 1850
Kate Smith Beard (daughter of Allen)
Irene Julia Hitchcock (daughter of Amos)
Emily Prince Hitchcock (daughter of Amos)
Ellen Jane Hitchcock (daughter of Amos).
Emogene Hitchcock (daughter of Amos)
Lucina Sperry

July 3, 1855
Sarah M Beard (daughter of Allen)
Grace Beard (daughter of Allen)

Nov. 29, 1857.
Willis Edwin Ward (adult).

Dec 6, 1858
Mary E Russell

July 14, 1861
John C French (adult)
Marietta French (adult).
Josephine French (daughter of John)
Gertrude French (daughter of John)

Sept 8, 1878
Edwin Nathan Clark
Ives David Lounsbury.
Frank Burnet
Lucretia Irene Robbins
Martha Ann Davis
Hannah Clark.

Harriet Adeline Johnson
Lydia Ann Peck

Sept 5, 1880

Isadore Sarah Sperry (child of Pearl)

Isabel Emily Sperry (child of Pearl)

Pearl Prince Sperry (child of Pearl)

Eugene Foster Clark (son of Edwin)

Walter Edwin Clark (son of Edwin)

Mary Alice Hitchcock (daughter of Ransom)

Carrie Louise Hitchcock (daughter of Ransom)

Annie Stella Hitchcock (daughter of Ransom)

March 6, 1881.

Henry Bigelow Peck
Nelson Justus Peck
Edwin Harry Peck
Burton Mitchell Wellman
Treat Baldwin Johnson
Wilfred James Megin
Martha Elizabeth Wel.man
Frederick Amos Wellman
Susan Urania Wellman
Harry French Peck

March 4, 1883

Minnie Rebecca McClure

March 21, 1886

Florence Betsey Munson
Clifton DeWitt Rosha

July 5, 1894

Lena Belle Clark
Ruby Basham Clark
Frank Joseph Clark
Harold Clark Sperry

Oct 22, 1899

Bertha Emily Lounsbury
Dorothy M Lounsbury

April, 1900

Dorothy May Lepper
Jennie Ellen Lepper
Margaret Josephine Lepper
Clarke Beecher Johnson
Frank Irving Johnson
Raymond Nelson Peck
Norman Harry Peck

Nov 25, 1906

Edwin August Clark

Sept 5, 1909

Warren Dwight Johnson

June 23, 1912.

Lawrence Edwin Peck

Feb 9, 1913

Edward Anderson
Harold Anderson

THE 150TH ANNIVERSARY CELEBRATION.

The celebration of the one hundred and fiftieth anniversary of the Bethany Congregational church was observed on Saturday and Sunday, Oct 11 and 12, 1913 A large part of the people of the town without respect to creed or church affiliation, were present, as well as an equally large number who arrived in automobiles and teams from adjoining towns Many present from out of town had hereditary or ancestral connection with Bethany and so showed their loyalty to the old town, as well as to the church which has been so large a factor in the best interests of the community On Saturday at 10 30 a m , Rev Sherrod Soule, of Hartford, gave a very interesting address on "The Debt We Owe to the Country Church" Dinner in Perry's hall followed, and it was served to about two hundred and fifty people

The afternoon was devoted to after-dinner speaking Hon William H Williams acted as toastmaster The speakers were Rev Charles B Toleman, of Woodbridge, Rev C F Luther of Westville, Rev George F. Abel, of Seymour, Rev Leonard E Todd, of Oakville, Rev C B Strong, of Prospect, Rev J W Newton, of Madison, Mr S G Davidson, and Rev John W. Wright

Charles Hoadley, of Naugatuck, presented the church with an old hatchet which was found in the steeple during the recent repairs, and which shows by its shape and its evident antiquity that it was left there when the church was built It is mounted in a plush-lined case and a plate bears the name of the donor and the dates 1832-1913

On Sunday, the exact date of the anniversary, services were held in the church, with a sermon by Rev H B Beach, followed by communion service and the four children of Mr. and Mrs Frank Read were baptized

At the afternoon service a historical sketch of the church was read by Wallace Humiston, and Rev Joel Stone Ives, of Hartford, whose mother was born in Bethany, gave an address

There was a large attendance, the other town churches being closed, and the people united in the service The pastor of the Methodist church took part in the morning service Much of the success of the occasion was due to the fact that everyone in town, without regard for denominational differences, gave their hearty support, making it an "Old Home Day" as well as an anniversary celebration

---

HISTORICAL SKETCH OF THE CHURCH.

BY WALLACE D. HUMISTON.

Nearly three hundred years ago a number of the wealthy residents of London conceived the plan of a settlement that should be governed with the Bible for its law They came to New England and in 1638 laid the foundations of New Haven For a long time it was deemed imprudent to settle far from the cluster of dwellings erected there, but as the years passed the danger from hostile Indians decreased and we find our hardy forefathers pushing out into the forests which surrounded New Haven in search of land fit for farming

Just about a hundred years after the founding of New Haven, a sufficient number of families had settled

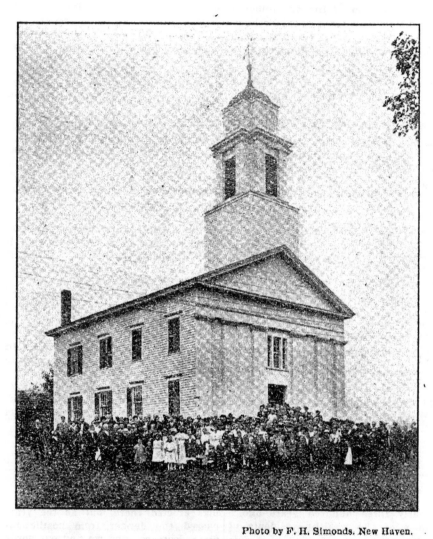

Photo by F. H. Simonds, New Haven.

BETHANY CONGREGATIONAL CHURCH,
OCTOBER 11, 1913.

In the region which is now included in Woodbridge and Bethany to warrant the organization of a church. Accordingly the region was formed into the parish of Amity. On the Lord's Day and other occasions our fathers, the hardy pioneers of this forest town, assembled at the Amity meeting-house For seven or eight miles in all directions these men of God descended from the breezy, life-giving hills, to the temple down in the valley, to pay this debt to the Supreme Ruler of the universe.

But the population of the northern half of Amity Parish was steadily increasing By 1750 a school house was needed, the first in this town It not only served as a school house but later, we learn, served as the house of worship for this community The first step toward separation from Amity Parish occurred in 1755 The General Assembly granted "winter parish privileges to the inhabitants of the northern parts of Amity" This means that during the cold months of the year the people were free to engage a minister During the summer they worshipped as of old at the meeting house in Amity

It was in 1762 that complete separation from Amity was effected and the name "Bethany" first appeared upon the map of Connecticut A charter was granted by the General Assembly, which made Bethany a distinct ecclesiastical society, with all the privileges and powers belonging to such parishes.

The first meeting of this society was held Nov 13, 1762. A few months later the society applied "unto the Reverend Association for their advice" concerning a candidate to preach in said society in order for settlement The association held its meeting in Waterbury May 31, and the minute on this subject as recorded by Rev Warham Williams, contains these words, "We, having maturely consid- ered the matter, unanimously advise said society to Mr Stephen Hawley as a suitable person, highly approving of him for that purpose" Eventually Mr. Hawley was invited to become pastor. His reply to the call has been preserved and may be seen in the vestibule.

At the society meeting in September it was voted that the ordination take place on the second Wednesday in October and that on the first Wednesday a fast preparatory to the ordination should be observed. At the same meeting it was voted that a committee apply unto the Rev Moderator of the Consociation of New Haven county in order to settle the church of Christ in Bethany, according unto the established ecclesiastical constitution of this colony, and to transact all the affairs of the society that are necessary in carrying on said ordination

The tradition is that the ordination services were performed in the open air, in a field where now stands the house of Mr Collins, Oct 12, 1763 The sermon was delivered by that eminent divine, Dr. Joseph Bellamy, of Bethlehem Mr. Hawley was a native of New Milford and was graduated at Yale College in 1759, in the same class with Dr. Trumbull, of North Haven

Three years after the settlement of Mr Hawley it was considered necessary to build a larger meeting house to accommodate the increasing congregation, and application was made to the county court for a committee to look over the situation and choose a site. Much difficulty was experienced in choosing a suitable location, and three successive committees were elected before a location could be agreed upon, and even then a third of the members were dissatisfied. The site was located on the north side of the road leading over the hill from the "shunpike," so called, near the residence of the late James Cotter.

Photo by F. H. Simonds, New Haven.

INTERIOR OF THE CHURCH,

As Decorated for the 150th Anniversary Celebration.

The meadow opposite his house was the meeting house green, the church being on the western side. On the north was the mansion of Dr Hezekiah Hooker, and on the south and east sides, respectively, the residences of Rev. Stephen Hawley and Capt. Ebenezer Dayton, of Revolutionary fame.

It was planned to build the meeting house of material furnished by the inhabitants. In December, 1767, it was voted that "we will provide the boards, clapboards, shingles, nails and glass, necessary for building the meeting house the year ensuing." A tax was laid and it was decided that one half might be paid in "flax seed or some other species that will answer in New York." The building was to be forty feet in width by fifty-five feet long. It was ordered "that those that score timber for the meeting house shall have two shillings sixpence per day; and those that hew shall have three shillings sixpence per day." Deacon John White and Deacon Hotchkiss were appointed "to cull the clapboards and the shingles for the meeting house." The building of the meeting house progressed slowly. It was occupied in January, 1770, but it was not entirely finished until many years after that date.

The steeple and bell were added in 1803. Now indeed the society had a church edifice in which a just pride could be taken. It was one of the largest and finest in this section. Besides the galleries and choir loft it contained nearly thirty large square pews, arranged in two central "square bodies" and in a row about the sides, with the exception of spaces reserved for the pulpit and the three entrances. The pulpit was on the western side of the meeting house and was reached by stairs. The whole was surmounted by a huge green sounding board. Beneath the pulpit was a long seat on which the deacons sat facing the people. The tall white spire rising high o'er the verdant hills of Bethany was one of the most conspicuous objects that met the sailor's eye as he entered New Haven harbor.

In 1783 the parishes of Amity and Bethany united their efforts in seeking to secure town privileges, but they could not agree as to the location of the town house or public hall. After Bethany had made many proposals, none of which were accepted by Amity, it was decided to petition the general assembly for the incorporation of Bethany as a separate town, but, however, the two parishes finally effected an agreement and they were incorporated as one town, called Woodbride, in honor of Rev. Benjamin Woodbridge, the first pastor. Similar attempts were made in 1802 and 1804 to have the parish incorporated as a town, and at last successfully in 1832.

Mr. Hawley became too infirm at about sixty to be able to preach constantly especially during the winter months. But he continued to officiate more or less until 1803, the year before his death. He was then a trembling old man with white locks. He was often led into the church and assisted into the pulpit, and was sometimes able to deliver only a part of his discourse. He was tall and very spare and his appearance made a deep impression on the young.

Mr. Hawley died in July, 1804, after a pastorate of over forty years. His grave is in the old cemetery, marked by a tombstone which was erected at the centennial celebration of the church in 1863.

When Mr. Hawley's health became so poor that he could no longer officiate, Rev. Isaac Jones was called by the church as a colleague pastor. He was born in New Haven Feb. 16, 1775, and was graduated from Yale in 1792 at the age of seventeen. He was ordained June 6, 1804, and the sermon which he preached soon after as his inaugural address was printed. Mr. Jones's short pastorate was a stormy one. Dissatisfaction with him arose among some of the members, and factions were formed which led to one of the greatest ecclesiastical wars that the rural towns of Connecticut have ever known. Matters reached such a magnitude that Mr. Jones was tried before the association, and his connection with that body was severed. He was later restored upon a public confession assented to before a three-days' session of the two consociations of New Haven county, but in 1807 the New Haven West association declared that Mr. Jones had not complied with the advice of the previous session and he was therefore without ministerial authority. His farewell sermon was preached in the hall of the Wheeler house in 1808. His text was from Jeremiah, "Many pastors have destroyed my vineyard." Mr. Jones became an Episcopalian and many of his congregation followed his example. He was the first rector of Christ church, Bethany for two years. Most of his subsequent life was spent in Litchfield where he died in 1850.

The third pastor of this church was Nathaniel G. Huntington, of Rocky Hill, Connecticut. He was born in 1785 and was graduated from Yale in 1806. He came to Bethany in 1809 and was ordained and installed on Aug. 22 of the following year. About two

years after his ordination Mr. Huntington had a hemmorhage and during the remainder of his pastorate his health was poor. As it continued to grow worse he asked to be dismissed in 1823. He remained in Bethany for a year or two, then he moved to Oxford and finally to Orange where he died Feb. 10, 1848.

The old meeting-house on the hill was torn down early in 1831 and the green was sold.

The present house of worship was built during the summer and much of the material of the old meeting house was incorporated into the new, so that much of this present structure dates from 1769. The dedication services occurred Oct. 13, 1831. Dr. Nathaniel Taylor, for years a noted professor in Yale Divinity school, was then the acting pastor of this church. He preached the dedication sermon from the text, "This is none other than the House of God and this is the Gate of Heaven."

It has come to us a heritage from the past, a good example of colonial architecture. Origina.ly there was a porch with two large pillars in front, as in the Woodbridge church which was built a year later than this. Also the old pews, with doors, were replaced many years ago. Some of the doors are preserved in the wainscot of the choir loft.

The bell of the old meeting house was placed in the steeple in 1803. One Saturday evening some young men turned it bottom-up and filled it with water. Their plan involved a shower-bath for the sexton when he rang the bell the next morning, but the night was so cold that it froze the water and caused the bell to crack. It was used for many years after that event, but it had a "dingle" in its voice. It was replaced in 1851 by the fine old bell which now calls the people to worship.

Since the time of Nathaniel Huntington many ministers have served this church. Some of the important pastorates, because of length or influence, were those of E. W. Robinson, S. C. Brace, D. M. Elwood and C. S. MacFarland. Mr. Brace was editor of the North American Review before he became pastor here. It was largely due to his efforts that the centennial was observed fifty years ago. He died in Philadelphia in 1897. It was in that year that C. S. MacFarland was ordained in this little church. He remained here three years. Dr. MacFarland has risen high in the ministerial ranks as an author and a preacher. He is at present executive secretary of the federal council of churches. Absence on the Pacific coast prevents him from being present today.

Thus have we traced the principal vicissitudes of this part of the church of Christ down the stream of time for one hundred and fifty years. At times ever since the incorporation the storm and whirlwind have passed over it, but by the kindness of Providence it still stands firm among its sister churches of the community.

THE BETHANY CONGREGATIONAL "MEETINGHOUSE,"
1769—1831.

NATHAN CLARK.

Nathan Clark born in what is now Bethany, in 1824, was a son of Isaac and grandson of Isaac, both of whom were natives of Milford, Conn. Isaac Clark, the father of Nathan, married Esther, daughter of Deacon Joseph Treat, descended from Robert Treat, who was lieutenant-governor of the State of Connecticut 17 years, and governor 15 years. Isaac Clark held the office of selectman of the town of Woodbridge for eight years in succession. Nathan Clark was elected town clerk and treasurer of the town of Bethany in 1855, and held those offices continuously until 1881. He was elected probate judge in 1862, and held the office continuously until his death in 1893. He was also postmaster of Bethany for eight years, from 1855 to 1863. He was a member of the Congregational Society and was a member of the Society's Committee for nearly thirty years.

DEA. THEOPHILUS SMITH.

Deacon Theophilus Smith came to Bethany while young and by the energy and uprightness of his character won prominence and influence in the community. He was received a member of the church by letter from Milford January 7th 1827. He taught a High School, the first in town, and later kept a store and an inn near the junction of the turnpike and Center street, and by reason of the great amount of travel over the turnpike was well patronized. It was the custom when the pulpit was supplied by ministers from New Haven for them to come out to his Inn and be his guests over Sunday. He was a deacon of the church for many years. He was very earnest and efficient in church matters and was thoroughly conscientious in all affairs of his business life. He died February 21st, 1849, aged 83 years. He married first, Elizabeth Beecher, daughter of Lysias Beecher, who died March 30, 1830, aged 31. He married second, Eliza L. Beecher, who died September 27, 1884. His daughter, Elizabeth B., was the wife of Rev. Edmund Puck.

JUSTUS PECK.

Justus Peck was one of the Society's Committee for many years and acted as fund agent until his death, Feb. 3, 1885. His son, Harry F. Peck, has acted as chairman of the fund committee and fund agent since 1885.

Rev. Joel S. Ives, Registrar of the Congregational House, Hartford, is a grandson of Richard Stone of Bethany whose name appears as holder of one of the pews in in the Congregational church in 1800.

Rev. John Thomas Andrew, son of Jonathan Andrew, was born in Bethany July 19, 1811, graduated from Yale College in 1839, and at Yale Seminary in 1842, and taught in Cornwall 1842-1844, being prevented from continuing in the ministry by throat difficulties. He married Sept. 9, 1839, Jane Ann, daughter of Caleb Jones of Cornwall, whom he outlived, and died there May 3, 1887, aged 76.

DEACON CLARK HOTCHKISS.

Clark Hotchkiss, born Mar. 25, 1803, son of Isaac Hotchkiss, was a deacon of the church for more than sixty years. He married Caroline, daughter of Chillon Sperry, and they had two sons and six daughters. Isaac, who married Mary Reid and lived in Michigan; Martha, married Lyman Gaylord, lived in Wisconsin; Mary, m. a Mr. Hicock; Sarah, died in infancy; Fanny E., 2d wife of Adrian Rosha; Julia, m. Thomas Higgins of Ansonia; Anna, m. Adrian Rosha, died in 1873; and Arthur, m. Julia P. Sperry. Deacon Hotchkiss lived in the house now occupied by his grandson, Dea. Clifton D. Rosha. His parents lived in a house which stood a little further south. Dea. Hotchkiss died July 3, 1890, aged 87 years.

HARRY FRENCH PECK.

Harry French Peck, chairman of the Church Fund Committee, has repeatedly been elected to a number of the most responsible offices in the gift of his townsmen. He has been Selectman, Assessor, member of the Board of Relief, and Town Auditor, and represented the town in the General Assembly in 1895 and was then the first and only Republican elected to the General Assembly since the town was incorporated, sixtytwo years before, receiving over two votes to his opponent's one. During his early years he followed farming on his father's farm, one of the best in the town of Bethany, and attended to the repairing of farming utensils, and finding this work one to which he was peculiarly adapted he built a shop near his house and contracted for repairs to farming implements, besides shoeing horses and oxen, work so much in demand in a farming community, and so favorably known did his shoeing become that frequently oxen were sent as much as ten miles over the hills to his shop. He owns a farm of 285 acres, sending therefrom large quantities of farm produce to the city.

EDWIN N. CLARK.

Edwin N. Clark succeeded his father as town clerk and town treasurer and filled these offices for thirty years, and that of judge of probate for sixteen years, and was clerk of the Congregational church 35 years, from 1877 to 1912, when he removed to Seymour.

Deacon Thomas Horsfall was a member of the Society's Committee for a number of years and was a member of the committee of arrangements for the 150th anniversary celebration.

DWIGHT L. HUMISTON.

Dwight L. Humiston is a native of Hamden but has been a resident of Bethany for many years. He has been one of the selectmen of the town for a number of years and in the fall of 1896 his fellow townsmen showed their appreciation of his sterling qualities by electing him to represent the town in the General Assembly of 1897, which he did with credit to himself and to the satisfaction of his constituents.

REV. JOHN W. WRIGHT.
Pastor in 1913.

Errata.

Page 147, instead of Rev. Philip J. Phelps should be Rev. Philip J. Ralph.

Page 174, for Charles Hoadley read Charles C. Hoadley.

Page 178, 1st column, 17th line, after objects, add—"on the distant horizon."

ELSON E. BEECHER.
Chairman Anniversary Committee.

WALLACE D. HUMISTON.
Historian of the Church,

150TH ANNIVERSARY COMMITTEES.

GENERAL.

Elson E. Beecher.   Rev. John W. Wright.
Dea. Thomas Horsfall.   Dea. Clifton Rosha.
Nelson J. Peck.   Wallace D. Humiston.

ENTERTAINMENT.

Mrs. May Peck.   Miss Alice Richards.
Mrs. Dwight Johnson.   Mrs. Chas. Booth.
Mrs. James Megin.   Miss Ruth Carrington.
Mrs. Kate Lacy.   Mrs. Elson E. Beecher.
Mrs. Abner Warner.   Mrs. Carrie Johnson.
          Mrs. Harriet Stahnke.

MUSIC.

Mrs. Harry Peck.   Mrs. Elsie Johnson.
          Miss Frances Booth.

FINANCE.

Dea. Clifton Rosha.   Mr. Abner Warner.
Mr. Ralph Carrington.   Mr. Harry F. Peck.

PUBLICITY.

W D. Humiston.   Mrs. Fannie Rosha.
Mr. Harry F. Peck.   Elson E. Beecher.

DECORATION.

Mrs Elsie Johnson.   Mrs. Elson E. Beecher.
Howard Doolittle.   Elton Doolittle.
Elsie Russell.   Clarke Johnson.
          Alice Payne.

SOCIETY'S COMMITTEE.

Clifton D. Rosha.   E. N. Clark.
          Nelson J. Peck.

FUND COMMITTEE.

Harry F. Peck.   Clifton D. Rosha.
          Nelson J. Peck.

DEA. CLIFTON D. ROSHA.

NELSON J. PECK,
Of the Anniversary Committee.

RESIDENCE OF H. F. PECK.

THE FREDERICK WARNER HOUSE, SOUTH BETHANY.

REV. ISRAEL PERKINS WARREN, D. D.

One of the clergymen whose name is recalled in connection with the recent anniversary celebration was Israel Perkins Warren, D. D., who was born in Bethany Apr. 8, 1814, in a house which stood near the old red schoolhouse of the Gate District. His boyhood was spent with his grandfather, Israel Perkins, who gave him a liberal education at Yale, where he was graduated in 1838, and from Yale Divinity school, class of 1842.

He served as pastor of the churches in Granby, Mt. Carmel and Plymouth successively. The remainder of his life was spent in editorial work From 1856 to 1859 he was corresponding secretary of the Seamen's Friend Society, New York City. Later he was secretary and editor of the American Trust Society of Boston, and then until his death he published and edited the Christian Mirror of Portland, Maine. Dr. Warren was the author of many books, among them, "Chauncey Judd," and "The Three Judges." Not long before his death he made a visit to Bethany and he wrote a very interesting account of his stay. He died in Portland, Maine, Oct. 9, 1892.

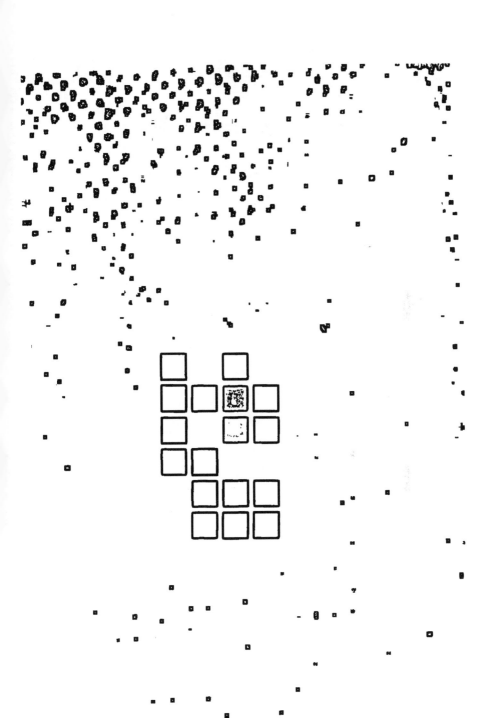

9 781360 673622